*Speaking of Soap Operas*

# SPEAKING OF SOAP OPERAS

## ROBERT C. ALLEN

The University of North Carolina Press

Chapel Hill and London

© 1985 The University of North Carolina Press

All rights reserved

Manufactured in the United States of America

First printing, April 1985

Second printing, January 1988

Library of Congress Cataloging in Publication Data

Allen, Robert Clyde, 1950–

Speaking of soap operas.

Bibliography: p.

Includes index.

1. Soap operas—United States—History and criticism.

I. Title.

PN1995.9.S3A44   1985     791.43'75'0973     84-21894

ISBN 0-8078-1643-4

ISBN 0-8078-4129-3 (pbk.)

*for Allison*

# Contents

Acknowledgments/ix

Introduction/3

CHAPTER ONE
The Meaning(s) of "Soap Opera"/8

CHAPTER TWO
The Current State of Soap Opera "Knowledge"/30

CHAPTER THREE
The Soap Opera as Commodity and Commodifier/45

CHAPTER FOUR
A Reader-Oriented Poetics of the Soap Opera/61

CHAPTER FIVE
An Institutional History of Soap Operas/96

CHAPTER SIX
Toward a History of Soap Opera Reception/130

Afterword/181

APPENDIXES
A: *Painted Dreams*, Episode 25 (1931)/187
B: *Today's Children*, Monday, January 3, 1938/192
C: *The Guiding Light*, Tuesday, January 10, 1950/199
D: *The Guiding Light*, Monday, March 5, 1956/204

Notes/213

Bibliography/231

Index/239

# Acknowledgments

This book's origins lie in an on-again/off-again fascination with soap operas that I can trace back at least to the late 1950s, when I first remember catching glimpses of the worlds of *Search for Tomorrow* and *As the World Turns* during summer vacation and when I was home sick from school. Like most males of my generation, I repressed whatever attractions those worlds might have held for me during adolescence and college. Acknowledging all those who have helped to rekindle and sustain my interest in soap operas over the last eight years would be impossible, but I do wish to thank some who have contributed in a direct way to this particular manifestation of that interest. While I was a graduate student at the University of Iowa, Chris and Linda Jackson were responsible for my becoming a full-fledged soap opera viewer. Sam Becker and Dudley Andrew allowed me to teach a course on television criticism at Iowa in 1977, which provided an "academic" rationale for all the hours I spent watching *The Guiding Light*. Over the last five years I have imposed my interest in soap operas upon hundreds of students at the University of North Carolina at Chapel Hill. I have learned much more from them than they from me. As students in some of those courses, Sally Johnstone, Rene Keever, and Sheri Castle helped to design, execute, and analyze the results of various soap opera audience studies conducted between 1979 and 1982. Professor Jane Brown of the School of Journalism at the University of North Carolina gave me the opportunity to participate in a national audience survey and helped on various occasions to locate graduate students who could translate my naive research questions into computer language. Mark West and Laurie Schulze helped me to comb through the trade and general press for material on the history of soap operas. Laurie Schulze also read and critiqued drafts of several chapters of the book, as did my colleague in the Department of Radio, Television, and Motion Pictures, Seth Finn. Ed Devlin and Janet Storm of CBS graciously helped me to set up interviews with the cast and staff of *The Guiding Light*, including Douglas Marland, Charita Bauer, Carrie Mowry, Denise Pence, Michael Laibson, and Nancy Franklin, whom I thank for their time and candor. Dean Leab enabled me to present some of my early work for the book to the Columbia University Faculty Seminar on American television, and he and his wife Kathy opened their home to me on my frequent research trips to New York. A Faculty Research Grant from the University of North Carolina gave me a summer off to begin writing. Russell Merritt and Maxine Flekner of the Wisconsin Center for Film and Theater Research facilitated my use of the Irna Phillips papers and allowed me to reprint several of Phillips's scripts. David Bordwell, Kristin Thompson, and Russell Merritt made four frantic days of research in Madison much more enjoyable than they might have been. It has been a genuine pleasure to work with Iris Tillman Hill and David Perry at the University of North Carolina Press. The former chose two outstanding readers for the manuscript, Jane Feuer and Horace Newcomb, whose comments and critiques were invaluable. As always, my family and family-by-marriage were enormously supportive and understanding. This book is dedicated to my wife, Allison, for reasons too numerous to recount.

*Speaking of Soap Operas*

# Introduction

Since the early 1930s nearly one hundred thousand hours of daytime dramatic serials—soap operas—have been broadcast on radio and television in the United States. These hours represent the unfolding of nearly two hundred different fictive worlds, many of them over the course of decades. Within nine years after the debut of the first network radio soap opera in 1932, the soap opera form constituted 90 percent of all sponsored network radio programming broadcast during the daylight hours. With but a brief hiatus in the mid-1940s, *Guiding Light* has been heard and, since 1952, seen continuously, 260 days each year, making it the longest story ever told. Today the audience for network television soap operas is estimated to be fifty million persons, including two-thirds of all American women living in homes with televisions; the cumulative audience for soap operas over the past fifty years is inestimable. This enormous audience today provides more than $900 million in revenues for the three commercial television networks—one-sixth of all network profits.[1]

In the preface to what remains one of the most useful analyses of soap operas, James Thurber described "soapland" in 1947 as "a country so vast and complicated that the lone explorer could not possibly hope to do it full justice."[2] Today, over thirty-five years later, the soap terrain is more vast than Thurber could have imagined. Not only does the soap opera continue to enjoy undiminished popularity among what we have presumed to be its traditional constituency, working- and middle-class American women, but new groups have "discovered" soap operas, including millions of college students (nearly half of all undergraduate students in the United States), five million non-college-age men, and as yet uncounted adolescents. Limited in Thurber's day to the "wasteland" of daytime broadcasting, the soap opera form today has been successfully adapted to prime-time television in such shows as *Dallas*, *Dynasty*, and *Falcon Crest*. Television soap operas are now as popular in Latin America as in the United States, and for the past twenty-one years the most-watched television program in Britain has been not an adaptation of a classic novel but *Coronation Street*, a twice-weekly working-class soap opera. As the economic hegemony of the three American commercial television networks has been challenged by new technologies, soap operas have become programming innovations used by cable television services to lure viewers. There are now "Christian" soaps, "R-rated" soaps, teenage soaps, and, in the offing, a soap for deaf viewers.

This book is an examination of the American soap opera as narrative form, cultural product, advertising vehicle, and source of aesthetic pleasure for tens of millions of persons. Like Thurber, I am perceptive enough to realize that I cannot "do full justice" to the soap opera as object of study. Like other complex cultural products, soap operas refuse to yield to simple explanations, either causal or hermeneutic. The goal of this book is not to have the "last word," to close off the soap opera from further analysis by exhausting its meaning or significance (as if that could be done), but rather to open it up, to map out some of its historical, economic, aesthetic, and cultural features, to reveal the full extent of its multiple determinations rather than seize upon simple explanations. Since *Painted Dreams* first constructed a fictional radio world that we can call "soap opera" in 1930, the soap opera form has been the object of an enormous amount of discourse, both popular and scholarly. But today the soap opera remains to us—to continue Thurber's metaphor—not unlike Egypt to the eighteenth-century French or China to the nineteenth-century British: a place about which much is said but little known. The "private lives" of soap opera stars are "exposed" (usually via press releases distributed by the star's publicity manager) in newspaper columns, television shows *about* soap operas, and a dozen or more fan magazines, while in more scholarly journals the (presumed deleterious) effects of constant soap opera viewing upon the fabric of American culture are enumerated. But commercially inspired hype and traditional sociological studies beg any number of more general and, in my view, important questions about soap operas. How do they not only give pleasure to millions of viewers but instill a sense of loyalty unknown in other forms of television programming? How did soap operas originate and why have they survived as one of the most prolific of broadcasting genres? How might we explain the curious fictive worlds that soap opera characters inhabit? What is the process by which soap operas are produced? What causes them to look and sound as they do? How have soap operas changed in the last fifty years and in the transition from radio to television? What is the relationship between the world of the soap opera and that of the soap opera viewer? How might we account for their enormous popularity and audience diversity? These are some of the questions I address in this book.

This book is also about how soap operas and their audiences have been and might be studied, and, by extension, how other types of broadcast programming might be examined. In this respect, my goal is polemical. I join those who argue for a thorough reassessment of the manner in which traditional mass communications research in the United States has attempted to "explain" the complex relationship between viewers and fictional programming and for a reconsideration of the consequences of forty years of domination by a single research paradigm upon the current state of "knowledge" about television and radio programming and viewing. My critique of the empiricist methods usually employed by American media researchers to study fictional programming is likely to be regarded as either a radical and undeserved attack or merely the latest and not very novel repudiation of a by now thoroughly discredited research philosophy. Such is the distance between the perspectives discussed in this book and from which some of its readers are likely to come. American and European cinema studies and British (and to a lesser degree other European) media studies have long embraced an antiempiricist position. The battles against exclusively quantitative analysis, the presumed objectivity of the investigator, and appropriateness of research models based on the natural sciences for the study of cultural phenomena, and other tenets of empiricism are no longer being fought; the war is over, and the antiempiricists now occupy the field. The frames of reference within which American media scholars train and work are quite different, however. There allegiance to the tenets of empiricism is still strong, and the antiempiricist refutation is registered as "discontent" among some scholars in the field. To be sure, there are signs of "ferment in the field," as the title of a recent issue of *Journal of Communication* put it. A new "mainstream" journal devoted to critical studies in mass communication has been launched, and such venerable figures as George Comstock and Lee Thayer have castigated their empiricist colleagues for being "the equivalent of the physician who can treat but not diagnose." Most who teach mass communications in the United States and contribute articles to the "leading" journals in the field, however, are more likely to agree with Gerald Miller when he says: "The time-honored epistemological tenets of empiricism, with their emphasis on the public nature of knowledge and the centrality of intersubjective reliability, have served students of communication well"—if, in fact, they have considered the possibility of there being alternative explanatory systems at all. For Miller the battle is as much political as philosophical: between the inherently egalitarian objective research model provided by "science" and inherently elitist challenges based upon "personal authority" and "idiosyncratic interpretation."[3] There is, I believe, a sufficient lack of recognition of the philosophical underpinnings of American empiricist mass media research among those who practice it to justify the detailed discussion in the first part of this book of their effects upon the study of soap operas. This discussion might also prove useful to the reader relatively unfamiliar with the tradition of media study in this country or the arguments raised against it.

Similarly, the alternative approaches I propose in later chapters are either ambitious and "foreign" or modest and "traditional," again depending upon the reader's perspective and expectations. Because empiricist mass media research is incapable of dealing with the complexities of narrative fictions as textual systems, I propose in chapter 4 a "poetics" of the soap opera, whose goal is not the elevation of the soap opera to the realm of Art or the search for hidden meanings but, rather, as Jonathan Culler expresses the goal of any poetic undertaking, "to advance one's understanding of the conventions and operations of an institution, a mode of discourse."[4] In part because empiricist mass media research has no theory adequately to account for the relationship between readers and fictive textual systems,[5] I explore the application of "reader-response" or "audience-oriented" criticism in literary studies to soap opera viewing, arriving at what I call a "reader-oriented poetics" of the soap opera. The fundamental insights of reader-response theory, particularly those of the central figures in the German *Rezeptionsästhetik* movement, Wolfgang Iser and Hans Robert Jauss, have been thoroughly absorbed into current literary and narrative studies, and my reiteration of those basic precepts may amount to belaboring the obvious for readers from that perspective. Yet what might be familiar territory to some is likely to be *terra incognita* to others, for whom the relationship between literary theory and the analysis of television programming is far from obvious.

In place of the historical variant of empiricism, which regards the historian's task as the collection and arrangement of all the "facts" of the past, I propose a historiographic orientation derived ultimately from the philosophy of science as an alternative means of dealing with the origins of the soap opera and its development over time. For the reader familiar with the ongoing and vociferous debates within the philosophy of history (especially in Europe) over the epistemological status of historical knowledge, realism, the historiographic position I adopt here, will hardly seem revolutionary. Indeed realism is a reaction against not only empiricist historiography but also the extremes of the antiempiricist position as well. To some the historical analysis in chapters 5 and 6 may appear quite conventional. Yet it is difficult to locate in histories of American mass media *any* sort of explicit historiographic position. With its recognition of multiple and uneven determinations of historical phenomena and its specification of generative mechanisms as the object of historical investigation, realism provides a good historiographic framework for a consideration of the history of soap opera as commercial vehicle, cultural artifact, textual system, and site of exchange (economic/aesthetic) between the institution of broadcasting and millions of (predominantly female) readers.

By addressing, among others, two such different constituencies—those who come to the study of broadcast narratives from cinema studies, literary criticism, or "European" media studies, on the one hand, and, on the other, those who approach television programming from the perspective of empiricist social science—my aim is not to effect some sort of synthesis. Nor is my goal merely to encourage American media researchers to "tolerate" what tends to be referred to as "critical studies." As the first two chapters will make apparent, I believe that the philosophical principles upon which empiricist social science (the foundations of American media research) is based preclude its ever accounting for phenomena that cannot be reduced to the investigatory simplicity of the independent variable in a laboratory experiment. The relationship between commercially broadcast narratives and their audiences certainly refuses any such reduction. In some respects the premises of empiricist social science and those of reader-response theory and realism render their respective projects "incommensurable," to use the terminology of Thomas Kuhn. As Kuhn points out, however, any possibility of resolving incommensurable positions requires engagement in activities that might allow the actors to "recognize each other as members of different language communities and then become translators."[6]

# The Meaning(s) of "Soap Opera"

What is meant by the term "soap opera" and how did it come to mean what (we presume) it does? Even for someone who has never seen an episode of a soap opera, it is impossible to approach that viewing experience or the reading of this book "naively." Rather, because soap operas and discourse on them have a history covering more than half a century, the soap opera (whether as a potential viewing experience or object of inquiry) comes already "encrusted" with the effects of previous viewings and readings. There is no "objective" position from which to regard the soap opera, no way to wipe our mental slates clean. Nor is there any way to "remove" the layers of discursive sedimentation around the soap opera and regard it as if it had not been listened to, viewed, studied, commented upon, criticized, defended, and otherwise engaged by countless numbers of persons on countless occasions.[1] Acknowledgment of our position as experienced or tainted readers and of our object of study as "always-already-read" is important at the beginning of any serious cultural investigation, and it is essential in the case of the soap opera. Here we have an object of study whose very name has always not only denoted a genre of broadcast programming (the daytime dramatic serial) but also carried with it an attitude toward that genre.

*American Speech* lists "soap opera" among its "New Words" in 1945, but it appears in *Newsweek* as early as 1939. The term probably originated in the entertainment trade press of the late 1930s. *Variety*, famous for its neologisms, is a likely candidate as its inventor. By 1939 "soap opera," along with "washboard weeper," had been taken up in the general press as a generic substitute for the less colorful and more cumbersome "daytime dramatic serial." The "soap" in "soap opera" derives from the sponsorship of daytime serials by manufacturers of household cleaning products: Procter and Gamble, Colgate-Palmolive, and Lever Brothers. "Opera" acquires

*The Meaning(s) of "Soap Opera"*

meaning only through its ironic, double inappropriateness. Linked with the adjective "soap," opera, the most elite of all narrative artforms, becomes a vehicle for selling the most humble of commodities. Also, yoking together "soap" and "opera" marks the distance between the opera's own thematic preoccupations (legend, myth, royalty) and presumed audience (the educated elite) and those of the radio serial: as the 1939 *Newsweek* article defines it, the soap opera brings "the hard-working housewife the Real Life adventures of Real People."[2] The domestic and culturally "unimportant" concerns of the serial drama are by the term "soap opera" made to bear odious cultural comparison with the "rightful" usage of the term. Since the 1930s the soap opera has been defined by what it pretends to be but is not, by what it lacks rather than what it is.

Ambiguity over what a soap opera actually denotes afflicts more recent definitions as well. The 1975 edition of the *Dictionary of American Slang* defines it as "a daily dramatic serial program broadcast by radio usually lasting fifteen minutes each day, concerning fictitious domestic crises and troubles and often characterized by little action and much sentiment." That in 1975 the soap opera was no longer on radio but was the staple of daytime television programming appears to have escaped the notice of these lexicographers; that it represented a debased dramatic form did not.

Ferdinand de Saussure provided us with the crucial insight that linguistic signs acquire meaning by occupying a space within an overall conceptual system of similarity and difference rather than through any direct connection with an extra-linguistic referent. "Cow" signifies "that which we mean by the concept of *cowness*" rather than any actual four-legged, bovine, farmyard animal. What a sign or word "means" is even more relative than Saussure indicated, however. A sign constitutes a set of "referential potentialities," the selection and organization of which in any particular "activation" of that sign depend upon the nature of the discourse in which the sign is being called upon to act.[3] In other words, grasping what "soap opera" has come to mean requires that we examine the discursive contexts within which it has been used.

We need also to recognize that some discourses carry more weight than others. This definitely does not imply that the meaning of "soap opera" within one discursive context is "truer" or more complete than that in another. Rather, by virtue of their visibility or by the authority assumed by or ascribed to them within a culture some discourses produce "encrustations" that are denser and more permanent than those of other discourses.

Put another way, there are asymmetrical power relationships between various levels of discourse. In the 1950s my mother occasionally talked with my Aunt Helen about the soap operas they both watched, while at the same time writers and editors at *Time* magazine also occasionally "spoke" to their readers about the same soap operas. However, the discourse of professional journalism could impose itself upon the meaning of soap opera in other discourses in a way and on a scale my mother's discourse could not. We shall return to the extremely important "silent" responses of millions of soap opera listeners and viewers in later chapters. At present we are concerned with the meanings of soap opera within those discourses that have exercised what might be called a supervisory or regulatory power over other discourses within American culture.

I would argue that the meaning of soap opera across discourses, and within "academic" discourse particularly, has been conditioned by the activation of "soap opera" within two separate but related supervisory discourses: criticism (aesthetic discourse) and sociological research. By examining historically the manner by which soap opera was taken up by these discourses, we can expose some of the "layers" of encrusted meaning that we confront today whenever we approach the soap opera as an object of inquiry. First, however, we should at least acknowledge the discourse into which soap opera was first inserted: that of commercial broadcasting.

## Soap Operas in Broadcasting Discourse

Ironically, although the term "soap opera" probably originated in the broadcasting trade press in the late 1930s, it was not a term frequently used in that press (with the exception of *Variety*, which assigned an insider's term to everything) even in the 1940s, by which time "soap opera" had become part of common parlance. Broadcasters and broadcast journalists stuck with the more awkward "daytime dramatic serial" rather than the more pejorative "soap opera," and for good reason. Broadcasters had no qualms about the "appropriateness" of soap opera subject matter, no confusion as to the purpose of soap operas or whose interest they should serve. Soap operas were a solution to an advertising problem: how might radio be used during daylight hours to attract the largest audience of potential consumers of certain products? Hence the discussion of the soap opera in such industry periodicals as *Broadcasting*, *Sponsor*, and *Advertising Age* is unapologetic. In a 1935 article entitled "Daylight and Drama—Salesmen for Flour," a writer for *Broadcasting* (the unofficial organ of commercial broadcasting interests) described an early soap opera as follows: "*Today's Children* differs from many women's programs in that each broadcast is a chapter or episode in the lives of a typical American family, their friends, and the sweethearts of the younger members of the family. . . . It is drama, homey drama of the type that appeals to 'just folks,' the mothers, the homemakers, the *flour users* of America" (italics added).[4] There is no condescension here, no odious comparison to "legitimate" drama, no doubt as to the standard to be used in judging the "quality" of the soap opera "product." The article continues, "The amazing allegiance of hundreds of thousands of women not only to members of the cast but to Pillsbury products [the show's sponsor] is a constant source of wonderment even among those professional people who for years have been working with radio."

## Soap Operas in Aesthetic Discourse

If the soap opera had been merely one of the legion of marketing innovations to arise from the economic vicissitudes of the Depression, the term "soap opera" would probably never have left the pages of *Variety* and the parochial discourse of the advertising industry. But the daytime dramatic serial represented not only a new vehicle for extolling the virtues of soap powder but a fictional world into which millions of listeners plunged every day. That fictional world was one constructed by writers, articulated by actors, and governed by principles of dramatic logic and narrative progression. Thus because it shared, however superficially, certain qualities with existing aesthetic forms (the theater, the novel, and films), the soap opera entered aesthetic discourse as well.

Until very recently the aesthetic discourse on soap operas has been marked by near unanimous disdain of the form. Certainly this was true of the critical response to soap operas in the general press of the 1940s and 1950s. Writing in the *Saturday Review of Literature* in 1940, Katherine Best called radio soaps "serialized drool." Also that year, Whitfield Cook described in the *American Mercury* the ordeal of subjecting himself to one day of listening to daytime drama.

> Through the long mid-afternoon, while I itched to listen in on Rep.
> Die's denunciations or Mr. Damrosch, Swansdown Flour, Bisquik,
> Dr. Lyon's Tooth Powder, Mazola . . . and Procter and Gamble kept

me drugged with the insidious fascinations of "Valiant Lady," "My Son and I" . . . "Orphans of Divorce," . . . and "Backstage Wife." . . . Then suddenly "Jack Armstrong, the All-American Boy," "Little Orphan Annie," and "Tom Mix" were upon me, and I realized it was the children's hour. Children's hour indeed! Hadn't the whole day been one long children's hour![5]

In short, until structuralist and semiotic theories began to influence aesthetic discourse on film and television in the 1970s, soap operas took on meaning within American critical or aesthetic discourse primarily through their exclusion from the referential field of that discourse: the field of "art." Indeed soap operas occupied a discursive space so far outside the boundaries of normative aesthetics that they could be used as the *sine qua non* of antiart, the parody of true art, the "soap opera." But simply to recount the derogatory comments made about soap operas and the manner by which the term was used to berate other narrative and dramatic forms would not enable us to understand the meanings of soap opera within aesthetic discourse. The manner by which a discourse activates a particular word or sign can be implicit as well as explicit. Thus we need to examine not only what was said about soap operas but also what was assumed and left unsaid.[6] Although it is well beyond the scope of this study to produce a comprehensive analysis of American discourse on art, in order to understand the ectopic discursive space to which soap operas were, and to a large degree still are, consigned, it is necessary to examine traditional aesthetic discourse, to borrow Foucault's phrase, "from the point of view of the rules that come into play in the very existence of such discourse."[7]

These "rules" will be here expressed as axioms, but it is difficult to find them articulated explicitly in any piece of criticism—whether of a soap opera, painting, or play. They constitute the substratum of traditional views of art: that which "goes without saying." To be sure the term "aesthetic discourse" covers a great deal of territory, and it would be simplistic to view this discourse as univocal. But while Clive Bell's position is distinguishable from that of Dwight MacDonald and his from the critic from the *New York Times* and all three positions from their bowdlerized versions in high school art primers in the 1940s and 1950s, certain assumptions about what art is, who makes it, and what it "does" hold true. It is at the level of these basic, unexamined, and largely unexpressed assumptions that traditional aesthetics cannot accommodate the soap opera. These assumptions about art in "mainstream" Western aesthetics undergird such chronologically and conceptually separated works as Laurence Buermeyer's *The Aesthetic Experience* (1924) and Murray Krieger's *Arts on the Level* (1981), as well as discourse at all levels of complexity in between—including that in which the soap opera figures.

1. *Traditional aesthetics presumes the definability of the aesthetic object.* In his study of the defining terminology used by contemporary aestheticians, analytic philosopher Joseph Margolis devotes an entire chapter to the definition of a work of art. After surveying the range of already proffered definitions of the artwork, Margolis ventures his own, least objectionable one: "A work of art is an artifact considered with respect to its design."[8] Underlying this discussion and Margolis's own definition is the assumption that, regardless of the nature of that object, the work of art is specifiable and delimitable *as an object*. At issue here is not the received impression of the work—that is, differences among spectators in the aesthetic experience provoked by the work—but an assumption about the ontological status of what is generally meant as a "work of art." The very term aesthetic *object*, and certainly its use in aesthetic discourse, implies an independently existing, intersubjective, empirical object whose temporal and spatial boundaries are fixed and known. While critics might argue as to what the work bearing the title *The Sound and the Fury* connotes, they presume a universal consensus as to the object denoted by that title. That the specifiability of the aesthetic object is a central tenet of traditional aesthetic discourse is also demonstrated by the infinite care taken by scholars to establish one version of a play, novel, or film as definitive.

But how does one go about specifying *Guiding Light* or *General Hospital* as an object of critical study? As the only narrative form (with the possible exception of the comic strip) predicated upon the impossibility of closure, the soap opera resists specification as an aesthetic object. *Guiding Light* has been broadcast continuously, 260 days each year, for more than forty-five years. "Reading" only that portion of the text represented by the television version of *Guiding Light* (since 1952) would require 233 days of nonstop viewing, during which time another 164 hours of text would have been produced. But this task is impossible because until the mid-1960s *Guiding Light* (like all soap operas) was transmitted live, and even with the advent of videotaping individual episodes are rarely saved. As Dennis Porter has pointed out, for thousands of years drama has been presumed to possess a beginning, middle, and end. The soap opera, however, "belongs to a separate genus that is entirely composed of an indefinitely expandable middle."[9]

Not only do soap operas lack any semblance of dramatic unity, but their lack of ultimate closure renders them narratively anomalous. Even the analogy made by soap opera defenders between the soap opera and the serialized novels of Dickens and Collins applies only superficially. Although Dickens might not have known how *The Old Curiosity Shop* was going to end when he began writing it, he did know that eventually it *was* going to end. Each chapter moved the reader one step closer to the novel's telos, closing off more and more sources of indeterminacy along the way. The soap opera has no telos from which meaning can be retrospectively constructed.

Another aesthetic problem created by the narrative openness of soap operas is suggested by the second half of Margolis's modest definition of a work of art: "A work of art is an artifact *considered with respect to its design*" (italics added). Because the soap opera cannot be objectified, it cannot be said to have a "form" in the traditional sense. Margolis says of design, "I have in mind only the artist's product considered as a set of materials organized in a certain way; to state how such materials are organized is to describe the design of some work." But to describe the organization of materials or relevant features in a work, is it not necessary also to describe the totality in relation to which they are organized? So many of the terms used in traditional aesthetic discourse—balance, symmetry, composition, volume, weight, emphasis, mass, theme, tension, unity, integration, essence—take on meaning only because of an implied relationship between some feature of a work and the work as a whole—as a discrete, autonomous, objectifiable whole. But in soap operas, as television critic Marya Mannes complained in 1961, all is "suffused, formless, unresolving, unending."[10] With a beginning that is only glimpsable as some point in the remote past and with no ending in sight, soap operas leave the critic with no point from which to regard the "work" as a whole. In dramatic terms, it is as if critics were to review a play the first act of which was performed before they arrived and the denouement of which was as yet unwritten.

*2. The work of art is the concrete expression of the personality and vision of the artist.* Since the Romantics, the twin notions of artist-as-genius and artwork-as-expression have been deeply ingrained in traditional aesthetic discourse. The determining effect of artistic vision certainly has been challenged over the years by art historians of various critical persuasions (formalists and the disciples of Taine, to name but two), but the communicatory and expressive function of the artwork continues to occupy a central position in traditional aesthetic discourse. For French critic René

Huyghes the very purpose of art criticism is the discovery of the psyche that hides within the work of art: "Soon one comes intuitively to the understanding that every painting is a sign and that one can discover in it the imprint of a soul. . . . It is the reflection of his own character that the artist seeks and transmits in the image that he makes of Nature." Less floridly expressed, the same view can be found in a quite different discursive context: an "art appreciation" textbook for high schools. "The artist must have something to say that he can make interesting because of his artist's vision. . . . [We ask of a painting] What is it the artist is trying to say? What does he want to express?"[11] As Tony Bennett notes, "It is thus no accident that hermeneutic procedures have scarcely ever been deployed in relation to forms of fiction where the name of the writer does not function under the sign of the 'author'; such texts have been regarded as, by definition, without 'real meaning.'" Nor is it surprising that early attempts to pull some of the products of popular culture into the field of aesthetic discourse took the form of the discovery of "authors" where none had been seen before. Such works were then legitimized because a "source" had been established for the text's "meaning."[12]

Soap operas, however, are marked by their authorial anonymity, and the soap opera production process has long been viewed as inimical to artistic expression of any sort. In the early 1940s, when soap operas first attracted the attention of the general press, the production of soaps was characterized as industrial assembly-line methods applied to broadcasting, and the writing of soaps as the epitome of hack writing. The only admiration expressed for soap opera writers by those who first wrote about soap operas is a grudging recognition of the sort of narrative cunning required in what is otherwise a subliterary task. A writer for *Fortune* noted in March 1946: "The work is hard; writers need staying power to keep a serial going for years. Ingenious writers have ways of stringing out material. In one instance, a woman character in a serial took seventeen days to get through a revolving door; the time was taken up by flashbacks to her past life." In short, the soap opera is seen as having no identifiable artist who embodies it with a personal vision. The closest thing to a soap opera author, the writer, "manufactures" his or her product in a manner depicted as identical to that by which the show's sponsor produces bars of soap. The goal of art, the creation of meaning "as revealed to the sensitive mind and soul of the artist," in the soap opera has been corrupted into the selling of a product and the legitimate skills of the storyteller perverted into "entirely mechanical and cynical techniques."[13] Here, as in other aspects of pretelevision soap opera discourse, soaps are represented not merely as nonart but as false art: the diversion that brainwashes rather than uplifts, the misappropriation of creative skills, and even the misuse of the public airwaves.

3. *Appreciating true art requires work on the part of the perceiver. The greater the art, the more "difficult" it is for the uninitiated to fully understand.* As novelist Mark Harris puts it, "There is easy reading. And there is literature. There are easy writers, and there are writers. . . . I resist, as *true* novelists do, the injunction to be clearer, to be easier, to explain, if I feel that the request is for the convenience of the reader at the expense of craft."[14] This precept of traditional academic and popular aesthetics is expressed in a wide variety of contexts: in the valuing of modernist and abstract painting over representational art, in the belief that the critic's task is to teach the naive spectator how to have a genuinely aesthetic experience, and in what has been called the "figure in the carpet" presumption of traditional literary criticism—that the true "meaning" of a literary artwork lies hidden below its ostensible surface meaning so that a gnostic critic is needed to trace this hidden pattern for the less astute general reader.[15]

In the "popular culture" debates of the 1950s and 1960s, commercial mass media in general, and in some cases soap operas in particular, were held up as prime examples of nonart because understanding them required a minimal amount of effort on the part of the listener/viewer. In his 1953 essay "A Theory of Mass Culture," Dwight MacDonald quotes with approval Clement Greenburg's statement that *kitsch* (mass art) "predigests art for the spectator and spares him effort, provides him with a shortcut to the pleasures of art that detours what is necessarily difficult in genuine art." Writing four years later, sociologist Ernest van den Haag argues that mass culture not only diverts the spectator from serious art but also renders him or her incapable of recognizing "the real thing." But the diversionary power van den Haag ascribes to mass culture extends well beyond the merely aesthetic: "All mass media in the end alienate people from personal experience and, though appearing to offset it, intensify their moral isolation from each other, from reality and from themselves. . . . [O]nce they become a habit, [mass media] impair the capacity for meaningful experience."[16]

The arguments of MacDonald, Greenburg, van den Haag, and their philosophical predecessor Jose Ortega y Gasset expose in particularly pointed fashion the incommensurability of traditional aesthetics with the perceived attributes of commercial mass-mediated texts. The attacks against mass culture in general apply with even more force to the soap opera as the essence of *kitsch*, demonstrating once again that from this view soap operas are not merely nonart but antiart. In his influential *Revolt of the Masses*, Ortega y Gasset in 1932 had detailed what he saw as the emergence of the new "common man," no longer subject to external norms and traditional sources of domination, politically in ascendance in western Europe, and totally unaware of the political and economic sources of his newfound freedom. Left to his own devices, the "common man" "makes no demands on himself, but contents himself with what he is, and is delighted with himself." MacDonald adopts this view of the "masses" (while disavowing Ortega y Gasset's solution to the problem: the restoration of the *ancien regime*) and sees the mass media industry as appealing to and fostering the lassitude, valuelessness, and depersonalization of the modern mass age.

> Like nineteenth-century capitalism, Mass Culture is a dynamic, revolutionary force, breaking down the old barriers of class, tradition, taste, and dissolving all cultural distinction. It mixes and scrambles everything together, producing what might be called homogenized culture. . . . It thus destroys all values, since value judgments imply discriminations. Mass Culture is very, very democratic: it refuses to discriminate against, or between, anything or anybody. All is grist to its mill, and all comes out finely ground indeed."

While art is communication between a perceptive artist and a perceiving individual spectator, mass culture is to MacDonald the mass production of false art distributed in bulk to mass consumers. He singles out the soap operas produced by Frank and Anne Hummert, originators of more than a dozen radio serials, as examples of why popular culture products cannot be art. "Unity is essential in art; it cannot be achieved by a production line of specialists, however competent." MacDonald might also have had soap operas in mind when he complained that mass culture threatened to inundate genuine culture "by its sheer pervasiveness, its brutal, overwhelming *quantity*."

Van den Haag shares not only Ortega y Gasset's view of the masses but also his political conservatism, making him, if possible, even more alarmist than MacDonald in his assessment of the effects of mass culture. Mass culture encourages the blurring of fiction and reality and the false investment of the qualities of one in the other. Mass media provide the masses with a comforting escape from modern realities and ultimately an evasion of them. Where true art deepens our understanding of the complexities of reality, mass culture veils reality and displaces it. Van den Haag leaves no doubt as to the eventual psychosocial consequences of mass culture. "Once fundamental impulses are thwarted beyond retrieving, once they are so deeply repressed that no awareness is left of their aims, once the desire for a meaningful life has been lost as well as the capacity to create it, only a void remains. . . . Diversion, however frantic, can overwhelm temporarily but not ultimately relieve the boredom which oozes from nonfulfillment."[17]

## *"Soap Opera" in Social Science Discourse*

To the popular culture critics of the postwar period, the consequences of mass culture were not merely aesthetic but fundamentally social as well. If, like MacDonald and van den Haag, one assigns important epistemological and moral functions to art—art helps us to know the world and fosters communication between individuals—and if, as van den Haag puts it, a "substitute gratification" has taken the place of art in the lives of the masses, then what has taken place is nothing less than a subversion of an important part of the social order. From this perspective, what makes mass culture so insidious is that it uses the techniques of art not to produce a genuinely aesthetic effect but to make a profit. When the notion of a manipulative antiart is combined with Ortega y Gasset's conception of the valueless "common man," the true extent of the danger of mass culture becomes apparent.

The postwar debate over the social consequences of popular culture was prefigured a decade earlier in the social scientific discourse on soap operas. The space occupied by soap operas in the aesthetic discourse of the 1940s, which I described above as ectopic, is more specifically a position 180 degrees removed from "real art." That "other side" of traditional aesthetics to which soap operas were relegated turns out to be not merely aesthetically irrelevant but, as MacDonald et al. are later to show, anti-aesthetic and hence socially threatening. Beginning in the early 1940s soap operas become the subject of intense social scientific scrutiny. Whereas in aesthetic discourse soap operas represent that about which nothing of substance can be said, soap operas reemerge in social scientific discourse as that which must be explained.

Since it began in the late 1930s, social scientific research on soap operas has been organized around three interrelated questions: (1) Who listens to (or watches) soaps? (2) Why? and (3) What are the effects of soap operas upon this audience? The first question was also the first to be asked, for what were rather straightforward reasons. Until the development of regular ratings services in the 1940s there was little hard information on how many people listened to a particular radio program or on demographic differences between the audiences for various types of programming, and thus no solid basis upon which to determine the price of advertising time. For nearly a decade advertisers were simply charged one-half the evening (prime-time) rate for ads run during daylight hours because it was presumed the audience before 6:00 P.M. was roughly half that after that hour. As we shall see in a later chapter, however, as perspicacious advertisers, such as Pillsbury and Procter and Gamble, discovered the advantages of daytime programming and as the scale of daytime listening became apparent, broadcasters increasingly needed more accurate quantitative and demographic information about the daytime audience. And since by 1941 nearly 90 percent of all advertiser-sponsored daytime programming consisted of serials, audience analysis of soap operas became of primary importance.

One of the first published studies to indicate the scope and constitution of the soap opera audience was a 1939 "secondary analysis" of the crude ratings data generated for the industry by the Cooperative Analysis of Broadcasting. The analysis, supervised by NBC research director H. M. Beville, was distributed by the first American academic research unit devoted exclusively to the study of radio, the Princeton Radio Research Project, headed by Paul Lazarsfeld. The study, later published in *Public Opinion Quarterly*, showed that while listening to serials (indeed, radio listening in general) varied among socioeconomic groups and was most prevalent among those at middle and lower income levels, the popularity of soap operas was by no means limited to any one social stratum. Furthermore, Beville found that some serials drew their audience primarily from one socioeconomic group, while others had broader appeal. The study's findings in and of themselves are less important for our purposes (although Beville's findings were, as we shall shortly see, confirmed in any number of later studies) than the fact that their publication was designed to attract the attention of readers both within and beyond the commercial broadcasting industry. In particular, Lazarsfeld used the Beville study to demonstrate the utility of this kind of research both to broadcasters and to academics interested in the social implications of radio listening.

The enormous influence Paul Lazarsfeld was to exercise over the course of audience research and more generally over the philosophical and methodological orientation of American mass communications research (an influence that will be discussed in more detail later) justifies the inclusion here of a brief discussion of the context of the publication of the Beville study.[18] In 1937 the Rockefeller Foundation funded the establishment of a center for the study of the effects of radio on American society. It chose as its director Lazarsfeld, an Austrian sociologist who had come to the United States as a Rockefeller Foundation Fellow in 1933, and who was prompted to stay in the United States after a fascist government assumed power in Austria in 1934. The Office of Radio Research, set up at Princeton University under the Rockefeller grant, moved to Columbia University in 1939 and became the Bureau of Applied Social Research.

Lazarsfeld quickly saw that the initial grant was not a permanent or sufficient funding source for the type of research unit he envisioned. He also saw that if "communications research" was to engender support from the academic community (both at Columbia and more broadly), it had to be cast in terms of a more established American discipline—in this case, empirical sociology (although empirical sociology itself was at this point but a fledgling academic enterprise). The solution Lazarsfeld arrived at was what he called "administrative research": studies that would serve the interests of commercial broadcasters but that would also form the basis for more disinterested sociological inquiry.

For Lazarsfeld, arriving at an accommodation with commercial broadcasters was a necessary evil for an academic research unit unable to secure adequate funding from university or philanthropic sources. Furthermore, the broadcasting industry was itself a primary generator of data about radio use—data that were of tremendous value to nonindustry investigators since no individual scholar or group of scholars could ever afford to duplicate such regular and large-scale data collection efforts. Realizing that no university at that time was likely to fully fund a national center for mass communications research, Lazarsfeld settled for an academic locus for his bureau within the Columbia University structure and an operating budget that came largely from commercial and governmental contract research. Most of these contract studies would have, in Lazarsfeld's words, "scientifically valuable aspects, but only surplus time and money could be devoted to completely scientific purposes."

The Beville study, published in November 1939 in the midst of Lazarsfeld's move from Princeton to Columbia, was part of a larger effort to establish the legitimacy of the bureau's work within academic sociological discourse and to present the results of a study involving the cooperation of the industry with the bureau. The inclusion of soap opera listeners in the study had less to do with the bureau's "scientific" interest in that audience than with its importance to broadcasters and the fact that the data on that group had already been collected (and for other reasons). As Lazarsfeld noted in a 1969 reminiscence, the Rockefeller project was originally designed to be oriented toward psychological laboratory studies. Lazarsfeld, however, was inclined more toward sociological field research than behavioral psychology. Because the foundation grant was not sufficient to allow for large-scale data collection, Lazarsfeld had to establish the bureau's research reputation, initially at least, on the basis of secondary analysis of data collected by others: the Gallup organization, ratings services, government surveys, and the broadcasting industry itself. We will speak more later about the consequences of Lazarsfeld's establishment of mass communications research as "administrative" in nature. For the present it is worth keeping in mind that from the beginning academic research into the relationship between soap operas and their audiences was conditioned by delicate relationships between the academic sociological apparatus, individual academic institutions, philanthropic foundations, and commercial interests.

By the early 1940s, the very pervasiveness of the daytime serial phenomenon spurred an academic interest in soap opera audiences that extended beyond the needs of broadcasters to determine advertising rates. (Of the sixty quarter-hour network time periods between 10:00 A.M. and 6:00 P.M. at least one serial was on the air in fifty-nine of them.) Gradually the dimensions of the soap opera "phenomenon" became apparent to those outside the broadcasting industry, and a vociferous and highly publicized attack on the purported effects of soap operas followed this recognition. It sprang from some of the same fears expressed by critics of a more aesthetic bent, who warned of the burying of authentic culture under the cumulative weight of mass antiart, but the discourse in which its charges were made was that of science rather than art. This attack did more than any other single factor to place soap operas on the agenda of social science discourse and to establish the terms by which soap operas and their audiences would be considered within that discourse.

In March 1942 a New York psychiatrist, Louis Berg, told the Buffalo Advertising Club that listening to soap operas caused "acute anxiety state, tachycardia, arrhythmias, increase in blood pressure, profuse perspiration, tremors, vasomotor instability, nocturnal frights, vertigo, and gastrointestinal disturbances." Berg charged that at a time when radio programming ought to be contributing to the war effort, broadcasters proffered a surfeit of daytime fare that "pandered to perversity" and played out "destructive conflicts." "These serials furnish the same release for the emotionally distorted that is supplied to those who desire satisfaction from a lynching bee, lick their lips at the salacious scandals of the *crime passionnel*, who in the unregretted past cried out in ecstasy at a witch burning." At his own expense, Berg published his "research findings" in two brochures, and his claims of the injurious effects of soap operas received extensive attention in magazine and newspaper stories.

Already concerned that the Roosevelt administration might impose wartime programming controls, broadcasters hurriedly commissioned their own studies of soap opera listeners. Within months, sociologists, ministers, civic leaders, social workers, doctors, and commentators were all debating the "effects" of soap opera listening. What got obscured in the resultant furor were the means by which Dr. Berg conducted his "research": he simply recorded his *own* blood pressure and pulse while he listened to radio soap operas.[19] The attention he and his "research" received was less a function of its validity than of the discourse within which it was positioned (that of the physical sciences) and the social status of Berg's profession in relation to that discourse (doctor/psychiatrist).

To a very large extent the sociological studies generated in response to Berg's allegations were informed by a very different research problematic. Berg claimed to examine the direct, immediate physiological effects of soap opera listening, and from these effects he extrapolated more general emotional, psychological, and, finally, cultural ramifications. The social-scientific rejoinders to his charges (many of which were commissioned by broadcasting interests) recast Berg's concerns as answers to the questions, Who listens to soap operas and why? This shift away from a perspective that focused on direct effects and toward a more descriptive and functional perspective is emblematic of a larger alteration in the paradigm governing mass communications research in the United States—a shift not unrelated to the position of the nascent discipline, which had one foot in the academy and the other in the industry. The shift also helped to "encrust" the meaning of soap operas within the discourse of mass communications research with a particular conception of its audience, which is felt even today.

Berg's attack on soap operas represents one of the more extreme expressions of what came to be called the "hypodermic" theory of mass media effects. In this view an isolated media message is capable of functioning in the manner of a virus that is "injected" into the psyche of the isolated, and hence susceptible, individual viewer or listener. Media messages are regarded as powerful molders of opinion and conditioners of behavior and the media audience as atomized, passive, and incapable of mediating the effects of these messages. The hypodermic orientation emerged in the 1920s in part as a response to the unprecedented use of print and electronic media in state-sponsored or state-sanctioned propaganda campaigns during World War I. The media, it was felt, had helped to persuade entire societies of the rightness of conducting the most barbaric warfare in centuries and had done so in the face of untold personal suffering and loss experienced by millions of people as a direct result of that warfare. The ascendancy of behaviorism as a research orientation within American psychology in the 1920s further encouraged a conceptualization of the media message as a "stimulus" and the research task as observing "subjects" (viewers) in order to ascertain their short-term "responses." The determination of the direct effects of media messages was also important to the American advertising industry, particularly following the advent of radio as a nationally based, commercially supported medium in the late 1920s. Press entrepreneurs, broadcasters, and advertising agencies all had a vested interest in demonstrating that a message (advertisement) had a direct behavioral effect (a change in purchasing behavior) upon a given audience. Furthermore, competition among media for advertising dollars fueled the demand for, in the words of pioneer American sociologist Robert Merton, "evolving rigorous and objective measures not easily vulnerable to criticism."[20]

The research paradigm Lazarsfeld and his associates at the Bureau of Applied Social Research were instrumental in posing against the hypodermic theory was one that preserved the notion of mass communications research as objective and quantitative, but substituted a view of the media as less powerful and a concept of media effects as indirect and mediated both by the needs of individual audience members and the social context of media consumption. Besides countering the views of the previous paradigm, the Lazarsfeld position also provided a better "fit" with the requirements of the commercial broadcasting industry. In 1942, in what remained the definitive study of the soap opera audience for over thirty years, Herta Herzog, a researcher for the bureau, examined not the effects of listening upon soap opera listeners but rather the psychological and social needs soap opera listening fulfilled. Especially for rural listeners and those with little formal education, soap operas were sources of advice, Herzog explained, but she refused to evaluate the power of this "advice" to change attitudes.[21]

What emerges from the studies of soap opera listening in the mid-1940s is the assumption that it constitutes a nonnormative mode of media consumption behavior most likely to be engaged in by a distinctive and "different" subaudience. Study after study attempted to establish the "typical" soap opera listener in terms of her demographic, psychological, and cultural difference from "ordinary" radio listeners. One of the first studies conducted in the wake of Berg's charges was sponsored by the bureau and conducted by Leda Summers. Some 9,000 Iowa men and women were interviewed, and, on the basis of 5,324 replies by women, it was determined that half of them were regular daytime serial listeners. Despite looking for them, Summers could find few significant differences between serial listeners and nonlisteners in age, education, place of residence, or any other demographic or psychological category. She concluded that there was no recognizable "type" of soap opera listener. Herzog, like Summers, found greater listening among lower education and income groups, but she found no significant differences between soap opera listeners and nonlisteners with respect to social participation, intellectual interests, personality profile, or interest in public affairs.[22]

In May 1943 NBC released the findings of a study of serial listeners conducted for its Blue Network by the advertising firm of Foote, Cone, and Belding. Five thousand "housewives" were interviewed in 75 cities. The researchers found that half the total daytime listening of those surveyed was devoted to soap operas and, once again, that the soap opera audience cut across income and educational levels. While listening to soaps was more prevalent among lower education and income groups, nearly 40 percent of college-educated women reported listening to serials. The NBC study's findings were confirmed the following year by a CBS-sponsored study based on 6,000 interviews conducted in 125 communities. It determined that 54 percent of female respondents were serial listeners and that while the largest proportion of listeners were from lower socioeconomic and educational groups, 40 percent of college-educated women and 35 percent of those from the highest economic group were listeners. Soap opera listeners were not significantly different from nonlisteners in "cultural level, club membership, magazine reading, Happiness Index, Index of Social Intelligence, or attitude toward family." A 1946 Lazarsfeld-supervised study, based on a national survey of attitudes toward radio, found no differences between soap opera listeners and nonlisteners of the same socioeconomic level.[23]

In short, the studies found over and over again that the majority of American women listened to soap operas and that while a higher proportion of that audience came from the lower end of the economic and educational scale, large numbers of "upscale" women also listened. Despite the clear indication that soap opera listening pervaded all groups, the methodologies of the studies suggested that soap opera enjoyment had to be explained as some kind of lack on the part of the listeners: the psychological need of women for advice, a social or emotional lack, educational deprivation, the inability to enjoy other types of programming, and so forth. "Ordinary" radio listening apparently did not need this kind of analysis. The relative lack of research on the "needs" met by other types of programming and on the demographic, psychological, and intellectual profiles of other audiences reveals the presumption on the part of researchers that the appeals of newscasts, variety shows, comedies, and "serious" drama were self-evident, while the appeals of soap operas had to be accounted for by reference to either a distinct subaudience or inherent differences between those who listened and those who did not within the same socioeconomic group. As we shall see in a later chapter, although the only "difference" between the soap audience and that for other types of radio programming was that the former was almost exclusively female, this fact alone was enough to mark soap operas and their audiences as a phenomenon that could not be regarded as "normal."

Despite the inability of these attempts to specify soap listeners as in some way different from the rest of the radio audience, the fact that the soap opera audience was seen implicitly as a group to be studied *in terms of its difference* had definite and long-lasting consequences. Overwhelming empirical evidence to the contrary notwithstanding, critics, commentators, and even other researchers advanced an image of the typical soap opera listener as an intellectually and imaginatively impoverished "lower-class housewife" whose interests extended only as far as her own front door and whose life of mindless tedium was relieved only by her daily immersion into a fantasy soap world which she frequently mistook for reality. Although the hypodermic view of media effects, and its concomitant view of the listener as passive and atomized, was rapidly being replaced in media studies by the Lazarsfeldian "personal influence" model, the soap listener continued to be viewed by many as isolated from meaningful social intercourse, unequipped to deal with the "real world," and forever vulnerable to psychic manipulation.

Ironically, this image was proposed by both critics and defenders of soap operas. Anticipating MacDonald, Merrill Denison, writing in a 1940 issue of *Harper's*, found the popularity of soap operas disturbing.

When one understands the entirely mechanical and cynical technics which have been perfected for the manufacture of these radio shows, and when one considers the whole-hearted acceptance with which millions of women listen to them, one cannot help wondering what would happen were the same technics used to serve political ends rather than the relatively harmless ones of promoting the sale of soap, breakfast foods, and tooth pastes.[24]

During World War II, Federal Communications Commission (FCC) Chairman Clifford Durr commissioned Charles Siepmann "to develop ideas on how the FCC could better work for higher broadcasting standards."[25] In *Radio's Second Chance* (1946) Siepmann cited soap operas as an example of the need for government intervention to protect the public from greedy advertisers and broadcasters. "The intense interest of the [soap opera] addicts, their morbid frame of mind, their pitiable credulity, make them a pushover for the advertiser. . . . Its [the soap audience's] low IQ and many other attributes which, from the standpoint of vigorous democratic health, mark it as a social liability mark it also as the perfect vehicle of sales suggestion."

But broadcasters had a vested interest in representing radio listeners—to advertisers, if not to the general public—as susceptible to persuasion. Otherwise the entire foundation of advertiser-supported commercial broadcasting would crumble. It was particularly important that women listeners be depicted as malleable, since they made (and make) a disproportionately large share of consumer purchasing decisions. Thus, in discourse less critical of the broadcasting industry the manipulator/manipulated image of the relationship between the soap opera and its audience is transformed into its "positive" obverse: teacher/student. Soap operas serve as a sort of remedial ethics and civics lesson for the socially retarded. In a direct response to the criticisms of Berg and others, Max Wylie, a soap opera writer, contends:

> Women of the daytime audiences are having physical and psychic problems that they themselves cannot understand, that they cannot solve. Being physical, they feel the thrust of these problems. Being poor, they cannot buy remedies in the form of doctors, new clothes, or deciduous coiffures; being unanalytical, they cannot figure out what is really the matter with them; and being inarticulate, they cannot explain their problem even if they know what it is. . . . [Soap opera] takes them into their own problems or into problems worse

than their own (which is the same thing only better). Or it takes them away from their problems. It gives listeners two constant and frequently simultaneous choices—participation or escape. Both work.[26]

The logical and, because of its status as an "academic" treatise, most disturbing extension of the soap addict image comes in a 1947 study conducted by two University of Chicago anthropologists, W. Lloyd Warner and William E. Henry, published in *Genetic Psychology Monographs*. Conceptualizing soap operas as symbol systems, Warner and Henry set about to determine how one soap opera, *Big Sister*, "stimulated" its female listeners as a group and as individuals, and to assess whether this stimulation was positive ("Does it assist the women who listen to adjust to the external realities of American society?") or negative (Does it "contribute to their inner emotional maladjustment and disorient their external relations with their families in general?"). Although acknowledging that soap opera listeners came from all socioeconomic levels, they restricted their sample to sixty-two soap opera listeners who were "commoners": ("lower middle and upper lower class"). To make the study even more "manageable," they limited their sample to women who were married "housewives" from urban environments (Chicago and Detroit). As a control group, Warner and Henry selected five upper-middle-class career women—presumed *not* to be soap opera listeners. This socioeconomic level was chosen "because they are easier to find in our population and easier to interview." Once the "personality" of each subject was assessed through her responses to the Thematic Apperception Test (which involves the construction of a narrative on the basis of pictures), she was given several plot situations from the *Big Sister* program and asked to extend them imaginatively (a "Verbal Projective").

On the basis of the former instrument, Warner and Henry concluded that the "listener" group could be characterized as having "dulled" imaginations, a fear of spontaneity, stereotypical views of interpersonal situations and the "outside" world at large, strained sexual relationships, and apprehension of the unknown—in short "their responses are psychologically stereotyped and repetitive and sociologically traditional and conventional." The women of the control group, on the other hand, "while showing greater intellectual and imaginative freedom, are more likely to have a higher rate of neurosis, and it is probable that the reveries of many of them will be filled with symbolic themes that are non-adaptive and frequently escapist." Warner and Henry saw *Big Sister* serving a positive social function in that it strengthened and stabilized "the basic social structure of our society, the family," by reinforcing the listener's view of the world outside the home as an evil and unfulfilling place and demonstrating that her proper place is in the home. They left no doubt as to their assessment of the value of the soap opera as an instrument of social control:

> The personalities of our listener group appear typical of the women who belong to the Common Man level of our culture. . . . As females in our society they have learned by rewards and punishment, from birth to sexual maturity, to conform to the rigid conventions of our middle-class culture. They have been trained by their families to be wives and mothers and, unconsciously, to carry out and maintain the roles, moral beliefs, and values of their social level. This they do most effectively. We shall have occasion to say later, but it is well to say it now, that should they fail in this behavior our society, as we know it, would not continue.[27]

## The Soap Opera and Its Audience

Whether listeners/viewers learn attitudes or behaviors from soap operas, and whether the life of the "common man's" wife in the 1940s was as rigidly rule governed and oppressive as Warner and Henry indicate, is not at issue here. The Warner and Henry study is but one further example of the penchant of investigators to collapse the entire soap opera audience into a single social and psychosocial category whose members could be regarded as "different" from everyone else and whose interest in soap operas is seen as deriving not from a genuinely aesthetic impulse but from a psychopathological (if, in Warner and Henry's opinion, sociologically necessary) need for role reinforcement.

Certainly Warner and Henry's assessment both of the soap opera audience and of the soap opera's function within modern society was extreme (although, as we shall see in the next chapter, this has not prevented it from being cited as "fact" in more recent studies). It is fair to say, however, that aesthetic and sociological discourses of the pretelevision era helped to encrust the soap opera with a particular notion of its audience. Given the "supervisory" power of those discourses, these encrustations were passed down to us as part of the likely meaning of soap opera. What we regard the soap opera as today is inextricably tied up with what we presume its audience to be and to have been. Like the Hollywood melodrama of the 1930s and 1940s, the soap opera signified a "woman's" form. This is not merely to say that women constituted its audience but also to mark the form as inherently different from "ordinary" forms. Unable to fathom the appeal of soap operas and regarding it as unaesthetic (if not antiaesthetic), researchers have frequently constructed a "typical" soap opera fan who is intellectually, socially, economically, and sexually "one of them." Displacing the soap opera viewer to a position "out there," paralleling the ectopic position to which the soap opera form has already been removed in aesthetic discourse, encourages a further reduction of the relationship between viewer and soap opera to one of stimulus/response or, in its more generous form, teacher/student.

Again, the point here is not to deny that many working-class women enjoy soap operas (they obviously do) or to rule out the possibility of "learning" occurring as a result of watching soaps (it almost certainly does) or to regard as aesthetically deficient anyone who does not enjoy watching soap operas (that would merely be to invert the aesthetic canon). Rather it is to remind us that the term "soap opera" carries with it a set of deeply embedded attitudes toward it, that it has come to "mean" because of its position within and across discourses—a position relative to notions of art, mass media, social status, gender, and culture. For the contemporary investigator, the position of soap opera within traditional aesthetic and social science discourses circumscribes the range of questions likely to be asked about it and the methods likely to be used in answering them.

# The Current State of Soap Opera "Knowledge"

For twenty-five years after the soap opera research boom of the 1940s, the daytime serial once again became invisible—except, of course, to its millions of listeners and, beginning in 1950, viewers. In a 1972 article in *Public Opinion Quarterly*, Natan Katzman noted that "despite the magnitude of the phenomenon, there has been no published research on television serials." All that social scientists (not in the employ of television networks or advertising companies) knew about the soap opera *viewing* phenomenon was derived from the "preliminary" and "outdated" radio research of the 1940s. By the winter of 1982, however, a bibliography of "scholarly writing" on soap operas could list seventy-six books, articles, and theses published in the ten years since Katzman's essay.[1] Although it listed some few works that address what we might loosely call "aesthetic" aspects of soap operas (and of course preceded the very recent work on soap operas from semiotic and feminist perspectives), this bibliography revealed that, by and large, soap operas have been conceptualized in recent scholarly literature as an object of social scientific research.

In the years between the pioneering radio research of Lazarsfeld, Stanton, and Herzog and the publication of Katzman's "Television Soap Operas: What's Been Going On Anyway?" a new academic discipline had emerged: mass communications. By 1972 the general research direction inaugurated by Lazarsfeld and his Bureau of Applied Social Research in the late 1930s had solidified into a dominant paradigm governing the questions that would be asked about the mass media and the methods that might be used to answer them. In the years since 1972, the adequacy of this paradigm in providing accounts of the relationships between audiences and media institutions has increasingly been called into question, and, as was noted earlier, it has been rejected entirely by some media scholars in both Europe and America. Despite these challenges, it remains the primary perspective from which mass communications research is conducted in the United States and the perspective from which most of the academic research on soap operas has been done.[2] As I will show, the *empiricist* assumptions behind most of the *empirical* research conducted on soap operas (and, by extension, on broadcast narratives in general) are not without serious ramifications for the "knowledge" that research claims to produce.

## The Empiricist Basis of Mass Communications Research

As a discipline, American mass communications research has been organized around an object of study, the "mass media." The means by which the processes and effects of the mass media have been explained in mass communications research derive almost entirely from other disciplines, notably, other branches of American social science. In borrowing "methods" from psychology, sociology, and political science, American mass communications research also took on the ontological and epistemological assumptions that govern those methods. Traceable ultimately to Mill and Hume and bolstered by much more recent work in what is broadly called "probability theory," these assumptions can be characterized as *empiricist*. As David Willer and Judith Willer point out, for many American social scientists empiricism is assumed to be *the* way by which the world can be known.

> Sociology and other social "sciences" have been committed for some time to a particular methodological approach—an approach so all-pervasive that, although commitment to it is only partially conscious, it enters unknowingly into the most diverse activities. It is a guiding force in the statement of "theory" as well as in the research process. It determines what is today sociologically legitimate and is even the basis of evaluation of historical works. It influences the manner in which we carry out our projects and simultaneously determines the meaning of sociology as it is taught and guarantees its continuance.[3]

Empiricism is predicated upon several ontological and epistemological axioms. An absolute distinction is presumed to exist between an objectively existing universe of "facts" or events and the knowing subject who attempts to explain those events. The subject is "knowing" because he or she generates knowledge about the world through sensory data derived from observation. In the empiricist view, the investigator is a disinterested, objective observer and accurate recorder of "what happens." Those observations must not be tainted by expectation, idiosyncratic differences between observers, personal interest in the outcome of scientific observations, or other sources of "bias." In the natural sciences, the demand for objectivity can often be met simply by replicability. In the application of empiricism to social science, however, elaborate procedures are often necessary to ensure that the investigator does not affect the observations he or she makes. If protecting the objectivity of the empiricist social scientific enterprise is problematic, its conceptualization of the relationship between the subject and object of that enterprise is not: the primary task of the investigator is to serve as an impartial observer, competent to record the truths of an externally existing realm of data as they are revealed.

In empiricism, these "truths" are expressed in regularities. Knowledge is equated with observed regularity, and ultimate knowledge with absolute regularity. Absolute regularity is expressed as a universal or covering law, which can be used to predict the outcome of future observations: In all cases in which X has been known to occur, Y has also occurred; Y has never occurred without X; and X has never occurred without Y; therefore we can predict that in the future whenever X occurs, Y will also occur and vice versa. These covering laws are inductively derived and are ad hoc in nature; they describe regularities among observations of data and not logical or causal connections between phenomena.

In order to observe a regularity between two events, it is necessary that the potential influence of all extraneous factors be eliminated or controlled for, so that, in the terminology of the "scientific method," we have only an "independent" and a "dependent" variable. In the natural sciences the investigator can generate regularities through the construction of the experimental situation, a closed system in which all factors save one have been set aside. The investigator can ask, "What would happen if I poured hydrochloric acid on zinc?" and construct a situation for observing the results. The situation of the social scientist is different in two key respects, however. First, since human beings think and change their behaviors on the basis of thought, it is difficult to conceive of a sociological "law" with the explanatory force of a covering law in physics.[4] Second, the closed system of the experimental situation is frequently inapplicable to the investigation of social phenomena. Hydrochloric acid can be expected to behave the same in the laboratory as it does in "nature," but human beings can be expected to behave quite differently "in the lab" than they do in uncontrolled and un-observed situations.

The effects of the latter difference between the natural and social sciences will be discussed shortly. One consequence of the difficulty of achieving absolute regularity in the observation of social phenomena has been the increasing reliance of the social sciences upon probabilistic explanation and, concomitantly, upon computers and sophisticated statistical procedures to detect and express partial regularity. The probabilistic explanation does not carry the same explanatory or prognosticatory weight as the covering law. It says, "There is a probability A that whenever X occurs, Y will also occur." The empiricist social scientist frequently finds himself in the position of explaining the relationship between phenomena not as an absolute regularity but as a regularity greater than that likely to be produced by chance. The "test of significance," "test of randomness," or "null hypothesis" results in a correlation coefficient, the assigning of a numerical value to the degree of correlation between two occurrences along a scale from $-1$ (absolute negative correlation) through 0 (no systematic correlation) to 1 (absolute positive correlation). The probability that any difference or similarity observed was not the result of chance increases as the correlation coefficient approaches $-1$ or 1.

Empiricists conceive of theory in one of two ways. They sometimes equate theory with as yet untested and sometimes untestable speculation. Empiricism's ontology is atomistic; it explains by discovering regularities, not interconnections between phenomena. Yet empiricist social scientists frequently desire to "go beyond their data" and make educated guesses as to the mechanisms responsible for the regularities they have observed. In doing so, however, they also exceed the limits of knowledge as posited by empiricism by pointing toward agencies that are not directly observable, and hence are "nonempirical" and ultimately unknowable in the empiricist view. All that empiricism can say about causality is subsumed under the concept of regularity. Recognizing the inevitable subjectivity of theory (that is, it cannot be derived from the direct observation of phenomena and recording of data), some social scientists eschew it altogether in the belief that ultimate knowledge will result not from theory but from the accumulation of facts. More and more studies, establishing more and more regularity, will eventually sweep speculative theory before them. In this view, if theory has relevance at all, it is as a statement of greater generalizability of regularity, as some overall statement of the high probability of regularity within which many separate instances can be subsumed but which still falls short of the predictive power of a covering law.

Regardless of which concept of theory is employed by empiricist social scientists, it occupies a marginal role in the construction of knowledge, as indeed it must, given the empiricist definition of knowledge as the observation of regularity and the demand that the investigator approach his or her study with a *tabula rasa*. To a large degree, mass communications research defines explanation solely as the collection of data and the advancing of logical generalizations that might follow from those data.[5]

## Investigating Soap Operas from an Empiricist Perspective

It is essential here to distinguish between *empirical* and *empiricist*, and between the view that quantification is a necessary but not sufficient procedure in social inquiry and the view that quantification is both necessary *and* sufficient. Far too often those making a distinction between empiricist researchers and nonempiricist researchers draw a false distinction between those who study "the real world" (empirical scholars) and others, who, presumably, do not. This spurious dichotomy makes it far too easy for empiricists to see their enterprise as unassailable (few scholars would bridle at the charge that they study some aspect of reality) and dismiss anti-empiricist objections and alternatives as "subjective" or merely polemical.[6] Yet it is important to remember that one can study the "real world" (and thus take up an *empirical* object of inquiry) without subscribing to the ontological and epistemological assumptions of *empiricism*.

The distinction between "empirical" scholars and other types of scholars is also frequently reduced to one of data analysis: "empirical" scholars use objective, replicable, quantitative methods, while "critical" scholars use subjective, and hence less "rigorous," qualitative modes of analysis. The central issue here, however, is not "counting" versus "interpreting" but rather the adequacy of the particular conceptualization and analysis to the phenomenon being explained. Few social scholars of whatever philosophical stripe would deny that data analysis expressed as numbers is useful in explaining some aspects of culture. It makes perfect sense to express demographic and geographical data on soap opera audiences, for example, in proportions of total households or households using television, relative frequency of viewing among various demographic categories, and so forth. By the same token, the complaint made by researchers oriented toward quantification that qualitative analysis is sometimes unnecessarily imprecise should not be dismissed out of hand. What is important here is the relationship between the nature of the object being studied and the manner by which that object is taken up ("operationalized" in social-scientific jargon) within a particular conceptual and explanatory framework and, *mutatis mutandis*, the effects of the latter upon "knowledge" generated about the former.

In an attempt to bring social inquiry into the model of research offered by the natural sciences, media researchers have attempted to break down complex social phenomena into their constituent parts, believing that aggregated knowledge about controlled aspects of the whole would eventually yield knowledge about phenomena too complex to fit the natural science model. As Gerald Miller puts the problem, "Generalizations referring to the conjoint influence of several dozen variables are neither scientifically satisfying nor practically useful."[7] This assessment of the epistemological status of knowledge of "generalizations" about complex social phenomena might well be accurate—that is, they might be neither "scientifically satisfying," in an empiricist sense of universal laws, nor "practically useful," in the sense of predictability. But this does not warrant the empiricist assumption that knowledge of complex social phenomena *can* be gained by forcing them to yield to the demands of quantitative analysis. The question for us then becomes, What is the "fit" between the complexity of the soap opera text and its reception as objects of social inquiry and the explanatory power of the analytical framework provided by empiricist mass communications research?

## Content Analysis

A few audience analyses of soap operas have been published since 1972;[8] analyses of soap operas as texts, however, have been more common. More than one-third of the seventy-six scholarly works on soap operas mentioned in the 1982 bibliography are textual analyses. Almost without exception, the method employed in these studies is *content analysis*. Bernard Berelson, one of the pioneers of content analysis in mass communications research, defined it as "a research technique for the objective, systematic, and quantitative description of the manifest content of communication."[9] The content analyst devises categories of "content" and counts the relative frequency of occurrence within the text. The text is thus transformed into quantifiable data so that it might be compared to something else—other texts, the occurrence of certain features elsewhere, the normative occurrence across a group of texts, and so forth. The aim of content analysis of soap operas is frequently to assess the degree to which they present distortions of the "real world." The "world" of the soap opera has been compared to the "real world" in such categories as occupational and sex roles, alcohol use, causes of death and disease, interpersonal communication patterns, and sexual behavior. It is easy to see that content analysis represents the application of empiricist social science to the study of texts and, as such, suffers from the same limitations that undermine empiricist investigations of other phenomena. In the case of content analysis of soap operas, as in other texts, however, the problems of empiricist research in general are compounded because what is being observed for its regularities is not some aspect of a real-life society but a fictional construction.

Since 1977 researchers at the State University of New York at Buffalo have conducted systematic investigations of various aspects of soap operas as part of "Project Daytime." Most prominent among these studies have been content analyses, which form the heart of one of the first scholarly books (if not the first) devoted entirely to soap operas, *Life on Daytime Television: Tuning-In American Serial Drama*, edited by Mary Cassata and Thomas Skill and published in 1983. As these studies represent the most recent and extensive textual analyses of soap operas conducted from an empiricist perspective, it is here that the strengths of content analysis should be most in evidence.

Representative of the content analysis in the book, and of those conducted by empiricist researchers elsewhere, is "Life and Death in the Daytime Television Serial: A Content Analysis," by Cassata, Skill, and Samuel O. Boadu. In it they ask, "What is the effect of all this sickness and death [in soap operas] on the audience? Does it have any impact at all? And if so, is it good or bad?" As a first step in answering these questions, the researchers conducted a content analysis of "all the health-related conditions reported to have happened in the serial dramas" in 1977. On the basis of plot summaries of thirteen soaps, 191 occurrences of health-related conditions among 341 characters were recorded, and the frequency of various types of conditions was compared to the statistical incidence of these conditions in the "real life" population. Mental illness was found to be the most common disease in soaps and murder the leading cause of death. The rate of fatal motor vehicle accidents in soap operas was 5.3 per 100 persons, compared with only .022 per 100 in real life. Among the "startling findings" of this study is the discovery that of the seven professional people who succumbed to mental illness five were doctors or nurses and two were writers.

The researchers concluded that in soap operas most people suffer because "they are unable to cope." "Most of their mental stress is tied to their specific life situation; the solutions they apply to solve their problems might possibly serve as guides to the viewer for solving similar problems." That death, suffering, and physical impairment in the soap opera world were visited upon characters and not real people was seen as irrelevant: "Whether the health problems portrayed are real or imagined is not as critical as their appearance of reality. At the very least, the problems, large and small, are happening to people who are real to the viewer." Since soap characters are perceived as real, soap operas can potentially serve as direct transmitters of values: "Generally, because physical impairment comes more often as a result of accidents rather than disease, and because soap opera people are more apt to die as a result of an accident sustained in the outside world rather than from illness, we believe that soap opera viewers who are hospitalized, institutionalized, or homebound because they are suffering from the same illnesses, probably feel secure not to be out in the real world where they might too sustain injuries and die."

This and other content analyses of soap operas operate on the basis of several undemonstrated assumptions. The first is that there is an equivalence in signification between the unit of content extracted from the text and the meaning of that unit as it functions as a part of the text. On the face of it, this would seem to be an unproblematic assumption: alcohol is alcohol; its function and consequences carry over from the real world to that of the soap opera unchanged, so that if a character drinks a fifth of bourbon we can expect him to get drunk, just as a real person would. But the construction of a fictional world from elements of the experiential world of the reader is not a process of transplantation but of transmutation. The text represents a selection of conventions from the "real world," but these conventions are recombined within the fictive context of the narrative. In this process of reorganization their functions in the real world are partially stripped away in order that they might "fit" into the world of the text.

In the study cited above knowledge of the function of a traffic accident, violent act, or coma within a particular text was irrelevant. The "texts" examined were not even the soap opera episodes themselves but plot synopses. In none of the content analyses in the Cassata-Skill book is there any indication whether the "encoders" (those who reduce the text to regularities) have ever seen the soaps they encode or not. And, in fact, within the framework of empiricist content analysis there is an argument to be made that prior knowledge of the text reduces the objectivity of the encoder and thus is to be guarded against. The meanings of accidents, sexual acts, conversations, occupations, disease, death, or birth are derived entirely from their functions in the real world and not necessarily from their functions in the texts of which they are parts. A content analysis of Shakespeare's tragedies, based on plot synopses, would no doubt find that they present a "distorted" picture of Elizabethan life, with more murders, accidents, infidelities, and domestic quarrels than were experienced by the population at large. Connected to the failure of content analysis to distinguish between fictive and nonfictive textual systems is the implicit belief that soaps function to represent the real world, that they are to be judged and are read as exclusively mimetic in nature. In another study in the book Cassata and Skill wonder: "How does she [the female soap opera character] compare to women in America today? Does she portray women as they really are, or is she an unrealistic product of some writer's imagination? Is she presenting women as they should be, or as they should not be?" And in another they ask, "How do these people in the soap opera world compare to their counterparts in the real world?"[10]

Every fictive narrative appropriates some aspects of the reader's world; otherwise it would be unintelligible. And it is no doubt the case that in some respects the world of the soap opera appears to be an asymptote of the "real world." But this by no means warrants the conflation of the one with the other or the assumption that viewers read soap operas as mirror images (funhouse or otherwise) of their own or anyone else's lives. In fact, one of the Cassata-Skill studies provides evidence to the contrary. In "Soap Opera Women: An Audience View" they collected the responses of 1,576 women to a survey in an issue of *Soap Opera Digest*. The women were asked to name their favorite female soap opera characters and to indicate if they portrayed "women" "as they really are," "unrealistically," or "somewhat between realistic and unrealistic." They hypothesized that since the southern United States was more traditional in its values, responses of southern soap opera viewers would "reflect a more traditional view of women through the selection of rather conservative 'favorite characters.'" When no differences in this regard were found between southern and northern viewers, they attributed it to "television's ability to homogenize our culture."

Of course a number of alternative explanations could be constructed, but one just as plausible is that this finding is an illustration of the difference maintained in soap opera texts, as well as in the minds of viewers, between fictive worlds and their own. Cassata and Skill were also surprised that many viewers (particularly younger ones) did not find their favorite characters entirely "believable": "It was our assumption that viewers would find it difficult to involve themselves with a favorite character who lacked believability." They attribute this discrepancy to the "lack of depth" in the portrayal of younger people on soap operas. They were similarly puzzled by the large number of respondents (38 percent of the total survey and 48 percent of teenage viewers) who had "no opinion" when asked whether their favorite character "represented women as they should be" and by the fact that viewers from certain demographic groups did not choose favorite characters who matched those characteristics. The first "anomaly" provides support for the view that experiential plausability cannot be equated with the pleasure viewers derive from soap operas; characters are read as characters by viewers and not as people from down the street. The "no opinion" response should have been a clue to the researchers that one of their basic premises—that soap operas hold a mirror up to society—is ill founded or at least unacknowledged by many viewers.

The insistence upon making soap operas an appendage of the "real world" is perhaps most telling in the empiricist refusal to distinguish "characters" in soap operas from "people" in the real world and in the assumption that viewers are equally unable to do so. In these studies, accidents happen not merely to fictional characters but to "people who are real to the viewer." In another study the researchers ask, "To what extent do people imitate the behaviors of those fictional characters who become so much a part of their lives that they seem closer than family or friends?"[11]

Much of the fear that soap operas serve as transmitters of values and molders of behavior is based upon the belief that soap opera characters are read as "people who are real to the viewer." Once again the complex relationship between soap operas and their viewers has been greatly oversimplified. Soaps do engender a high degree of loyalty in many viewers, and because of the constant interaction between viewers and characters over years and, in some cases, decades, it might seem that some viewers know their favorite characters better than they know real persons in their immediate environment. We frequently speak of fictional characters, televised and otherwise, as if they were endowed with volition and enjoyed a life beyond the limits of their fictional realms, but this does not mean that in so doing we cease to recognize that they are but fictive constructs, either words on a page or actors in roles, and not flesh-and-blood human beings.

Much is made of letters sent by overly-ardent fans to warn soap characters of impending danger and of actors who play villainous roles being accosted in department stores by outraged viewers. Yet there is no reason to believe that the proportion of soap opera viewers unable to distinguish fiction from reality is higher than that of the audience for any other form of narrative entertainment. Given the fact that, as content analysts frequently point out, soap opera characters are endlessly subjected to an "unrealistic" amount of pain, suffering, tragedy, disease, and death, regarding them as real people would render soap opera viewing a psychically intolerable ordeal on the order of spending every afternoon at the emergency room of the local hospital watching the ambulances being unloaded.

What is denied to soap opera viewers in content analyses is the possibility of aesthetic experience, for central to that experience is an essential distance—however small—between the reader and the world of the narrative. However close the reader or viewer pulls the fictive world toward him or her by endowing it with aspects of the "real world," this pull toward reality is counterbalanced by the text's fictional status. Thus its inherent and necessary unreality is preserved.

## The Limits of Empiricist Knowledge

Restricted to explanation by quantification and dependent upon a spurious equivalency between the "real world" of the viewer and the fictional world of the soap opera, content analysis winds up telling us little about the relationship between soap opera texts and their viewers. Without some conception of what a narrative fictive text is and how it operates and without a corresponding conception of how that text is read and incorporated in and by the reader, the world of the soap and that of the evening news become indistinguishable—which they clearly are not. This brings us back full circle to the refusal of both critics and social scientists to acknowledge the soap opera as aesthetic object and to an image of the soap opera viewer that is directly descended from one of forty years before.

In the absence of aesthetic mediation, the relationship between viewer and soap continues to be seen as one of teacher/pupil, role-model/emulator, manipulator/manipulated. In the first essay in their book, Cassata and Skill, along with coauthor Michelle Lynn Rodina, cite as "a psychological formula which underlays the typical soap opera" Arnheim's 1944 assessment that "radio serials attract the listener by offering her a portrait of her own shortcomings, which lead to constant trouble, and of her inability to help herself." They even enlist Warner and Henry in support of one of their modeling hypotheses, quoting that portion of the conclusion of their 1948 study which claims that soap operas "contributed to the integration of their [listeners'] lives into the world in which they live." This perpetuation of a notion of the soap opera viewer that was already problematic when it was formulated in the early 1940s can be ascribed in part to the empiricist subject/object dichotomy, in which the ostensible object of study and "facts" about it are presumed to be entirely separate from the conceptualization of that object and the manner by which it is investigated. Thus what Warner and Henry or Arnheim conceived soap operas and soap opera listeners to be is not seen as having a predispositional effect on the "facts" they "find" about them. Empiricism, in its desire to be a cumulative science, encourages the piling up of "facts" and the assumption that the referents of these facts—the meanings attached to soap operas and their viewers in language and discourse—are themselves objective and unchanging. Everyone "knows" what a soap opera is. The complex interchange between conceptualization and conceptualized, object in discourse and object of discourse, becomes merely an accumulation of facts. In the process this peculiar formulation of what a soap opera is or is not and of what it means to be a soap opera listener or viewer is unwittingly handed down intact from year to year, study to study, "fact" to amassed "fact."

Based upon an epistemology that admits only of explanation as an expression of regularity and confronted by an object of study (the relationship of the mass media to the social and cultural worlds of which they are a part) that adamantly refuses to be reduced to such regularity, empiricist mass communications research faces a dilemma. One response has been to develop more and more subtle statistical procedures in an attempt to describe "hidden" regularities among complex data sets. But even when such procedures result in the discovery of "significant" regularities, they also produce greater uncertainty as to the meaning of those regularities. The complexity of statistical operations in social science increases in direct proportion to the degree of "openness" of the system being investigated. But since "significance" in a statistical sense refers only to a negative probability (that a regularity was *not* the result of chance) and says nothing about what that regularity actually signifies, the more variables represented in the object of study, the less can be said, beyond the observation that part of the operation of the system occurs by some mechanism or interaction of mechanisms that is nonrandom. Furthermore, the more open the system being investigated, the less likely the same description of regularity will apply to "similar" systems or to the same system at a different point in time. While the model of empiricist social science might be based upon that of laboratory science, the latter, as Lee Thayer puts it, "predicts nothing that it does not control or that is not otherwise fully determined. . . . One cannot successfully study relatively open systems with methods that are appropriate only for closed systems." Thayer provocatively asks: "Is it possible that this is the kind of mentality [empiricism] that precludes its own success?"[12]

Another response to the limitations of empiricist explanation in mass communications research has been to circumscribe its object of study, leaving one that more readily yields to explanation by regularity. However, this strategy quickly becomes the social science equivalent of what David Hackett Fischer calls the "quantitative fallacy" in historical inquiry: the belief that "unless a thing can be measured quantitatively, it does not exist significantly." Fischer compares this mode of thinking to the behavior of the man in a story told by Abraham Kaplan in his book *The Conduct of Inquiry*: "There is a story of a drunkard searching under a street lamp for his house key, which he had dropped some distance away. Asked why he didn't look where he had dropped it, he replied, 'It's lighter here!'"[13] George Comstock's metaphor is different, but his point is the same, one directed specifically toward American mass media research:

> There is a tendency to avoid the reality of the media in favor of that captured by theory and empiricism. It is as if we had before us a double-column page, with research on one side and the mass media, in all their phenomenal reality on the other—the sitcom, the *film noir*, Francis Ford Coppola, the *New York Post*, the *Los Angeles Times*—and read with a hand over that media column. There is reductionism in research that implies a continuing conceptual anxiety among those who practice communications research, and which that hand covers up to avoid it.[14]

The harnessing of elements of an open system so that they might be examined in isolation (free from confounding variables) is, in the extreme case, tantamount to studying the operation of the automobile engine by taking out each component, one by one, and staring at it for awhile. Many mass communications researchers share an implicit faith that however insignificant the object of analysis in any given study, their findings, when placed among those of thousands of other researchers, will automatically add up to an understanding of the whole, but this faith is misplaced. Thayer suggests that the explosion in mass communications research since World War II

> is not attributable to great achievements but to ever more fragmentation. We "gain" by knowing more and more about less and less. Fragmentation also comes from the delusion that the analytically smaller unit is somehow "realer" and more empirical. Actual people in actual life circumstances make for a situation that is much too messy and complex. Not only is it more scientific sounding to deal with fragments; it is also a whole lot safer.[15]

But let us suppose that the goal of empiricist knowledge of the mass media were to be reached, and researchers were able to formulate a set of covering laws on the basis of which future developments could be predicted. What then has been gained in our knowledge of the phenomena these laws account for? As Russell Keat and others have pointed out, empiricists confuse predictive power with knowledge.[16] The ability to subsume a set of events under a covering law does not mean that we understand how and why those events came about.

It would be shortsighted to dismiss out of hand the entire body of research generated by mass communications researchers working within the empiricist problematic. The issues addressed (What is the effect of soap operas upon their viewers? How is the soap opera world like or different from that of the viewer?) are important ones—even if the questions are framed in ways that reveal preconceived notions regarding "who" those viewers are and what those "effects" are likely to be. It would be equally shortsighted, however, to accept unquestioningly the "results" of these studies as knowledge of the phenomena they claim to explain. The claims of empiricist research must be considered in relation to the activation of its object of study within its discourse (in this case, the soap opera in all its encrustation), the correspondence between that object and its "operationalization" in particular studies, the likely effects of the research method employed, and the ontological and epistemological assumptions made by empiricism in general.

Regardless of how much can be salvaged from empiricist research on soap operas, they represent one of those "messy and complex" phenomena that for the most part will remain inaccessible to, and, hence, unexplained by, research under that model. We need to reconceptualize soap opera as an object of study, accepting rather than combatting its complexity and acknowledging our limitations in grasping that complexity. The following chapters represent not the application of a single "alternative" approach but several different lines of inquiry corresponding to some of the more prominent features of the relationship between soap operas and their audiences. These lines of inquiry converge upon and lead out from the point at which the individual soap opera reader confronts and chooses to engage the narrative world represented through sounds and images on the television screen. The reading moment represents an interaction between text and reader, between the results of specific encoding practices that cause the reader to recognize a soap opera *as* a soap opera and decoding practices that endow those sounds and images with meanings.

These sounds and images do not arrive on the viewer's television screen magically, of course, nor are they innocently presented merely to entertain. The enormous resources of the commercial broadcasting industry are brought to bear upon individual viewers and their readings of the soap opera, and it would be difficult to consider soap operas without looking at how they function within the social and economic institution that produces them. Moreover, the viewer comes to the reading act not only as an individual viewer but also (and in the case of soap operas, perhaps more importantly) as an individual occupying a particular position within society. Soap operas have long been considered a "woman's" form and viewers to be for that reason "different" from other viewers; thus it is only a short leap from looking at the act of soap opera reading to a consideration of the social meaning of that act. Finally, the act of soap opera reading exists within history and, in part at least, as a result of historical forces that have conditioned both the production of the soap opera text and its "consumption" by readers. This directs us "back" from any particular instance of soap opera engagement to an attempt to specify those forces (or "generative mechanisms," as I shall call them) and their interrelations.

# The Soap Opera as Commodity
# and Commodifier

The soap opera is hardly unique among narrative forms in having an economic raison d'être. Our access to novels and films is in large measure regulated by the forces of the marketplace: only those likely to make a profit for some person or corporate entity are likely to be published or produced. In both cases we purchase an opportunity to engage in the reading act. The economic exchange involved in watching American commercial television, and more particularly the soap opera, however, is more subtle than that which occurs when one buys a book or a ticket for a movie. Since the advent of cable television, network broadcasters have taken to calling their medium "free" television, as opposed to the pay-for-service system of cable. And in a sense commercial television is free, in that it involves no direct payment by the viewer for programming. But in return for being provided with programming, the viewer becomes a commodity: he or she is "sold" to advertisers in lots of one thousand. One does not have to be a cynic to hold the view that television transforms viewers into units of economic exchange. Perhaps the most cogent description of what motors commercial television comes from veteran television journalist Les Brown:

> The game of television is basically between the network and the advertiser, and the Nielsen digits determine what the latter will pay for the circulation of his commercial. The public is involved only as the definition of the number: so many persons 18–49, so many others, all neatly processed by television.
>
> In day-to-day commerce, television is not so much interested in the business of communications as in the business of delivering people to advertisers. People are the merchandise, not the shows. The shows are merely the bait.
>
> The consumer, whom the custodians of the medium are pledged to serve, is in fact served up.[1]

Viewed in this light, the soap opera text is but a context for the messages of the corporations that "sponsor" the soap opera's presentation. Obviously, however, it is that "context" which attracts the viewer and sustains his or her attention between commercials. What the viewer experiences as the world of *Guiding Light* or *One Life to Live* is not only the result of stylistic and narrative conventions but also, if not primarily, the product of institutional imperatives—imperatives not felt so directly in the production of narratives less fully penetrated by capital. Thus before discussing the processes by which soap operas are read, we would do well to review the processes by which they are constructed as texts and produced as economic vehicles.

## Soap Opera's Mode of Production

As we have seen, early aesthetic discourse on the soap opera emphasized the similarities between soap opera production and the manufacture of other "products." This is both an insightful and a misleading analogy. The production of soap opera texts does represent an application of the organizational and management strategies of industrial capitalism to textual production—strategies also applied to almost every other sphere of cultural production in the twentieth century as well—but it is highly reductionistic then to equate the manufacture of bars of soap with the production of soap operas. The absolute standardization required for the mass production of consumer items is inapplicable to the production of narratives. The consumer expects each bar of Ivory Soap to be exactly like the last one purchased, but he or she expects each new movie or episode of a television program to bear marks of difference.

### MASS PRODUCTION AND TEXT CREATION

Janet Staiger has investigated the transformation of early film production from a cottage industry in the 1890s and early 1900s to Hollywood's rationalized and standardized "factory" system of the late 1910s. She identifies three key components of this change: mass production, detailed division of labor, and the development of a written blueprint (the script) from which individual films were constructed.[2] In its mode of production, the contemporary soap opera can be seen as the end point of this historical process: the industrial system of production control loosely employed by the Holly-

## Commodity and Commodifier

wood studios is, by institutional necessity, fully embraced in the production of soap operas.

The economic structure of American commercial television is predicated upon habitual viewing. Advertisers learned long ago that a single "impression" (one exposure of the reader to an advertising message) usually had little impact upon purchasing behavior. In order for the prospective consumer to remember a product at the purchase point, the name and superior qualities of a product must be repeatedly reinforced. And in order for this to occur, the viewer must be available to the advertiser on a regular and predictable basis. Thus, beginning with network radio and culminating in network television, the regularizing of viewer attention has been an axiom of programming policy. The viewer must be encouraged not just to tune in for a single program but to submit to the "flow" of programming throughout an entire evening. The viewer must also be able to anticipate that next Sunday night's fare will be the same, but different: the Cartwrights will once again be found in Virginia City, but they will face a "new" problem. The demise of showcase drama is testimony to the primacy of regularization over innovation in television programming strategy. The series format can exploit viewer interest in a set of characters and a basic plot situation week after week; the self-contained drama or comedy cannot.

In the soap opera advertisers and broadcasters have found the ideal vehicle for the reinforcement of advertising impressions and the best means yet devised for assuring regular viewing. In a single week *General Hospital* can deliver more advertising impressions than *M*A*S*H* could in over two months. After twenty weeks or so the prime-time viewer knows he or she will be subjected to as many weeks of reruns or "replacement" fare; the viewer of *Ryan's Hope* can confidently look forward to a new episode every weekday for as long as the show is on the air. Once a soap opera has become established, its audience is remarkably loyal. For a prime-time series to run ten years is considered extraordinary; for a soap opera it is the norm. Soap operas provide such a stable profit base that were it not for their predictable profitability, commercial television networks would be hard pressed to finance much more expensive and risky prime-time ventures. Thus, the soap opera is by nature and function a mass-produced narrative form. A soap opera presented in one-hour episodes requires the production of 260 hours of text each year, the continuous presentation of which is interrupted only by an occasional holiday or preemption for news coverage.

### DETAILED DIVISION OF LABOR

As Staiger discovered, the mass production of narrative texts requires a high degree of centralized control over the production process. In American film history, films could not be mass produced until fictional films shot in studios replaced the filmic coverage of news events as the industry's staple. In soap opera production, the demand that an hour's worth of text be produced each working day further demands that the world of Henderson or Oakdale be constructed in the space of two television studios, that each working day be utilized as efficiently as possible, and that all major production decisions already be made by the time of the shooting of a particular episode.

Such efficiency is not possible without detailed division of labor. The production process is divided into a series of tasks, and workers trained to perform each of them. The cameraman of the early film industry, who shot, edited, and at times projected films, had by the late 1910s been replaced by the production unit: producer, director, writer, cameraman, actors and editor. Sixty years later, the production of Hollywood films and network television episodes, and soap operas in particular, is even more fragmented, with craft union agreements assuring that workers perform only a limited range of tasks.

Inherent in a detailed division of labor is the separation of conception from execution. The product is conceived and designed at the management level and fabricated by "workers." Responsible for only a small portion of the overall production process, an individual worker need not have a grasp of the concept behind the product, nor will that worker be called upon to make design decisions or possess the skills required for any other production task. He or she merely implements decisions made well before his or her job begins.

Although the soap opera "worker's" task is more complex than that of the assembly-line laborer and the decision-making latitude greater, there is still a sharp division between the conception that governs the shape and direction of the soap opera world and its embodiment as a series of broadcast episodes. Decision-making power rests with a small group of persons perched at the top of the production hierarchy and purposely isolated from those who work beneath them.[3] In the six soap operas still owned by Procter and Gamble, conceptual and decision-making power emanates from its offices in Cincinnati and is exercised through the manager of daytime pro-

## Commodity and Commodifier

grams of its production subsidiary, Procter and Gamble Productions, Inc.[4] The manager of daytime programs hires key production and writing personnel for all six soaps, deals directly with the programming and business departments of the three commercial television networks, and is responsible for the overall financial and creative management of the shows. An associate manager directly oversees the operations of the six separate soap opera production companies. He (both positions have been filled only by men) is assisted by five supervising producers, who represent Procter and Gamble's interests in the management of each show. The person actually responsible for the day-to-day operation of each production company in New York (where all six Procter and Gamble soaps are produced) is its executive producer, who serves as liaison between the production site and management in Cincinnati. For those soap operas not owned by Procter and Gamble, ultimate control rests with the television network itself, exercised through its daytime programming department.

Muriel Cantor and Suzanne Pingree maintain that the source of creative control in soap opera production is the head writer: "It is generally recognized that prime-time television is a producer's medium, and that soap operas are a writer's medium. . . . All sources report that the head writer has the power, within the limits of the genre, to determine content."[5] But the head writer–as–auteur theory of soap opera production needs serious qualification. First, as Cantor and Pingree point out, the head writer is an employee of the network or Procter and Gamble and must either conform to programming policy or risk being fired. A writer's tenure with a particular soap may be brief indeed. The contractual agreement under which most writers operate binds them to their employer for a multiyear period, but allows the employer to dismiss a writer at the end of any thirteen-week period. In the summer of 1982, Pat Falken-Smith, the highest-paid writer in the history of broadcasting, left *General Hospital* and a reported salary of $1 million per year to assume the head writer position at *Guiding Light*. She was replaced after thirteen weeks. In the case of the six Procter and Gamble soaps, the head writer must submit the plans for the narrative and character development of the soap to company executives for their approval. In his memoirs, Harding LeMay, former head writer of *Another World*, details the sometimes stormy story conferences at which his plot outlines were scrutinized. There is little doubt that the changes that resulted in *General Hospital*'s dramatic leap in the ratings in the late 1970s were effected by executive producer, Gloria Monty, and not by any particular writer. At present, *Guiding Light* has no one bearing the title "head writer"; story projections are determined by producers and merely implemented by staff writers.

What Cantor and Pingree regard as "interference" in the creative process by producers is, from an institutional standpoint, the necessary exercise of "quality control." No soap opera writer operates under the delusion that the soap opera is a canvas upon which to bare his or her creative soul. The writer's job is to generate the largest possible audience of potential consumers of the sponsors' products. Narrative craft and artistry are certainly involved in this process, but it is craft measured in Nielson ratings points and advertising dollars, not in degree of creative freedom. Ironically, the very fact that so many viewers derive aesthetic satisfaction from soap operas precludes any romantic conception of the soap opera writer as expressive artist. To Procter and Gamble its soap operas represent a primary advertising vehicle, one capable of reaching tens of millions of their most important customers: women between the ages of eighteen and forty-nine. To the networks soap operas are a crucial profit base, generating nearly $1 billion in revenues and one-sixth of all network profits. With a single thirty-second commercial time slot selling for nearly thirty thousand dollars, *General Hospital* earns over fifty thousand dollars per week in profits for ABC-TV. Any definition of "art" that does not have as its goal the satisfaction of as many viewers as possible and concomitantly the most cost-efficient use of broadcast airtime is, in this context at least, irrelevant. The producer's job is to assure that narrative form follows economic function.

Network and Procter and Gamble executives also monitor the effectiveness of narrative developments and attempt to anticipate the effects of future plot and character decisions. With tens of thousands of dollars riding on each ratings point, Nielson survey results are followed closely each week. Given the sophisticated quantitative techniques that have been developed to measure and attempt to predict audience response, it is somewhat ironic that the commercial television networks and soap opera sponsors also place great stock in much less rigorous means of gauging audience preferences. Letters written to soap opera actors become the property of the production company, and each month tallies are kept on the number of pieces of fan mail each actor receives. An actor whose fan mail increases markedly is likely to figure more prominently in future plotlines; one whose popularity, as measured by viewer mail, declines precipitously might be consigned to the outskirts of the soap community or become a candidate for a fatal traffic accident. "Focus groups" are also employed to measure viewer likes and dislikes. A dozen or so women at a suburban shopping mall might be asked into a meeting room to view an upcoming episode of a given soap opera and then to discuss what they liked and disliked about it with a network or sponsor representative. Data thus derived about subplots, characters, and situations are likely to be used at story conferences in evaluating present and future narratives.

A writer is also constrained by the fact that the setting and community of characters have already been determined before he or she begins writing. Writing an ongoing soap opera is like contributing a few chapters to an already half-written novel whose first chapters have already been published and read by millions of eager readers. Whatever popularity the soap opera enjoys when a new writer takes over is based upon the audience's acceptance of the setting and character relationships to that point. The new writer cannot do violence to the expectations generated on the basis of this history without also risking the loss of that audience. Producers would not be acting in their own best interests if they allowed a writer's desire for innovation to destroy what the audience perceives as the essence of a given soap. Writers might be able to play fast and loose with the narrative entanglements of individual characters (particularly "outsider" characters brought into the community to fulfill a given plot function and then written out) but the deep-structural community basis of the soap opera world must abide.

Producers also take it as their responsibility to see that writers do not antagonize the viewing audience by presenting as acceptable within the soap opera world values and behaviors the producers believe to be unacceptable to a sizable portion of that audience. We will return to this issue again later, but suffice it to say at this point that producers, particularly those of Procter and Gamble soaps, are extremely sensitive to the relationship between mores of the soap world and what they perceive to be the mores of the real world.

### SCRIPT OUTLINE AS PRODUCTION BLUEPRINT

Working within the parameters outlined above, the soap opera writer extends the world of the soap opera into the future: developing new subplots, adding and deleting characters, activating portions of the network of character relationships. The head writer usually plans story lines six months ahead. Once approved, these subplots are broken down into outlines for each episode, indicating the action and dialogue to occur in each "act"—

that portion of text that occurs between commercial breaks. The outline for the "teaser" and first act of episode 1993 of *One Life to Live* (aired 21 April 1976) reads:

*Prologue*: We're going to a new day. We open on Carla in the cafeteria reading the Banner. It's 6:35 A. M. Carla sees the opening night ad for Tony Lord's Place. Cathy comes in with a cup of coffee. We'll establish that she's filling in for Anna on some volunteer work. Cathy sits with her coffee and sees the ad. Carla assumes she's going to the opening. (Ed and Carla are). Cathy has to admit she isn't. She and Tony still aren't seeing each other. Carla senses her ambivalence about it. She then suggests that Cathy should get a date and come with her and Ed. On Cathy's thoughtful reaction, we go to black.

*Act I*: This is a direct continuation in the hospital cafeteria. Cathy tells Carla she's practically become a spinster—she wouldn't even know where to start finding an escort at this point in her life. Peter suddenly appears, tray in hand. Carla makes some comment *sotto voce* about him before he approaches and asks if he can join them.

Carla asks Peter to sit down. We'll establish that he has not seen Cathy since the funeral and, while he has talked with Jenny on the telephone, he's interested in finding out how she really is. Cathy tells him Jenny seems to be doing all right. Cathy understands the terrible sense of loss Jenny feels, etc. Peter, of course, says he would do anything he could to help Jenny, but he realizes there is nothing he can do now. Only time will help.

Carla leaves, after reminding Cathy to let her know about tonight. Left alone with Peter, Cathy begins asking about his life here—is he enjoying himself, etc. Peter tells her it's not an easy time for him—all work, no play. So many bad things have happened. Cathy nods and says they have been for her, too. She then mentions the opening of the club tonight. Peter hasn't met Tony but has heard about the club from Dorina and/or Victor. Cathy asks him if he would like to go—dutch, of course, with Ed and Carla.

Peter laughs and makes some comment to the effect that in San Carlos it would all be different—the roles reversed, that is. But since he's in America, he had better begin living like an American. He'd love to go—but he's not willing to go dutch at all. As they smile at each other, she tells him they'll argue about that later and we—

Cut to Tony's place. It's now 10 A.M. and it would seem impossible that the place is going to open that night. The bartender is working behind the bar as Tony talks one-way to Wanda on the phone. (She's at the wholesale market to get some last minute items). An U/5 person ["under-five character": one with fewer than five lines of dialogue] is tuning the piano—in other words, there is a slight atmosphere of bedlam.

Tony has barely put the phone down when it rings again. Tony picks it up and, one-way learns from Chapin that Victor wants a reservation for four that night for dinner. Tony puts the phone down smiling. Will wonders never cease? With this—

We cut to the Lord library. Victor is there as Dorian enters. No matter how it's written, we want the audience to feel there is no way she will go to Tony's tonight. She would not say this outright. She would start perhaps by saying that Senator and Mrs. Charlton are in town and she told Olivia they'd dine with them at the country club. On Victor's gentle reminder that he told her he wanted to go to his son's opening, we go in on her face as she turns from him so he cannot see the fury she feels. Fade out.[6]

With only a few exceptions, the head writer works in isolation from other members of the production staff, rarely visiting the studio where the episodes are shot, and sometimes, in fact, living in another city. For the thirteen weeks that Pat Falken-Smith wrote *Guiding Light*, she lived in Los Angeles, although the show was shot in New York. The separation of the writer from the production process is as much by design as for the convenience of the writer. Douglas Marland, who has written four soap operas, says, "There's always been a big thing about keeping writers, particularly head writers, away from the actors." Producers believe that writers might be less willing to kill off characters portrayed by actors they have gotten to know personally.

Nor does the head writer usually work collaboratively with the associate writers, whose job it is to translate the script outlines into finished scripts. David R. Sirota's ethnomethodological study of soap opera writing began with the premise that soaps were the result of a group writing effort—all members of the writing team contributing ideas to the narrative outline. He chose *One Life to Live* as the object of his investigation, and telephoned Agnes Nixon, the soap's originator, to ask her permission to observe her interaction with other members of the writing team. "Clear enough were my intentions so as to prompt Mrs. Nixon to (unknowingly) shatter a basic assumption upon which our communication was based. It had never occurred to me that Agnes Nixon worked alone. There was no collaborative dimension to her writing."[7]

By the time the script outlines reach the associate writers (sometimes called "dialoguers"), a great deal of the conceptual decision-making power has already been exercised. The script outline has become that third element necessary for the mass production: a blueprint on the basis of which the final product is assembled.

## EXECUTION

The job of the associate writers is not so much to add anything to the outline as to translate it from narrative précis to action and dialogue that will fill the logistical and temporal requirements of soap opera production. A one-hour script for *Guiding Light* is 30½ pages long, beginning on line 17 of the first page, using 29 lines per page. Nancy Franklin, who has worked as an associate writer since 1976, says of the relationship between herself and the head writer (in this case, Douglas Marland): "I think of it as an architect and a builder; Douglas is the architect, he gives me the plans and then I build it." The analogy is also apt in that most associate writers are employed directly by the head writer: he or she is paid a salary to produce the scripts needed for the soap opera; whether the work is then partially subcontracted to associate writers is of no concern to the producers. Like the head writers, associate writers usually work alone, apart from both the head writer and the studio. Although she had been one of three associate writers on *Guiding Light* for nearly two years, Nancy Franklin did not meet her fellow dialoguers until they were awarded an Emmy for best writing on a daytime dramatic serial in 1982.

Franklin's analogy of her job with that of a builder's must be qualified in one key respect: she is like a builder who seldom, if ever, visits the building site. Associate writers would probably not be recognized by the actors whose lines they write. The associate writer's task is clearly bounded. He or she moves one chunk of the soap opera narrative (an episode) several steps closer to realization on the television screen. The nature and direction of narrative movement within that episode, however, have already been determined before the associate writer begins work, and the writer is powerless to influence its actualization on the set. While writing dialogue for *Guiding Light*, Nancy Franklin talked with head writer Douglas Marland almost every day on the telephone, but she has never been asked for a story idea, nor has she proffered one. "It's not my place to suggest and I never have," she says. "This is not a committee."[8]

Once a script has been returned to the head writer for approval, it is ready to be produced. It goes first to the show's producer, who notes any special logistical requirements, the sets called for, which actors will be involved in what scenes, and so forth. The producer is responsible for overseeing the costs of production as well. One of the reasons for the longevity of the soap opera form and its successful transition from radio to television is its low cost relative to other narrative forms. Hour for hour, soap operas are much less expensive to produce than prime-time programming. The script is then duplicated and distributed to the actors. Although this varies from soap to soap and from month to month within a given soap, actors usually do not receive their scripts until a week or so before they will be shot. An episode is generally aired a week or two after it is shot. Shooting an hour-long episode of a soap opera requires two "shifts" of workers, two studios, and a twelve-hour day. Scenes are grouped so that all of those involving the same set can be shot in one studio either in the morning or in the afternoon and so that a given actor will be required only for one shift. The first-shift actors arrive at the studio around 7:30. There is a brief line rehearsal before makeup and costuming. Once everyone is on the set, a blocking run-through enables the director to finalize camera positions and editing cues. The scene is then shot "live-tape" (each scene recorded by multiple cameras in real time) and, it is hoped, only once. The second shift arrives around noon in time for mid-afternoon shooting in a second studio. While shooting is taking place in studio 2, carpenters and set decorators are readying studio 1 for the following morning's scenes. The episode is "in the can" by early evening.

Unlike the director of a Hollywood film, the director of a soap opera is allowed only an extremely limited repertoire of visual flourishes. As can be seen in the extract from the *One Life to Live* script outline, some shots are called for in the script itself. Soap opera's adaptation of the stylistic conventions of the Hollywood cinema (to be discussed in the following chapter) further restricts the range of directorial "innovation." Our conception of the expressive, visionary artist, inherited from the Romantics, leads us to regard such stylistic limitations as the suppression of artistic creativity. Aesthetic effect proceeds from artistic freedom. In the direction of a soap opera episode, however, as in the writing, authorial intervention can detract from the text's aesthetic effect rather than contribute to it. In order to "work" on us most effectively the soap opera world must appear to be autochthonous—an unauthored, autonomous, self-generating realm existing alongside the world of the viewer. Its driving mechanisms must appear to be internal and not imposed upon it by the exertion of forces beyond or behind it; it must be "another world."

Authorial anonymity is also a requirement of the soap opera production situation. Because creation of the soap opera text is ongoing, its world and characters cannot bear the mark of a particular creator. Central characters and relationships must survive changes in writers. Furthermore, there may be as many as four or five dialogue writers working on a single soap—all writing lines for the same characters but in different episodes. If the character is not to be perceived by the audience as schizophrenic, idiosyncratic differences in dialogue writing styles must be eliminated; the character must speak with a single voice. Similarly, no one director could withstand the pressures of directing five hour-long soap opera episodes each week; hence, several are employed, each directing an episode or two each week. Their styles must be indistinguishable, since if viewers were aware of directoral interventions, their attention to the events unfolding in the soap opera world would be distracted.

Perhaps because the soap world appears to be unauthored, the role played by soap opera actors in the construction of that world is the most misunderstood facet of soap production. The open-endedness of the soap opera narrative, combined with the extra-textual "visibility" of many soap opera actors, helps create the impression that actors might be able to influence, if not determine, the fates of their characters. Fan magazines, *Soap Opera Digest*, and the actors themselves are usually careful to leave the relationship between an actor and his or her soap opera character vague, in order to preserve the possibility in the mind of the viewer that characters are, in part at least, products of the volition of actors. In fact, soap opera actors play no determining role in deciding the actions of their characters. They "know" about their characters' fates only as much as each script tells them.

Soap opera acting is but another example of detailed division of labor: the execution of actors' tasks does not depend upon their knowing the conception behind them. It is rare that a soap actor meets the writers who write his or her character's dialogue and even rarer that that actor will be asked for an opinion of it. Charita Bauer, who has played the character of Bert Bauer on *Guiding Light* since its television debut in June 1952, has been consulted twice in those thirty-plus years about a projected story line concerning her character: once when her character's (presumably) dead husband was written back into the story and, more recently (1984), when Bauer agreed to use the amputation of her leg as the basis for a plot line involving the same tragedy befalling Bert Bauer.[9]

Illustrative of the limited control an actor exercises over his or her character is the present controversy over improvisation. Several years ago actor Tony Geary persuaded producers and writers at *General Hospital* that the impulsive nature of his character required that he be allowed to depart from the exact lines written for his character. The overall meaning of the lines would be preserved, but his "improvisation" of their delivery would lend a convincing spontaneity to his role. Geary's success with this strategy has prompted other actors to request the same degree of "freedom" in their performances. For the most part, writers and producers have been adamant in their opposition to this trend, arguing that there is no time on the day of shooting to experiment with the delivery of dialogue. But this logistical objection belies a deeper resistance. Opening up the production process to change on the studio floor would threaten the entire system of production control so carefully maintained at each stage of text creation. The head writer depends upon the script outline "blueprint" being followed at each production level once it leaves his or her hands. An actor's unwitting nuance or slip of the tongue might inadvertently sabotage a plot line. "Quality control" cannot be assured if product design is altered on the shop floor.

The power of actors is also greatly limited by the nature of the soap opera text itself. Although recent years have seen the development of soap opera "stars," the soap opera remains a textual system dependent upon not individual characters but an entire community of characters for its aesthetic effect and popular appeal. Actors, like writers, are bound to the production company for several years, but the company can release them during the first year of the contract after any thirteen-week period and thereafter at twenty-six-week intervals. Actors and producers alike know that the loss of any given actor will not irremediably harm the ratings of a soap opera; the community will survive any individual tragedy. When Eileen Fulton, who had played a central character on *As the World Turns* for two decades, decided to leave soap operas, her role was simply assumed by another actress, and life in Oakdale went on as usual. The community-centered nature of the soap opera world gives soap actors much less leverage in their dealings with production companies than their prime-time counterparts. In 1980, Larry Hagman, star of the successful prime-time serial *Dallas*, used his deathbed hiatus (the "Who Shot J. R.?" summer) as a convenient opportunity to negotiate a new contract. Hagman effectively argued that to many viewers his character *was Dallas*, and that his leaving the show would cause irreparable damage. No soap actor has ever been able to make the same case or extract the same contractual concessions.

## The Soap Opera as Text and Commodity

Each soap opera episode simultaneously represents two textual hierarchies, depending upon whether it is viewed from the perspective of its viewers or from that of its producers. To the viewer, the primary textual system of the soap opera is the fictive world it creates and maintains. Periodically, this world is suspended and a secondary textual system, the commercial, inserted. To the institution of commercial broadcasting, however (subsuming networks, local stations, advertising agencies, production companies, and sponsors), the world of the soap opera is but a pretext (both in the sense of preceding and of serving as an excuse) for the presentation of commercial messages. It would be silly to argue that the soap opera is either one textual hierarchy or the other: if the soap did not serve an economic function as an advertising vehicle, it would certainly vanish overnight, and unless many viewers derived aesthetic pleasure from the world of the soap opera, its economic utility would be nil.

Early writers on the soap opera viewed its unabashedly mercenary nature as some sort of aesthetic sedition. The soap opera was to them a narrative form whose aesthetic possibilities had been completely undermined by capitalism. Their insistence upon identifying this mercantile "brainwashing" with a female "mentality" is symptomatic of their inability or unwillingness to see that for American commercial broadcasting narrative forms *could serve no other function*. By turning broadcasting over to commercial interests in the 1920s, the state had established profits as the force determining how the public utility would be used. The soap opera has attracted notoriety in part because it happens to be the most effective and efficient means yet devised to generate those profits. It is not economistic to declare that the soap opera "exists" for one purpose: to sell consumer products.

We can deal with this paradox in several ways. One is to refuse to admit soap operas (and, by extension, all commercial broadcasting programming) to the realm of aesthetic experience, accounting for their appeal instead on the basis of personality deficiencies, morbid curiosity, gender, or some other factor that distinguishes "them" (soap viewers) from us. We might also simply consign soap operas and all other forms of commercial broadcasting to the category of capitalist cultural production, assuming that since all such programming serves the same function, it all has the same effect.

There are certainly other ways of reducing the conceptual tension of this paradox, but how much better it would be to regard this paradox as something not to be explained away but to be accepted as an accurate, if intellectually uncomfortable, description of cultural production under modern capitalism. Viewers ("we," not "them") both enjoy soap operas (and other forms of commercial broadcasting) *and* are commodified in the process. This does not mean that as critics we must simply accept this situation as an unchallenged "given," but if we are to understand what the soap opera "is," and why it looks and sounds as it does, it will not be by suppressing its paradoxical nature. Both the fact that audiences enjoy watching soap operas and the fact that they are advertising vehicles by which huge corporations derive equally huge profits must be taken into account.

A related paradox presented by the soap opera is the apparently inverse correlation between individual artistic intervention and aesthetic effect. The more unauthored the world of the soap appears to be, the greater is its effect. We might deal with this puzzling situation by denying aesthetic status to the soap opera, since there is no "artist" whose vision shapes its world and to whom the audience refers meaning. Conversely, we might recognize that modern technology and the application of principles of industrial production to cultural production have further constricted what were always inherent limitations of artistic invention in any work, and we might conclude on the basis of the soap opera that our conception of the role of the artist in the aesthetic experience needs to be revised.

The soap opera brings to the forefront important facets of both cultural production and cultural reception that traditional aesthetics has tended to ignore. First, no artist creates ex nihilo. Artists work within aesthetic, social, ideological, and economic contexts that condition and severely limit the nature and extent of their contributions to artistic production. Second, texts are not simply endowed with meaning by their creators; readers construct their own meanings through their interactions with the text. In the case of the soap opera, the role of any particular participant in the creative process is so circumscribed, the text created so immense, and the reading process so crucial that the Romantic view of the artist is rendered conspicuously anachronistic. Again, the soap opera is not unique among modern cultural products in this regard; it is just that it confronts us with these issues in a particularly direct fashion.

# A Reader-Oriented Poetics of the Soap Opera

The term "encrustation," which I have borrowed from Tony Bennett and others to describe the accretion of meanings around soap operas, needs here to be qualified in order to reflect not only the discursive loading that has occurred in aesthetic and social science discourses but also the concomitant "unloading" of other potential meanings of soap operas. Specifically, soap operas have been denied any status as fictive textual system, even though they are an aesthetic phenomenon of sufficient subtlety and complexity to have successfully engaged the imaginations of millions of readers for over half a century. Content analysis denies the soap opera's textuality by reducing it to quantitative data, while it denies the soap opera's fictive status by assuming that readers regard episodes as they would aspects of the "real world." The critic working within the problematic of traditional aesthetics refuses to engage the soap opera as aesthetic object. Even writers on popular culture who have elevated some categories of television programming to the status of art have found it difficult, if not impossible, to admit soap operas to the new canon—even where it would be logical for them to do so.[1]

In light of the detextualized status of the soap opera in social scientific and aesthetic discourses, it is necessary to reestablish its textuality, even at the risk of overemphasizing formal properties that probably would not be recognized as such by most readers who are not "professional" readers (that is, academics). This retextualizing operation will be a poetic one in that it will seek to give an account of the soap opera as textual system in terms of the general laws that govern its production and reception. Where the goal of traditional aesthetics is the evaluation of individual works according to their correspondence to an aesthetic canon, the goal of poetics is the establishment of the normative features of particular types of aesthetic products. Thus our examination of the soap opera as aesthetic object focuses on the distinctive features of the soap opera form in general, rather than on individual episodes. Furthermore, the problem of defining that autonomous, isolated aesthetic object, so important in traditional aesthetics, is for our purposes obviated by a poetics of soap operas. As Todorov notes with regard to literary poetics:

> Each work is therefore regarded only as a manifestation of an abstract and general structure, of which it is but one of the possible realizations. Whereby this science [poetics] is no longer concerned with actual literature but with a possible literature, in other words, with that abstract property that constitutes the singularity of the literary phenomenon: literariness. The goal of this study is no longer to articulate a paraphrase . . . but to propose a theory of the structure and functioning of literary discourse, a theory that affords a list of literary possibilities, so that existing literary works appear as achieved particular cases.[2]

My insistence in this chapter upon the soap opera as a governing set of structural principles by which the reader is able to recognize any specific instance as a soap opera and through which the reader engages with the soap opera as a textual system transcending any specific episode is to some degree a strategic maneuver, a deliberate attempt to force attention upon aspects of the soap opera that have been hidden for so long. More than forty years ago Adorno encountered the refusal of empiricist mass communications research to regard "art as something objective in itself," rather than merely a stimulus, a set of statistically (if not behaviorally) measurable responses, or an "inaccurate" copy of reality. Forty years later the assertion of the distinctive and quantitatively irreducible textuality of the fictive narratives audiences encounter on television is still, unfortunately, necessary. "Critical studies" in American mass media does *not* indicate a concern for the analysis of textual production and reception, but rather points out a general orientation that is "critical" of the dominant empiricist model.[3]

If the elaboration of the soap opera as textual system is to be more than a mere formalist exercise or rhetorical counter to the antitextualism of empiricism, however, it must be tempered by a concern for both the functions the soap opera is designed to serve by the institution that produces it and the manner by which it is engaged by its readers. In recognition of the latter, the poetic operation conducted here will be a reader-oriented one. To Jonathan Culler poetics is inherently concerned not only with texts but with reading strategies as well, since poetics constructs hypotheses regarding the "conditions of meaning" within texts and "hypotheses about the conditions of meaning are claims about the conventions and interpretive operations applied in reading."[4] In bringing to bear upon soap operas a reader-oriented poetics this analysis is not so much applying a single critical model as it is taking into account the insights of a number of critics and theorists who have contributed to a general reorientation of literary studies away from the "work" and the "author" and toward the "text" and its "readers."[5] Thus it will be advancing hypotheses regarding what Wolfgang Iser calls the *verbal* and *affective* dimensions of the soap opera textual system.

Obviously referring to literary, and not televised, texts, *verbal* describes the text's "intersubjectively verifiable instructions for meaning production," or what might be called its formal properties. The verbal aspect guides the reader's response, encouraging certain meanings and eliminating others. As a verbal structure, the text exists as a signifying potentiality, analogous to a peculiarly tuned musical instrument: a range of sound production is possible, but some sounds are easier to produce than others. Not until this verbal structure is engaged by the reader, until its potential is actualized, is meaning constructed. This fulfillment of "that which has been pre-structured by the language of the text" Iser calls its *affective* aspect. The meanings produced by the interaction of the reader and textual structure are neither totally private and arbitrary nor totally determined by the verbal aspect of the text, but are situated somewhere between the two. The text initiates "performances" of meaning, in which both text and reader play crucial roles. The verbal aspects of the text prevent its realization in the mind of the reader from being entirely idiosyncratic; *General Hospital* is not fifteen million different texts because it has that many readers. At the same time, however, the relative indeterminacy of the text's verbal structure produces a range of actualizations, and it is this indeterminacy—the part of meaning production not controlled by the text—that allows us to say that *General Hospital* means different things to different viewers. Thus, understanding how the soap opera signifies and gives aesthetic pleasure requires that we consider both its "verbal" structure—its formal properties—and the mechanisms by which readers of soap operas construct meaning on the basis of those properties.[6]

## Visual and Auditory Style

To the content analyst, the visual and auditory articulation of the soap opera's narrative is a transparent and hence insignificant feature. Content analysis presumes not only that events and objects in the soap opera world mean the same as they do in "real life" but also that the viewer experiences them as if they were real. Yet the apparent transparency of soap opera style renders it neither natural nor meaningless. For the viewer there is no preexistent soap opera world that is represented on television; it is only as sound and images on the screen that the world of *General Hospital* or *As the World Turns* is known. Soap opera style represents the crystallization of a set of stylistic conventions taken over from Hollywood filmmaking practice (called by film scholars the classical Hollywood narrative style). While every type of American narrative television has adapted the Hollywood style to some degree, the soap opera has reproduced that style in what is perhaps its most austere form.[7]

The hallmarks of the Hollywood style are economy, transparency, and accessibility. Its overall aim is to produce a seamless, possible world, detached from our own yet governed by a real-world sense of plausibility. It is into this world that we are immersed for the duration of the film. The Hollywood style positions the spectator as the ideal, quasi-omniscient observer of the events in this complete fictional world, or diegesis. Our interest in this world is secured through the story that unfolds within it. The Hollywood style focuses our attention on the story by hiding the patently artificial means by which the story is related and its world constructed on the screen. Every element of style functions in the Hollywood cinema not for its own sake but as part of this reciprocal process of perfecting the illusion of the "reality" of the narrative world while simultaneously disguising the techniques of illusion making.

The Hollywood style can be expressed as a set of rules governing every category of cinema style—rules derived not only inductively, through their observation in individual films, but deductively from normative precepts laid down since the 1920s in various manuals, guidebooks, and periodicals in which the "pros" related the techniques of "good" (read, "Hollywood") filmmaking practice. For example, one basic difference between the narrative diegesis as constructed in film and that in literature is that a filmic narrative possesses an explicit spatial dimension, while the "space" of a literary narrative is purely imaginary. Hence a number of rules prescribe how space should be used in Hollywood films. Space functions primarily to

contain narratively significant elements; the greater the narrative significance of the element, the greater the space it occupies on the screen and the
less "other" space there is to look at. In the shot construction of a typical
scene in a Hollywood film the amount of space represented on the screen
diminishes rapidly from shot to shot, while the relative scale of objects depicted increases proportionally. In a dialogue scene set in an Empire State
Building office, the first shot (the establishing shot) might well be the exterior of the building. The second shot (the master shot) is likely to be the
office in which the dialogue is to take place, with both characters shown in
the same shot. As the dialogue begins, we can expect alternating close-ups
of each other as he or she delivers lines, varied occasionally, perhaps, by a
reaction shot. By the time we have reached the narratively significant dialogue in the scene, the only space represented is that of each character's
head and torso. Our attention might be even further directed toward this
space by rendering out-of-focus what little background space is contained
in the shot. Certainly, not every Hollywood scene is constructed in this way,
but the above description does represent a paradigm of normative spatial
representation and object scale in Hollywood films and dramatic television. The effect of this paradigm is to focus the attention of the viewer on
that information necessary to propel the narrative forward, even if in the
process it depicts space in a manner entirely different from how we perceive it in "real life."

In the soap opera the conventions of diminishing space and increasing
scale are maintained, but operate within a greatly compressed range. The
production situation of the soap opera (studio television) and the econom-
ics of soap opera production (the need to turn out the equivalent of several
feature films each week as cheaply as possible) greatly restrict the spaces
represented. It is a commonplace to refer to the soap opera as a world of
interiors. Although *Ryan's Hope* is set in Manhattan and *Capitol* in Washington, the only views we regularly get of these cities occur in the title se-
quences. The development of portable broadcast-quality video recording
equipment in the 1970s enabled soap operas to "open up" their interior
worlds, but the locations to which audiences have been taken in these "re-
motes" have been exotic rather than domestic, carefully bracketed and seg-
regated from the depiction of ordinary space in Port Charles or Henderson.
So long as exterior space is kept offscreen, the spatial worlds of soap operas
can be represented as an aggregate of atomistic interiors whose relationship to each other in space is constructed in the mind of the viewer. To
"open up" these domestic worlds, however, would necessitate the creation

of explicit geographic connections and, hence, spatial congruities. The British soap opera *Coronation Street* has solved this problem by constructing a standing exterior set of the one-block section of the street on which all of the regular characters live—a solution more feasible in the depiction of a British working-class neighborhood than of an automobile-dependent, middle-class American suburb. In American soaps establishing shots of exterior locales are frequently eliminated and their function collapsed with that of the master shot. Thus the world of the soap opera is represented spatially through the close-up and the two-shot, a strategy that has the effect of focusing viewer attention almost exclusively on facial expression and figure relationships, respectively.

Editing is potentially the most disruptive of all cinematic elements. Each cut breaks spatial and temporal continuity and threatens to evoke the difference between cinematic convention and "real-life" perception, thus distracting the viewer from the narrative. For this reason, Hollywood editing conventions constitute an elaborate regulatory system, whose aim is to produce "invisible" editing. Changes in camera location are disguised by cutting on action. Screen direction and background are kept constant through the 180-degree rule (two successive shots of the same action must be from camera positions less than 180 degrees apart). Eyeline-matches link one character's offscreen glance with the object of that glance and both with the gaze of the viewer.

Editing in soap operas is, if anything, more "invisible" than in the typical Hollywood production. In Hollywood films and in prime-time dramatic television programs shot on film, the continuous space and time of a scene is an illusion constructed in the editing room. The entire scene is acted out in master-shot, then in a two-shot, then in individual close-ups, and so forth, so that the appearance of continuity must be reconstituted by the editor. Broadcast live until the mid-1960s, soap operas are now recorded "live tape," meaning that while scenes might be recorded out of their eventual sequence in the episode, each scene is enacted and recorded on video tape only once. Editing is done at the time of recording, by switching between the shots being simultaneously taken by three television cameras. Thus, unless something goes awry (an actor flubs a line, for example) the time of enactment is the same as that of presentation, its continuity represented rather than reconstructed.

Another important function of Hollywood editing is to indicate changes in point of view. Most of the time in Hollywood films the viewer is an unseen, nonparticipating observer of the action in the diegesis, the camera acting as the viewer's eyes. Occasionally, however, point of view will switch to that of a character in the diegesis, and, while in this "subjective" mode, the viewer's vision and that of the character are synonymous. Obviously, it is essential that third- and first-person perspectives are clearly differentiated, so that our visual relationship vis-à-vis the narrative is not called into question. A Hollywood editing convention called glance/object editing brackets subjective point of view, visually announcing the restriction of "our" sight to that of a single character and then reassuring us with an unambiguous return to a more omniscient vantage point. Glance/object editing involves a three-shot strategy. In shot 1 we see a close-up of a character looking into offscreen space. Shot 2 shows us the object of that glance as the character would see it. In shot 3 third-person point of view is restored with a close-up of the character. The subjective shot is sandwiched between two objective shots, leaving no doubt as to whose eyes we are looking through and when that visual doubling ceases.

Because the glance/object editing strategy requires the intrusion of the camera into the diegetic space of the scene, its use is even more severely restricted in soap operas than in Hollywood films. The alternation between objective and subjective vision in such "mainstream" Hollywood films as *Psycho*, *Notorious*, and *Stagecoach* is extremely rare in soap operas. Subjectivity is more frequently achieved auditorally through interior monologue. We might "hear" the character's inner speech, but we see the facial expression of that character from our omniscient and undisclosed point of view. Visual subjectivity is reserved in soap operas for prolepses (flashbacks), but even there what we see from a character's memory is almost always rendered in third person, so that we see the character in his or her own recollection. The more complete bracketing of subjectivity from normative representation in soap operas endows its use with all the more significance. Because we so seldom experience the world of the soap through the eyes of a character in that world, subjective vision endows both the subject and the object of that vision (the character and what he or she sees) with special meaning.

The soap opera's distillation of Hollywood style is also apparent in camera movement. Although not as potentially distracting as editing (since spatial and temporal continuity are preserved), camera movement can call attention to the means of cinematic representation and away from the diegesis. Hence camera movements in Hollywood films are usually "motivated" by figure movement within the shot. Two characters are depicted walking down the street talking to each other, and the camera tracks along in front of them to enable us to see their faces in frame. Their movement hides the fact of "our" movement. Hollywood films are full of examples of elaborate unmotivated camera movements, however: the opening shots of *Scarface* and *Touch of Evil*, the between-the-legs tracking shot in *42nd Street*, swooping crane shots in several Hitchcock films, among many others. All but the most acrobatic of them go relatively unnoticed by the viewer, however. Camera movement as such is probably more prominent in soap operas than in Hollywood films (a convention of "live" television practice carried over into "live-tape"), but it is very seldom unmotivated. Shots are "reframed" to allow for figure movement; pans tie one acting area to another. In soap operas, though, the unmotivated camera movement, like the subjective point of view shot, is meaningful because of its marginalization within normative practice. Its rarity immediately privileges the "content" of the shot: an unmotivated camera movement usually signifies "something important and unusual is about to happen."

The auditory component of Hollywood style assures that sounds will be limited to those that are narratively significant—again, even if this means violating laws of physics. For example, the establishing shot of a dialogue scene set in Times Square might contain a high level of ambient noise. By the time the dialogue has begun in two-shot or close-up, however, that ambient noise level has dropped to an almost inaudible level in order that the narratively significant dialogue can be heard. The soap opera's infrequent use of location shooting obviates the problem of unwanted diegetic noise, while its studio production situation assures that all dialogue will be clearly heard. As in the movies, the soap opera's nondiegetic musical score supports the narrative: smoothing transitions, covering ellipses, and helping to reduce indeterminacy in a particular scene by encouraging one reading over another. The serial nature of soap operas, however, enables music to function differently from Hollywood scores in two respects. Music can be used as an auditory signature, announcing each episode of a soap—a convention widely used in other types of television programming and dating back to the early days of radio. Also a piece of music can be associated with a particular character or relationship (sometimes called "theme" music). This is common enough in movie scores, but the serial nature of soap operas enables a "theme" to be woven through many episodes over a period of weeks or months, musically linking a given scene to its paradigm.

In most other respects soap opera style can be seen as a continuation, if not condensation, of Hollywood stylistic practice, in which elements of style function in support of diegetic illusion. Objects exist as aspects of decor or as props. Settings are utilitarian. Hollywood lighting is subtly nuanced compared with the necessarily flat television lighting style of most soap operas.[8]

## Soap Opera Narrative Structure

One frequently hears that soap operas are constructed not to be watched but to be listened to. This is another way of saying that the "zero-degree" visual style of soap operas carries no meaning, that dialogue is all. It is also said, usually by those trying to watch soap operas for the first time, that the elongation of plot lines over months, if not years, renders any given episode virtually static in narrative terms. Why, they ask, would anyone want to watch a soap opera five days each week when watching one episode per month is sufficient to "keep up with the story?" If one regards what Barthes calls the hermeneutic code—the causal chain of events that eventually leads to the "end" of the story—as the sole source of appeal for soap opera viewers, then it is difficult to explain why anyone would want to watch or even listen to soap operas more than once each month.

One of the fundamental insights of structural linguistics is that language and narrative are structured along two axes: a syntagmatic (combinatory) axis and a paradigmatic (associative) axis. As noted previously, one of the distinctive syntagmatic features of the soap opera is its absence of ultimate narrative closure; it is, in fact, one of the few narrative forms predicated upon the impossibility of closure. More will be said about the consequences of the syntagmatic openness of the soap opera shortly. But what is frequently overlooked in discussions of the soap opera is its paradigmatic complexity—a complexity that makes the soap opera unique among visual narratives and unmatched in literary narrative except for the most elaborate of epic novels.[9]

### PARADIGMATIC STRUCTURE

The source of the soap opera's paradigmatic complexity is its large community of interrelated characters. The Hollywood film or traditional novel is structured around a limited number of characters, a few of whom are marked more specifically as protagonists or antagonists. The events of the narrative "happen" to them, and the fates of minor characters hinge on that of the heroes and heroines. Soap opera narratives, on the other hand, contain upwards of forty regularly-appearing characters, and while some are more prominent than others at any given time, none can be singled out as the motor of the narrative. A great deal might happen to individual characters—multiple marriages, pregnancy, amnesia, temporary blindness, disabling accidents, and so forth, but very little happens to alter the nature of the community. The soap opera community is a self-perpetuating, self-preserving system little affected by the turbulence experienced by its individual members or the fate of any one character. The naive viewer might attend only to the constant state of crisis experienced by individual characters, but the experienced viewer is watchful for the paradigmatic strands that bind the community of characters together and the sometimes glacially slow but far more significant alterations in this network. "Who a character is" is as much a function of his or her place in this paradigmatic system as what he or she "does" in a syntagmatic sense.

It is only by reference to the paradigmatic complexity of the soap opera that some of its most distinctive narrative features can be explained. Consider, for example, the high degree of redundancy in soap operas. What we might call interepisodic redundancy—the reiteration on Tuesday of plot developments from Monday—is to a large degree explicable as a device to keep nondaily viewers "up" on narrative developments. Such redundancy is also a function of the fact that soap operas must negotiate a narrow path between moving the story along too quickly, and thus "using it up" too soon, and stretching subplots out for longer than the audience will tolerate. But soap operas also contain a great deal of intraepisodic redundancy: the repetition of information from character to character within each daily episode. Unless we presume that soap writers and producers feel required to refresh the memories of the viewers every ten minutes, intraepisodic redundancy cannot be explained as a syntagmatic device. As an illustration of intraepisodic redundancy, let us presume that in scene one of a soap episode we learn from a conversation between Lucy and her friend Debbie that Lucy is pregnant with Rick's child. In scene three, Debbie tells her husband Chris of Lucy's pregnancy. In scene five, Chris warns his friend Billy against becoming too involved with Lucy.

Such references to Lucy's pregnancy might continue for days or weeks without anything "happening" to move this subplot closer to resolution. The same information—Lucy is pregnant with Rick's child—is passed along from character to character to character. In terms of the syntagmatic, or story, dimension of the soap, such exchanges *are* redundant, since the audience already knows that Lucy is pregnant and Rick is the father, and since such redundant dialogue scenes do not move the story forward at all. Paradigmatically, however, such exchanges are far from redundant. The experienced reader of the soap is able to read these exchanges as invokings of the paradigmatic network. It makes a difference that Lucy chose to confide in Debbie about her plight because Debbie was once married to Rick. Debbie's telling Chris of Lucy's revelation is read against the background of Debbie's inability to conceive a child and Chris's recurrent infidelity, and so forth. Reduced to its syntagmatic axis, the soap opera becomes an endless string of excruciatingly retarded subplots, related in episodes whose redundancy gives them an almost Sisyphean tiresomeness. To the experienced reader, however, soap operas' distinctive networks of character relationships open up major sources of signifying potential that are simply unreadable to the naive reader.

Thus our previous discussion of soap opera's adaptation of the classical Hollywood narrative style and its narrative function needs to be qualified in light of the soap opera's paradigmatic complexity. Obviously, one function of the close-up in soap operas is to concentrate our attention on dialogue and the narrative information contained therein. In addition, the style of the soap opera, built on close-ups and two-shots, functions paradigmatically to a degree quite unnecessary in Hollywood films. A pause, gesture, glance, or facial expression rendered in close-up may be syntagmatically insignificant but laden with potential paradigmatic meaning. To give but one example, in August 1981 Kelly and Morgan, two young characters on *Guiding Light*, were married. Nearly one entire episode was devoted to the wedding ceremony, which was attended by most of the show's regular characters. Throughout the wedding scene shots of the nuptial couple were intercut with close-ups of various wedding guests. Some of those characters given close-ups during the scene had played little or no part in the Kelly-Morgan subplot that had brought about their marriage. Nor was there any indication that a character's being singled out in a close-up functioned to anticipate his or her subsequent involvement in the Kelly-Morgan "story." How then was the viewer to read the relationship between shots of the wedding ceremony and close-ups of various other characters? To the naive viewer these characters were simply "there"—at the ceremony, but the experienced viewer knew that what tied these characters to Kelly and Morgan was their own relationship, past or present, to the institution of marriage. Without a single word of dialogue to indicate it, this particular plot event was plugged into *Guiding Light*'s extensive paradigmatic system. To be sure, this strategy at the "verbal" level may or may not have been "affectively" engaged by an individual viewer. The scene still had meaning even to the most naive viewer at the syntagmatic level. Still, to the competent reader, listening to this scene would hardly have been the same experience as viewing it, and in this case the function of the close-up was to stimulate a very different kind of narrative response from that usually evoked by the close-up in Hollywood films.

The complexity of the network of character relationships in soap operas derives in large part from the fact that, unlike characters in prime-time series, soap opera characters have both histories and memories. Thus the soap opera's paradigmatic system possesses both synchronic and diachronic dimensions. Certainly, character relationships change during the course of other types of narratives as well. Paul's relationship with his mother at the end of *Sons and Lovers* is read against the background of that relationship's history as it has evolved to that point in the book. The text might initiate this movement back across portions of the text already read by a reference to an earlier event, but it cannot specify what will be recalled. The text provides the reference, but the reader provides the context in which the recalled event is embedded. In soap operas, this reservoir of relational possibilities is more extensive than in any other narrative form. A viewer may read current relationships against the background of their status a year ago, five years ago, or, in some cases, more than thirty years ago. And unlike *Sons and Lovers*, that thirty-year period is not just text time but reading time as well, since it has literally taken thirty years for the viewer to "read" the text of *Guiding Light* up to that point.

The diachronic "depth" of the paradigmatic structure of the soap opera suggests another fundamental difference between it and other forms of narrative. Summarizing recent research on the temporality of fiction, Shlomith Rimmon-Kenan (following Genette) discusses two types of duration: story-duration (the days, months, years depicted in the narrative) and text-duration (the "amount" of text devoted to the relating of various "pieces" of story-time). She alludes to a third kind of duration against which the first two might be measured—the actual time it takes to read the text—but this "reading-duration" is not taken up because it "varies from reader to reader, providing no objective standard."[10] (This is, of course, a key difference between the experience of reading a novel and that of watching a film. The temporal dimension of the cinema or television is specific; running-time is the same as reading-time.)

Reader-response theorists have only begun to explore the concept of reading-duration except to note that we can never perceive a narrative text "all at once," except when we are no longer reading it, and then the events depicted in the first chapter (or reel) are separated from us by the time it took to get from there to the end of the story. But whether reading-duration is approximate, as in the case of the novel, or exact, as in the case of a film, it is presumed to occur at one historical moment. Iser points out that our understanding of the text changes as we "travel" along from beginning to end during the reading process, because the horizon constituted by our knowledge of the text to that point changes and with it the relationship between any particular narrative event and the rest of the text.[11]

The soap opera raises the possibility, unanticipated by Iser, that the reader's own extratextual horizons might change during the course of reading a narrative text. Our memory of the death of Joanne Tate's first husband in *Search for Tomorrow* is of a previous point in the text, but it can also be a memory of ourselves as readers of that text some twenty-years ago. And, to make matters even more complex, in this case it is also a memory of the actress as she portrayed the same character twenty years before—Mary Stuart has been playing the role of Joanne Tate since *Search for Tomorrow* began in 1951. The context of a recalled portion of a soap opera text is twofold: the "verbal" context within the text and the affective context of the reader's initial encounter with that textual segment. The relationship of a reader to a soap opera text is in the truest sense of the term a diachronic one, in which not only does the text change with each daily episode but the reader and his or her world changes *while* the reading act occurs. We often divide literature, television shows, and films into genres on the basis of their appeal to readers of particular age groups—as in "children's literature," the "teen novel," "children's programming." With the soap opera, we have a text that might have been begun by a reader in adolescence, but which, thirty years later, is still being read *by the same reader*, who is now a mother of adolescent children. This does not make the soap opera different in kind from other narratives, but it does mean that what can be assumed away in the case of the novel or the film must be regarded as an important constituent element of the soap opera.

We have already noted the complexity of the relationship between the soap opera and its "real-life" social context, and more will be said about this relationship in subsequent chapters. At this point we might notice that, to some extent, the paradigmatic dimension of the soap opera text helps to explain what many have seen as the peculiar social structure of its diegetic world. As content analysts have pointed out, the number of middle-class "professional" people (both men and women) is disproportionately high compared to their distribution in American society. One study found that over half the adult males in soap operas are doctors. Not surprisingly, the workplaces depicted in soap operas are those associated with middle-class occupations and leisure: hospitals, doctor's offices, law firms, corporate headquarters, restaurants, bars, and nightclubs. Because of the importance of interpersonal relationships in soaps, the work places depicted in them must allow for frequent contacts with other characters and opportunities to discuss matters not directly related to work—specifically, to invoke the paradigmatic network of character relationships that binds any single event in the text to the community at large. This helps to explain the preference for hospital nursing stations, waiting rooms, executive suites, and night clubs as regular settings for interaction between soap opera characters. Soap operas are, in a sense, "about" talk, and in the working world of the soap opera the opportunity to talk is associated with middle-class occupations.

The paradigmatic function of the middle-class work environment of the soap opera is itself an effect of larger, essentially ideological forces. The compression of social reality in the soap opera into a middle-class universe facilitates a suppression of material concerns in general. The economic exchanges that are so much a part of the lives of its viewers have little or no part in the soap opera world. Money seldom changes hands as a part of everyday life in the soap opera world; the cost of products is almost never mentioned; the businesses for which soap opera characters work (or, more likely, which they own) seldom actually produce goods; characters almost never worry whether there will be enough money at the end of the month to pay bills.

Similarly, soap operas' emphasis on paradigmatic structure is not unrelated to their notorious exclusion of minority-group characters. Despite the inclusion of black families in some soaps, the world of the soap opera is overwhelmingly white. The problem of including blacks and other racial groups in soaps is one not of working them into plot lines but of dealing with the paradigmatic consequences of their entry into the community of the soap opera world. There are three major types of relationships between soap opera characters: kinship, romantic, and social. Much of the appeal of soap operas resides in the complexity and overlap among these categories of actual and potential relationships for any particular character. Mistaken parentage has been a stock device in soap operas for decades. On *Guiding Light* the revelation that Quintin McCord was actually the son of Henry Chamberlain reverberated throughout the entire network of character relationships: Vanessa Chamberlain, for example, was transformed from a potential romantic partner to Quintin's half-sister. Enemies can become brothers; sisters, merely close friends; fathers, foster-fathers; and so on—all at the drop of a discovered birth certificate.

Unless a particular soap were to embrace interracial romance, marriage, and parentage as a community norm, the admission of a nonwhite character into full membership in the soap community would be impossible, since two of the three relational modes would be all but closed to him or her. Some soaps have teased audiences with actual or potential interracial romances—in one case effecting an interracial marriage only to dissolve it before consummation—but in all soaps black characters are relegated to a paradigmatic ghetto, always marked by their relational impoverishment. Once again, the paradigmatic dilemma as regards race in soap operas is itself an effect of external forces—specifically the producers' desire not to "upset" large numbers of their target audience (white women) by extending the normative boundaries of the soap opera world too far.

### SYNTAGMATIC STRUCTURE

The soap opera trades an investment in an ultimate narrative telos—the most characteristic feature of traditional narratives—for a series of overlapping "mini-closures," which resolve a particular narrative question but are in no way read as moving the overall story toward its eventual end. This absolute resistance to final closure is illustrated by the termination of *Love of Life*, one of the first successful television soaps, which was canceled by CBS in 1981. Even as the show drew toward its final episodes, there was no attempt to impose an overall ending; *Love of Life* did not so much end as it expired defiantly in medias res. Given the decentered nature of soap opera narrative and its diffusion through a network of interrelated characters, any attempt to pull all the paradigmatic strands together in some sort of synthetic grand finale, à la Wilkie Collins, would have smacked of the most transparent sort of deus ex machina.

Although I doubt that either Iser or Jauss anticipated its application to soap operas, reader-response theory does provide a means of positioning the reader and the reading process relative to the syntagmatic openness of the soap opera form. Drawing on Husserl, Iser contends that each sentence in a literary narrative can be said to contain a "retrospective section," which answers the expectations aroused by previous sentences, and a "hollow section," which creates new expectations to be confirmed, modified, or frustrated in subsequent sentences. At any given moment, the reader's relationship to the text constitutes a "wandering viewpoint," an intersection between protension (expectation) and retention (retrospection). Each sentence prefigures a horizon of expectations, which, as it is read, immediately becomes the background for the next sentence, over and over again in a syntagmatic chain of questions and answers, which are themselves new questions. As the reader encounters more and more pieces of text, those already read retreat further into the background. But the retained significance of that background is constantly being restructured in light of new text. "That which is remembered becomes open to new connections, and these in turn influence the expectations aroused by the individual correlates in the sequence of sentences." The wandering viewpoint of the reader of a fictional narrative—his or her participation in the dialectic of protension and retention, determination and expectation—positions the reader not outside the aesthetic object contemplating it but at a constantly changing point somewhere within the text constructing it.

> There is no escaping this process, for—as has already been pointed out—the text cannot at any one moment be grasped as a whole. But what may at first sight have seemed like a disadvantage, in comparison with our normal modes of perception, may now be seen to offer distinct advantages, in so far as it permits a process through which the aesthetic object is constantly being structured and restructured. As there is no definite frame of reference to regulate this process, successful communication must ultimately depend on the reader's creative activity.[12]

In the case of the soap opera, then, we have a text that not only is ungraspable as a whole at any one moment but is also a "whole" only by reference to a given moment. The traditional narrative privileges a reading position just "on the other side of" the text: the moment of teleological insight toward which all protensions have been directed and in light of which all ambiguities are retrospectively dissolved. The classic example is the closed-room murder mystery with its stock revelation scene, beyond which there is in a very real sense nothing left to be said. The soap opera privileges that ever-changing moment when the reader comes to the text once again. The "text" of *Guiding Light* comprises all the episodes ever broadcast since 1937—a text probably no one has ever "read" in its entirety and which today one could not reread, even if one had the months to devote to the task—but it is a text the last page of which is never the final page. The final page never comes, nor does the reader read on in anticipation of its coming. If, with Juri Lotman, we can characterize a literary text as acting like "a sort of living organism, which is linked to the reader, and also instructs him by means of a feedback system," then we can characterize the soap opera as functioning not only like a living organism but one which grows by regular increments to enormous proportions.[13] The syntagmatic openness of the soap opera creates a higher degree of what we might call protensive indeterminacy than is the case in many other types of narrative, particularly where the fate of individual characters is concerned. In the traditional narrative, the hero or heroine functions with respect to the narrative's point of closure; thus, our expectations of what will happen to that character are governed by that relationship. We do not expect Hercule Poirot to be the victim of the murderer it is his "job" (in both an occupational and narrative sense) to unmask. Certainly our expectations in this regard can be violated: the murder of the heroine of *Psycho* in the first reel has all the more shock value because we do not expect *her* to be killed. But because our perspective on the world of the traditional narrative is usually tied to that of one or two central characters, we expect, at the very least, that they will survive as long as the story itself does.

Protensive indeterminacy is perhaps most limited in the prime-time television series format. Our expectations of what will happen to Lucy Ricardo or Kojak during the course of any given episode is rigidly bound by our knowledge that that character will return next week totally unaffected by whatever happened this week. In the soap opera, however, because our wandering viewpoint "wanders" not only syntagmatically but paradigmatically as well (from character to character to character) there are no such limits to what can "happen" to a given character and thus none to our expectations. Soap operas regularly kill off even the most central of characters: Adam Drake on *Edge of Night*, Nancy Hughes on *As the World Turns*, among others. Nor does apparent death necessarily mark absolute determinancy where a particular character is concerned: characters can die or they can *die*. On *Edge of Night* several years ago, Nicole Drake disappeared after a boating mishap in the Caribbean, only to be discovered alive and well in Paris more than two years (reader time) later. Bill Bauer has now "died" three times on *Guiding Light*, and on the same show Roger Thorpe was resurrected twice before being given his "final" (?) death. A soap character can also be kept in a sort of protensive limbo—a potential but not active character. On *As the World Turns*, Penny has been absent from the world of Oakdale for more than a decade, but she is kept "alive" by having her call home occasionally, usually on a holiday. Similarly, the character of Laura Spencer on *General Hospital* disappeared into one of the most famous of soap-opera limbos when the actress who plays her, Genie Francis, signed a contract with another television network. Is she dead? Will she return? Tune in next week.

The syntagmatic movement of the reader's wandering viewpoint along the forward frontiers of the text is not that of the driver of a sportscar down a superhighway but rather that of the uncertain tourist provided with a rather sketchy map, who frequently stops to look back where he or she has been, occasionally takes a side road, and constantly tries to glimpse what lies around the next bend. The textual space the reader traverses in this process is not that of the superhighway but rather the rural backlanes, where the pavement suddenly stops and then starts back again, where the journey forward is halting rather than continuous. It is precisely at these places where the textual "pavement" is broken that the reader's active involvement in the text is most clearly seen. What the text leaves unsaid is, nevertheless, made to signify within the imagination of the reader.

The reader inserts himself or herself into the text through these necessary gaps, filling them in part—but only in part—according to his or her own frames of reference. The structuring gaps of the text, then, mark the point of intersection between the horizon represented within the text and the horizon brought to the text by the reader. Put another way, there the "reality" of the reader confronts the pseudoreality of the fictive text. But just as the text does not merely take over "real-life" conventions in the construction of its world, the reader cannot simply impose his or her referential system upon the text. The process of "gap-filling" is regulated by the text itself.

Syntagmatic gaps are constituent parts of any communication. The spaces between words mark necessary textual potholes to be negotiated by the reader/listener. In the literary text, structuring gaps occur at all syntagmatic levels (between words, sentences, paragraphs, scenes, chapters), and the "size" of these gaps range correspondingly from the seemingly insignificant and, to the reader, unnoticed to those which require a considerable and conscious "filling-in" process.

The role of gaps in the construction of textual meaning is most clearly seen where those gaps are large and regular features of a text, and where they are imposed upon the reader and controlled by the text. In the serial novels of Dickens or Collins, for example, textual segments were separated not only spatially (a partially blank page marking the gap between the end of one chapter and the beginning of the next) but temporally as well: the reader could not "jump over" the gap until the next serial installment was published. The serial story results in a special relationship between reader and text, one in which, in Iser's words, "the reader is forced by the pauses imposed upon him to imagine more than he could if his reading were continuous." The narrative anticipation that causes us frantically to flip from the last page of one chapter to the first of a new one was, in the serialized novel, attenuated, as New Yorkers anxiously and eagerly awaited the arrival of the ship from London carrying the episode of *The Old Curiosity Shop* in which Little Nell succumbs. Iser points out that readers in the nineteenth century found serialized novels read in installments more enjoyable than the same text published as a whole. He attributes this curious fact to a sort of *narrativus interruptus*: the strategic suspension of the text at crucial narrative nodes. "The result is that we try to imagine how the story will unfold, and in this way we heighten our own participation in the course of events."[14]

Syntagmatic gaps play an even more important structuring role in the soap opera. Each episode of a soap opera is, of course, separated from the next by a twenty-four-hour "gap" during the week and an even longer one over the weekend. Soap opera writers take advantage of this hiatus in reading activity by leaving a major narrative question unanswered at the end of each episode, saving the greatest narrative indeterminacy for the end of Friday's episode. The anticipation thus provoked produces in some soap opera readers the modern-day equivalent of Dickens's American readers greeting the packet at the dock: when Pope John Paul II was wounded in an assassination attempt in May 1981 the Associated Press reported that a St. Louis television station received three hundred calls from irate soap opera fans protesting the preemption of regular afternoon programming in favor of press coverage of events in Rome.

Within each episode the syntagmatic structure of the soap opera is regulated by the gaps inserted in the text at regular intervals to allow for commercial messages. Unlike the gaps between chapters of a novel, however, the commercial gaps of a soap opera are of a specific temporal duration beyond the control of the reader and, moreover, are "filled" with another textual system, that of the commercial advertisement itself. Sandy Flitterman has suggested that one function of some soap opera ads is to provide a text with a tight and closed narrative structure to offset the effects upon the reader of the soap opera's resistance to such closure. The ultimate answer to the question posed in the soap opera text just before the commercial might be weeks or months in coming (if it ever does), but the reader can take comfort in the knowledge that the mini-narrative launched by "ring-around-the-collar" will be satisfactorily resolved before the indeterminacy of the soap opera text is resumed.[15] One disadvantage of the closed structure of a narrative advertisement for sponsors is that once a commercial is "told," it loses much of its narrative appeal; the sixteenth retelling of the *Wisk* story ends exactly like the first. Thus the repetition of ads leaves plenty of room in the commercial gap for soap opera readers to fill it with retensive and protensive ruminations about the soap opera text. In a literary narrative, opportunities for such ruminations can be created by the reader just by lifting the eyes from the page for a moment or pausing at the end of one line before beginning the next. The viewer of a film or television program has no such "gap-creating" power. One can look away from the screen, but the text continues.

Within these gaps the viewpoint of the reader is free to wander both syntagmatically and paradigmatically. Previously related portions of a subplot can be reviewed in light of more recent events and expectations formed as to future developments. To a degree subsequent textual segments of a given subplot carry the reader across the gaps between them, guiding his or her viewpoint toward the subplot's eventual, if only partial, resolution. Much less guidance is provided by the text in relating an event from one subplot to one in another. Given the paradigmatic complexity of the soap opera, however, there are always many virtual relationships to be actualized by the viewer if he or she chooses to do so. The mere syntagmatic juxtaposition of two apparently unrelated scenes represents a paradigmatic indeterminacy for the reader: could the relationship between them be more than sequential? The text is frequently silent in this regard, but sometimes it encourages the construction of specific relationships between scenes or entire subplots. An example is provided by the 1981 *Guiding Light* Kelly-Morgan subplot. The 18 August 1981 episode is devoted largely to informing various members of the community of their wedding plans. Scattered among these scenes, however, are scenes of another couple's wedding plans, to which those of Kelly and Morgan are implicitly contrasted. The Kelly-Morgan marriage represents the fulfillment of young love, initially thwarted by another's deceit. Noela, who regarded Kelly as a ticket out of her drab working-class existence, tried to trick him into marrying her by making him believe he had fathered her child one night when he was drunk. When the ruse is discovered, Noela settles for marrying Floyd, a hospital janitor, with whom she had been carrying on a secret liaison for months and who is the real father of her baby. The two weddings are related oppositionally throughout the episode, principally through alternating scenes depicting the reactions of other members of the *Guiding Light* community to each of them. The news of the Kelly-Morgan wedding occasions unmitigated joy; that of Noela and Floyd's elicits shock, anger, or indifference.

The textual role of the commercial "gap" brings to light another key difference in reading situation between commercial television and literature or film—a difference particularly pronounced in the soap opera. In both literature and cinema the relationship between reader and text is essentially a private one. Unless the text is read aloud, the reader of a novel does not immediately share the reading experience with anyone else, even if the reading act occurs in a public place. Public viewings of films are made into private reading situations by shrouding the reader in darkness. Television, however, allows for public *or* private viewing, public *or* private reading. Soap opera audience research indicates that some audience groups—most notably college students—prefer to watch soaps with other viewers, thus making a public viewing situation in a dorm lounge or union television room into a social reading act.

Interpretation of a particular textual segment may be "assisted" by vocalized responses. Commercial "gaps" provide additional opportunities for the development of an interreader social discourse. More competent readers can acquaint new viewers with portions of the text the latter might not have seen. A reader's private interpretation of an action, scene, or line of dialogue can be compared to that of other readers, with the result that new expectations are formed and new paradigmatic relationships actualized. Ironically, the subjects of many soap opera commercial messages—laundry products, diapers, household cleaners—encourage the use of commercial gaps for social soap opera reading among college-age viewers, since these products are largely irrelevant to their life-styles.

## The Soap Opera Text: Closed or Open?

Semiotician Umberto Eco distinguishes between "open" and "closed" narrative texts. Closed texts, says Eco, "apparently aim at pulling the reader along a predetermined path, carefully displaying their effects so as to arouse pity or fear, excitement or depression at the due place and at the right moment. Every step of the 'story' elicits just the expectation that its further course will satisfy. They seem to be structured according to an inflexible project." The open text, on the other hand, has built into it multiple levels of interpretation. Whereas the closed text is a straightforward, linear pathway of stimulus and anticipated response, the open text is a "structural maze" of possible readings. The closed work offers an extremely limited set of interpretive possibilities, but the very narrowness of the text's interpretive pathway means that readers for whom the text was not intended or who are oriented toward the text by assumptions other than those of its author frequently stray from its "path" and produce aberrant readings. In the open work, while the possibility of pluri-signification is built in, so is the notion of the Model Reader—the reader with sufficient knowledge of the codes at work in the text to be able to read it competently. The open work is not open to any interpretation, for the reader, says Eco, is "strictly defined by the lexical and syntaxical organization of the text." So while the possibility of aberrant interpretations of the closed text remains always open, the multiple interpretations of the open text have been foreseen by the author and are hence to some extent closed off. To Eco, the novels of Joyce and Woolf are "open," while those of Ian Fleming and Harold Robbins are "closed."[16]

Ellen Seiter uses Eco's open/closed dichotomy as the basis for a feminist reading of soap operas. Accepting Eco's inclusion of the soap opera in the category of closed texts, she suggests "possible ways that women can read soap operas subversively—ways which do not exclude or negate the widespread negative interpretation of soap opera viewing as escapist fantasy for women working in the home."[17] Seiter's suggestive critique once again raises the issue of the relationship between aesthetic structure and social effect—an issue to which we shall return later in this chapter and in later chapters, particularly as regards historical changes in the soap opera's textual structure. Of immediate interest to us here is the closed text model of the soap opera upon which this bifurcation of preferred versus subversive readings is based.

While it is certainly possible for women (and others) to construct readings of soap operas "against the grain," the limiting of "allowable" readings to a unitary decoding, anticipated by the text and its authors, overlooks the television soap opera's signifying complexity. Eco's notion of the closed text presumes its orientation toward narrative closure: the interpretive pathway constructed by the author for the reader leads in a straightforward manner to "the end." Each reduction of indeterminacy brings with it a corresponding reduction of "allowable" interpretive possibilities. As we have seen, though, the soap opera is not governed by an ultimate telos, and, hence, protensive possibilities always outrun plot resolutions. Furthermore, the elaborate network of character relationships in the soap opera builds in the very pluri-significative possibilities Eco reserves for the open text. The complex paradigmatic structure of the soap opera outlines its Model Reader "as a component of its structural strategy," even though this is a term Eco reserves for open works. It is just that the Model Reader of *Guiding Light* is more likely to be a working-class woman than a male literary critic.

The reading competencies Eco speaks of with regard to the Model Reader of *Ulysses* or, we might suppose, his own novel, *The Name of the Rose*, involve three types of codes: textual, lexical, and intertextual. The more adept the reader is at the operation of these codes, the better he or she is able to negotiate the "structural maze" of the open text. Obviously, the lexically impoverished high-school student finds many passages of *Ulysses* unintelligible. Understanding that novel also requires the reader to "decode" certain textual strategies—shifts in narrational perspective, for example. And the Model Reader will be able to "plug into" the many intertextual codes employed in *Ulysses*: Irish history and legend, Catholic liturgy, Greek myth, other literary and nonliterary genres, and so forth.

The aim here is not to elevate the soap opera to the status of the elite artwork—the place, intentionally or not, Eco reserves for the open work— but rather to show that the soap opera shares with works Eco designates as open (and hence complex) certain constitutive features. Eco's analysis of such "open" works as *Ulysses* does help to point out the plural interpretive strategies employed by the reader in understanding any narrative work. Following Barthes and others, Eco calls the strategies codes—a term used here in a loose sense to indicate the interpretive mechanism linking signifier to referent. The process of reading soap operas, like that of reading *Ulysses*, involves the operation of multiple codes. As does *Ulysses*, the soap opera most fully engages its Model Reader, and, conversely, the soap opera (like *Ulysses*) contains an interpretive threshold below which the reader cannot fall and still "understand what's going on," except in the most superficial sense. This minimal interpretive threshold in the soap opera is based upon intratextual familiarity rather than extratextual lexical and literary skills—the soap opera is, after all, designed to reach the largest possible audience. Above this threshold, however, the reader may engage in multiple decoding strategies—plugging soap opera events and relationships into personal frames of reference via the operation of a number of different codes.

Like the open texts Eco speaks of, the soap opera text anticipates, to some degree, this pluri-signification, but it cannot totally control which codes will be engaged by the reader at any given moment or the interaction of those codes. It is what Iser calls the "overflow of possibilities" inherent in the decoding of any narrative work carried to a remarkable degree in the television soap opera that must account in large measure for its longevity as a form, the size of its audience, and the diversity of that audience. In fact, the soap opera represents an "over-coded" narrative form: characters, events, situations, and relationships are invested with signifying possibilities greatly in excess of those necessary to their narrative functions.

## The Variety of Soap Opera Codes

The notion of codes helps us to recognize that the pluri-signification of the soap opera, like that of other complex narratives, is achieved not willy-nilly but via certain generalizable interpretive pathways. Through these codes, the reader relates the text to his or her own world and experience, relates features of the text to one another, and relates the text to other texts.

### STYLISTIC CODES

As we have seen, the stylistic codes of the soap opera represent the distillation of the classical Hollywood narrative style, a tightening of stylistic conventions to the point that a marginal or nonnormative usage is immediately marked as significant by the viewer. The transparency of this style draws the viewer into the world of the soap opera and draws attention away from both authorial intention and the means of representation of this world. Through the soap opera's adaptations of the stylistic codes of Hollywood representation, individual images on the television screen are firmly anchored to the textual diegesis and that diegesis endowed with a visual and auditory "fullness." These codes also assure the stability of the relationship of viewer to text; our knowledge of the world of the soap opera may be always limited, but it is never problematic. The occasional excursions into subjective point of view and duplicitous narration made within the framework of the Hollywood cinema (represented by *The Lady in the Lake* and *Stagefright*, respectively) would be unthinkable in the soap opera. Such stylistic license would irremediably rupture the contract between viewer and text—although, as we shall see in another chapter, this relationship did not become solidified until the advent of televised soap operas. Thus, these stylistic codes encourage the reader to read the audio and visual signifiers of the soap opera text in terms of their referents within the diegesis of the text.

### GENERIC CODES

Other codes encourage the viewer to read a particular text or textual feature as one belonging to a larger category of texts the viewer knows as "soap operas." To the soap opera viewer the soap opera genre constitutes a portion of his or her horizon of expectations against which any particular text is read, in the same way that labeling a film a "musical" evokes certain characteristic features of that genre. Obviously, these "codes" are more at the level of specificity of conventions than linguistic or cinematic codes. Included in this category would be the soap opera's characteristic use of time and space—the attenuation of events (rather than their compression, as in most other narrative forms) and the construction of a world that is for the most part an interior one; a community-centered rather than character-centered fictive world; a serial narrative punctuated by commercial "gaps"; lack of overall narrative closure; and a complex network of character interrelationships. These conventions or codes are what enable any new "soap opera" to be read as such by its viewers, and they provide the basis upon which normative judgments about a new show or developments in an old one are formed.

### TEXTUAL CODES

One misconception soap opera nonviewers often have is that all soap operas are alike. Although all soap operas do share certain stylistic and generic traits, each has its own narrative patterns, community of characters, history, and stylistic peculiarities. These marks of difference between one soap opera and the next may be imperceptible to the naive viewer, but they are unmistakable to the competent reader. Far from being undiscriminating, most soap opera viewers express strong likes and dislikes for certain soaps. Each soap opera generates its own set of expectations, its own parameters in narrative, paradigmatic relationships, and style recognized by the audience and used by them to derive meaning from each episode.

The most obvious example of what we are calling here textual codes is that which governs the system of character relationships in a given soap. At one level a marital infidelity "means" the same thing whether it occurs in

General Hospital or One Life to Live, but the superficial meaning of a situation common to all soap operas is instantly overwhelmed by the deeper significance of that event in the specific character network in which it occurs. Some soap operas bear stronger marks of visual difference than others. Sets on The Young and the Restless are lit so that much of the decor is in shadow. This stylistic strategy is read by its viewers as "normal," while viewers of other soaps often find The Young and the Restless "gloomy."

Because the soap opera text has a history, it can be said to construct—to borrow terminology from Jauss—a textual horizon of expectations for its readers: the sum of its textual codes against which any new textual feature is received. The textual horizon of the soap opera appears largely undifferentiated to the reader, but it is what gives each soap opera world its specificity. Each episode, each new character, each new plot line becomes a "theme" to be assessed against the horizon supplied by the reader's perception of the text to that point. The importance of this horizon in the construction of meaning can best be seen when there is a considerable distance between it and a theme. Soap opera viewers can easily sense when a new development in a soap opera does not seem to "fit," which, given frequent changes in writers and producers, is not uncommon. The responses provoked by the distance between horizon and theme may be several. The soap's textual horizon might be expanded or altered to accommodate the theme. For example, a character who had been portrayed as a villain gradually takes on more and more redeeming qualities, so that over a period of time a marked personality change occurs. The viewer refigures the textual horizon of the soap so as to include not only that character change but the possibility of such character changes as features of the soap's world. Soap opera texts are full of such character transformations.

On the other hand, the theme might be at such odds with the soap's horizon that some viewers stop watching or switch to other soaps. In recent years some soap operas have introduced whole groups of new, younger characters in an attempt to cash in on adolescent and college-student interest in soap operas. In the process these soaps have no doubt lost some older viewers for whom such demographic shifts in the soap opera community represent too drastic a change. But in the case of the soap opera—unlike most other categories of narrative texts—a further response to theme/ horizon distance is possible. The writers and producers of a particular soap can respond to the feedback they receive from viewers by expunging the "theme" from the soap opera text. A plot line that was to last for several months can be foreshortened; a new character can be written out; or a familiar character scheduled for departure can be resuscitated.

## INTERTEXTUAL CODES

Like all cultural products, soap operas exist within networks of other texts to which they inevitably in some way refer, so that the reader is constantly comparing the text being read with the encyclopedia of other texts he or she has experienced. What I have referred to thus far as the generic code, which allows readers to place a text within the general category of the soap opera, might be seen as one type of intertextuality. Chapter 6 is largely devoted to a discussion of the intertextual horizon against which the first soap operas were read, particularly that portion of the horizon constituted by popular discourse aimed at American women.

In more recent years soap opera writers have exploited intertextual relationships in several ways. In their never-ending search for new plot twists, writers have based plotlines on popular movies, novels, other television programs, press reportage of the Mafia, religious cults, and terrorism, among other topics. Well-known actors from television and the movies have made cameo appearances in soap operas, either as "themselves," or, in the case of Elizabeth Taylor in *General Hospital*, as a soap opera character.

One of the most notable instances of soap-opera intertextuality occurred during the 1980–81 television season on *General Hospital*. Producer Gloria Monty introduced a major subplot that made reference not to any particular intertext but to an entire narrative genre: science fiction. An archvillain obtained a weather-altering device (the "Ice Princess") with the power to turn the climate of Port Charles into that of Siberia. After an elaborate global search, the device was found and the plot foiled by two of the show's most popular young characters. The success of the "Ice Princess" plot (or its perceived success, since Monty has always insisted that the audience was primarily attracted by the love affair between the two characters and not by the trappings of science fiction) fostered imitation, and soon other soaps were featuring diabolical dwarfs, rescues from desert islands, and treks across Africa.

In setting up resonances between soap opera characters and situations and those in other texts, however, writers risked bringing the intertextual codes being employed into conflict with the textual codes that keep any new event anchored in a world familiar to the viewer. For example, *Guiding Light*'s response to *General Hospital*'s intertextuality was to institute a gothic-romance subplot, complete with mysterious mansion, intimidating housekeeper, handsome-but-enigmatic master of the house, and poor-but-willing ingenue. But the world of the gothic romance is not that of the soap opera. The gothic romance isolates the heroine in an alien environment controlled by forces she cannot, at first, understand. The soap opera world is that of the community, governed by the dynamics of human interaction. While the gothic subplot was prominent, *Guiding Light* was split into two worlds with few connections between them. Eventually, the gothic plot was absorbed into the world of *Guiding Light*, but most of its gothic elements had to be jettisoned in the process: the ingenue and the master of the house marry; he turns out to be the long-lost son of a prominent Springfield family; the Mrs. Danvers character is sent to live with her sister in Scotland, and so forth. In short, the pull toward intertextual meaning meets a corresponding resistance from textual codes, whose function it is to preserve the autonomy of the soap opera world so carefully constructed for so long.

The soap opera "renaissance" of recent years has produced a new form of soap opera intertext: information about soap opera actors and the "behind the scenes" world of soap opera production in newspaper columns, specialized magazines, and television shows. Since the mid-1970s, an entire industry hyping the soap opera has emerged, one which rivals in scope, if not in size, the promotional infrastructure of Hollywood in its heyday. Several syndicated newspaper columnists now cover the soap opera "beat." Soap actors regularly make public appearances at shopping centers, arranged by agencies that do nothing else. Some soap actors have their own publicity agents. A half-dozen fan magazines are devoted largely to soap operas. In 1982 a half-hour, syndicated, "magazine-format" television program on soaps, *Soap World*, was introduced.

Representative of the function served by these soap intertexts is *Soap Opera Digest*, a biweekly magazine. It was begun in the early 1970s as a means of keeping viewers who worked outside the home up to date with plot developments on their favorite soaps. Today, in addition to plot summaries of all daytime soaps, *Soap Opera Digest* contains articles on and interviews with soap actors, photographic essays, articles on how soap operas are produced, and a readers' forum in which viewers can express their views about soap operas, among other features. Its focus is the soap opera actor and the character he or she plays.

*Soap Opera Digest* reflects and contributes to the transformation of some

soap actors into "stars." Richard Dyer defines a star as a "structured polysemy" constructed around a performer. Essential to the polysemic nature of
stardom is the development of a persona beyond that assumed by an actor
in his or her roles.[18] From the beginning of soap operas in the 1930s
through the 1950s, soap opera producers (particularly Procter and Gamble)
actively discouraged actors from developing off-screen (and, earlier, off-
speaker) images, perhaps believing that this would detract from the "realism" of the soap world, but also realizing (as did early film producers) that
the more a character became known to the public also as an actor, the
greater his or her potential leverage at contract renewal time.

More recently, however, networks, production companies, and sponsors
have realized the offsetting benefits of promoting soap actors and through
them the soaps in which they star. Rick Springfield, Dr. Noah Drake in *General Hospital,* is equally well known as a rock-and-roll performer. Other
soap actors (Tony Geary and Genie Francis among them) have firmly established extra–soap opera personas. *Soap Opera Digest* provides a prime
vehicle for promoting both the character as star and the actor as character.
Because of that magazine and other sources, the referentiality of some
characters is doubled: Dr. Noah Drake can be read as that character and as
Rick Springfield, the separate but related persona constructed from other
images. Although stories about soap opera actors in *Soap Opera Digest* are
frequently written as exposés of the "real" person behind the character, the
intertext used by the soap opera viewer is not the actor as person but
merely another image of an existing image. Obviously, there is a "person"
behind the character/actor/star, but this person is almost never known directly by the viewer; both character and performer's persona are constructed textual images that comment upon one another. Their difference
lies in the codes employed in understanding them.

### IDEOLOGICAL CODES

As we have seen, one of the primary ways any narrative text is made to
"mean" is the filling in of textual gaps by the reader, the imposition of the
individual's frames of reference upon the world of the text. The term "ideological," as applied to this process, designates the structured but largely unarticulated body of beliefs, assumptions, and values which forms the basis
upon which the reader fills in textual gaps. Eco calls this set of codes "common frames." The viewer constantly compares soap opera actions with
"what should happen" in such a situation: what is plausible, veristic, mor-

ally correct, and so forth, according to both the textual codes of the soap opera world and the viewer's own world of experience and values. For content analysts, ideological codes are the only ones employed in understanding soap operas, but in fact they are but one set of codes among several simultaneously employed by the viewer. The viewer realizes that even when his or her expectations are based upon experience, they are being applied *not* to a real-life situation but to a fictive construct.

In 1975, Sari Thomas conducted extensive interviews with a sample of forty soap opera viewers. Working from a theoretical model developed by Sol Worth and Larry Gross, Thomas suggested that soap opera viewers employed two distinct frames of reference in decoding them: attributional and inferential. According to this model, when readers encounter what they believe to be a fictional text, they decode it by attempting to assign patterns of signification (the "message") found in the text to its author. When, on the other hand, readers encounter what seems to be a nonauthored text (a natural phenomenon or a piece of unedited newsfilm, for example), they decode it by attributing meaning to it by reference to "real life," or, more accurately, their experience of real life.

Thomas does not suggest that the employment of an inferential frame of reference means those viewers regard soap operas as reality, but that they tend to rely more on what are called here ideological codes in their decoding. The viewer makes sense of soap opera characters and situations by imposing his or her own frame of knowledge, values, and experience. For example, Thomas asked her respondents to predict what would happen in a given plot line in *All My Children*. One viewer responded: "I think Chuck and Tara will stay together for the sake of the baby. Even if it is Phil's child, Chuck has really acted as the father. I don't go for that. I mean irregardless of who actually made the baby, it's the parents who raise the child that counts." Other viewers tended to base their expectations upon what Thomas would call attributional, and I would call textual, codes. (Given the invisibility and often plurality of soap opera authorship, it seems unlikely that viewers imagine a unitary communicating force behind the text itself.) For example, another viewer responded: "Chuck and Tara will stay together because this way there's always room for complication later on. If Tara and Phil actually did stay together, the whole story there would be kaput."[19]

Integrating Thomas's findings into the theoretical framework of this chapter, I would argue that attributional/inferential orientations of soap opera readers do not represent realistic/unrealistic or informed/uninformed decoding practices. Rather, the semiotic operation of the soap opera text not only allows for but encourages both these and other codes to be employed. To a greater extent perhaps than any other fiction, the soap opera text constantly walks the line between one that can be read as fiction and one that spills over into the experiential world of the viewer. The operation of the ideological codes pulls the world of the viewer and that of the text together; other codes keep them pushed apart. It is the possibility of simultaneously employing a range of codes, not in substitution for one another but in addition to one another, that renders the soap opera text "overcoded" and complex.

## The Female Reader

Both Iser and Jauss have been criticized—and rightly so—for constructing an ideal reader suspiciously like themselves: educated European males.[20] Neither would deny that differences in class and gender among readers condition the activations of texts by those readers, but neither concerns himself very much with the nature of those differences or their likely or even possible effects. Obviously, in the case of the soap opera we cannot afford to presume either a genderless or a male reader, since for as long as there have been soap operas, women have constituted their primary readership. The issue of the soap opera as "woman's fiction" will be taken up from a historical perspective in chapter 6. Here we need to examine the soap opera's *differently* gendered audience in its possible relationship to both textual structure and the position marked out for the reader within that structure. As we have seen, Ellen Seiter uses Eco's open/closed text distinction to argue that soap operas allow for the possibility of "alternative" readings unintended by their producers. In her book *Loving with a Vengeance*, Tania Modleski goes much further, suggesting that the soap opera represents a "femininely" structured textual system that engages the female reader in a unique fashion, with the result that "soap operas may be in the vanguard not just of T.V. art but of all popular narrative art."[21]

Modleski uses soap operas, along with romances and gothic novels, to point out that our notions of narrative pleasure and response to popular works remain overly narrow. Even in contemporary feminist criticism, it is frequently presumed that narrative pleasure is essentially "masculine" in nature because it involves identification with a single protagonist (usually male) and because of its orientation toward action leading to ultimate resolution, knowledge, and hence spectator/reader power.[22] The soap opera, however, is for Modleski an example of a narrative form whose structuring principles are essentially "feminine" and whose reader is positioned quite differently than in the mainstream Hollywood film or James Bond novel. Rather than make narrative closure the point from which narrative pleasure derives, the soap opera, which is predicated upon the impossibility of closure and constantly delays resolution, "makes anticipation of an end an end in itself." Whereas masculine narratives might "inscribe" in the text a reader whose omniscience is secured by the end of the book, the soap opera gives us a reader as ideal mother: one whose narrative interests are diffused among a large "family" of characters and whose power is always limited by her helplessness to bring their problems to ultimate resolution.

Thus the "immortality" of the soap opera speaks to the contemporary situation of the housewife/mother, whose life is given purpose and meaning by and through the family. The never-ending tensions and traumas suffered by soap opera families assure the continuing need for the advice and consolation of the mother. The soap opera asserts the centrality of the family, but does so by keeping its families in a state of constant disarray, always in need of the understanding of both its diegetic mothers and its mother/reader. Although denied ultimate knowledge that comes with resolution, the mother/reader is endowed with greater knowledge at any given moment than any of her "children" in the soap opera world. She is called upon not to pass judgment in most cases but, by being given "all sides" of an issue, to exercise maternal tolerance and sympathy.

To Modleski the soap opera represents a narrative form whose construction is diametrically opposed to that of the "male" film and novel. The latter favors action over dialogue and ruthlessly reduces indeterminacies in order to arrive at a single moment of closure, solution, and knowledge. The soap opera makes the consequences of actions more important than action itself, introduces complications at every opportunity, and denies the desire for ultimate control by assuming its own immortality. In the male narrative dialogue is motored by plot and serves to explain, clarify, and simplify. In the soap opera, dialogue increases indeterminacy and retards resolution. The self-knowledge that is frequently expressed through dialogue as the Hollywood film approaches resolution is largely absent from the soap opera. Talk bespeaks multiplicitous motives, the unintended ramifications of every action, and, concomitantly, the limits of self-awareness.

The work of Modleski and Seiter is complementary in several respects to the reader-oriented poetics of soap operas presented here. First, both interrogate the notion of narrative pleasure in general and the pleasures to be derived from popular texts in particular. In doing so, they demonstrate that the nature of that pleasure may differ greatly between men and women. This suggests that both the peculiar status of the soap opera as object of social science investigation and the disdain it has engendered among most critics are in part attributable to a misrecognition of this difference. The soap opera has been illegible as an aesthetic object partly because the terms by which it could be aesthetically engaged seemed foreign to most men. Feminist criticism of the past decade has raised the possibility that the narrative strategies and central stylistic features of "mainstream" fiction and film are sexually loaded, that a male reader/spectator is "inscribed" in the text. This does not mean that a female reader cannot enjoy such texts, but rather that her response is mediated by her difference from the text's implied reader. If this is the case, then the values that critics privilege in such works are likely to be sexually loaded as well.

Modleski acknowledges that criticism by sexual analogy can rapidly deteriorate into silliness, and neither she nor I would claim that the popularity and aesthetic appeal of soap operas can be explained by their attunement to the patterns and rhythms of female sexuality. As Julia Kristeva has argued, however, the feminine experience of temporality might well be different from that of male time. "Female subjectivity," says Kristeva, "would seem to provide a specific measure that essentially retains *repetition* and *eternity* from among the multiple modalities of time known through the history of civilizations."[23] Yet these temporal modalities—characteristic of the soap opera—are those least likely to be associated with works of narrative art within the discourse of traditional aesthetics. Indeed, it is their obverse—innovation and progression—that are revered in narrative fiction. Regardless of how far we might wish to go in regarding gender as a determinant of narrative pleasure, feminist criticism of the sort exemplified by the work of Modleski and Seiter proposes the *reception* of cultural texts as an essential category of critical analysis. As such, its concerns overlap to a significant degree with those of a reader-oriented poetics in general.

While her description of the soap opera reader as ideal mother is useful in differentiating the soap opera reading experience from that of other texts, Modleski comes close at some points in her analysis to reducing the soap opera reading situation to a metaphorical correspondence with the presumed life of a "housewife" and mother. Married women not working outside the home have long constituted the core of the soap opera audience, and the size and loyalty of this audience indicate that soap operas have long addressed the narrative and aesthetic needs of women working in the home and raising children. However, several important qualifications must be made to this association of the soap opera reader with the "average American housewife." First, neither the structure of the soap opera text nor the social situation of its audience has remained static—as we shall see in chapter 6. Although Modleski seems to present the "mother/reader" as a textually inscribed position to be taken up by whoever the actual reader happens to be, she comes close at times to conflating the two. What Modleski discusses as the decenteredness of soap opera form we have called here its paradigmatic complexity. The diffusion of interest and identification in the soap opera may well provide the housewife/spectator with "training in a decentered existence," but, viewed as paradigmatic complexity, it also opens up the soap opera text for a variety of responses from a number of different readerships. The soap opera represents an "over-coded" narrative form, in which characters and relationships are endowed with pluri-significative possibilities far exceeding that required by narrative function alone. It is this very indeterminacy created by the soap opera's over-coding that helps to account for the form's longevity and the breadth of its contemporary appeal. This is not to say that the soap opera is ideologically neutral or that it can be read in an infinite number of ways, but we must not confuse presumed ideological intent with either reader response or ideological effect.

As we shall see shortly, soap operas since their inception have been concerned with aspects of American life that have been marginalized in mainstream fictive narratives: parentage, family, the emotional consequences of romance, conflicting female role expectations, and so forth. Regardless of how the viewer might feel about the *way* in which these issues are addressed in soap operas, she knows that at the very least she will find that they *are* addressed there. Modleski's conclusion that the soap opera form is "not altogether at odds with a possible feminist aesthetic" stems from her recognition of that form as an alternative to "male" narratives. As such, it provided a point of departure at least for the development of narrative strategies that "make explicit the criticisms of masculine power and masculine pleasure implied in the narrative form of the soap opera." Quite aside from its potential as a possible proto-feminist form, however, the soap opera represents an alternative basis for narrative aesthetic pleasure in general—one that values complexity, repetition, and speech over simplicity, telos, and action. A soap opera viewer might find some aspects of a soap silly or uninteresting, but she knows that the nature of narrative engagement to be found in the soap opera is different from that to be found in any other form of commercial television—perhaps in any other form of narrative.

# An Institutional History of Soap Operas

## Writing a Soap Opera History

Since the inception of the soap opera in the early 1930s, nearly one hundred thousand hours of text have been broadcast on radio and television, and each year some twenty-six hundred hours of new text are added by network daytime soap operas alone. By any measure, soap operas constitute one of the most striking features of the history of commercial broadcast programming.

Yet models drawn from American mass communications research are of limited usefulness in studying the soap opera as an object of historical investigation. Broadcasting history, as it is taught and studied in this country, tends to be technological, economic, and regulatory history: the rise of broadcasting corporations, battles between them for control over technological innovation, government regulation of commercial broadcasting, relationships between broadcasting and other media (newspapers, in particular), and the impact of political and social change upon the economic structure of commercial broadcasting are among its primary concerns. Programming is relegated to a position of subsidiary importance, unless it can be seen as part of one of the above issues. The growth of radio news programming in the 1930s, for example, becomes one aspect of the "radio-press war."

Furthermore, as one might imagine, soap operas manage but a mention in standard histories of broadcasting. In his *Tube of Plenty: The Evolution of American Television*, Eric Barnouw, the most thorough and thoughtful of American broadcasting historians, devotes eight sentences out of his five-hundred-page history to both radio and television soap operas. Of radio serials he says:

Meanwhile [in the 1930s] daytime serials had developed an extraordinary hold over home audiences. Sociologists studying the phenomenon found that women looked to such serials as *Ma Perkins* and *Just Plain Bill* and *The Romance of Helen Trent* for guidance on personal problems. Many expressed a dire dependence on serials. Thanks to this devotion, many businesses were making a financial comeback through radio sponsorship.

Televised serials, at least, receive their own paragraph.

Weekday mornings and afternoons were increasingly profitable [in the early 1960s]. Daytime serials had at first seemed a failure on television. But when they were expanded from the 15-minute form inherited from radio to a 30-minute form, success followed. By 1964 daytime serials were an addiction comparable to the radio-serial addiction at its zenith, and were the mainstay of New York activity in television drama. They were especially profitable for CBS-TV.[1]

Barnouw's treatment of soap operas tells us much more about their peculiar position in academic mass media discourse than it does about them as historical phenomena.

There has been one serious book-length historical study of soap operas, Raymond William Stedman's 1959 dissertation, "A History of the Broadcasting of Daytime Serial Dramas in the United States."[2] It is valuable as a sort of prehistorical, year-by-year chronicle of individual soap operas and of the critical response their popularity engendered, but Stedman's historical analysis is much less illuminating. Basically, he attempts to explain the "lastingness" of the daytime serial form, and he concludes that "the durability of the form of the daytime serial drama seemed to be related strongly and principally to the continuing narrative." This is accurate enough, but not exactly a blinding historical insight.

Stedman's work, along with much of American writing on broadcasting history, is informed by the historiographical variant of empiricism. Empiricist history depends for its explanatory force not so much on regularity as upon the empiricist separation of subject and object. To the empiricist, history consists of the collection and arrangement of "facts." These facts are presumed to exist entirely apart from the consciousness of the historian who collects them (they are extradiscursive). The historian's role is that of disinterested, "objective" recorder. Knowledge is directly related to the amount of facts presented us by the historian: the more facts we have about a historical phenomenon, the more we "know" about it and the more it has been explained, since, properly arranged, the facts "speak for themselves." A "theory" of history is unnecessary, and interpretation is to be avoided as an unwarranted intrusion of subjectivity into the historian's objective project.

Empiricist history is frequently couched in narrative terms, a story related to the reader by the historian/narrator. Narrative has been a mode of historical writing for thousands of years, of course, and to the extent that historical explanation involves the description of a sequence of events bound by cause-and-effect relationships, all history is narrative history. As Hayden White has shown, however, empiricist history often takes on the trappings of traditional *fictive* narratives as well.[3] The historian retreats into the position of narrator, and the relationship of the historian to the events described is rendered unproblematic. The reader is asked to presume that the narrator, through whatever means, "knows what happened." History is presented as precast and already known, as a tale to be told with a beginning, middle, and end. Narrative transitions are allowed to displace causal explanations. History becomes a story "about" a finite set of characters, whose actions constitute the stuff of history.

The combination of empiricist ontology and epistemology and narrative historical form produces what we might call naive empiricism, to distinguish it from the philosophically informed empiricist history proposed by Carl Hempel, William Aydelotte, and others.[4] Both, particularly the former, have been thoroughly critiqued for more than fifty years. As early as the 1930s, Charles Beard challenged his colleagues in the American Historical Association to rethink their empiricist assumptions:

> History, as it actually was, as distinguished, of course, from particular facts of history, is not known or knowable, no matter how zealously is pursued the "ideal of effort for objective truth." . . . The historian seeking to know the past, or about it, does not bring to the partial documentation with which he works a perfect and polished neutral mind in which the past streaming though the medium of documentation is mirrored as it actually was. Whatever acts of purification the historian may perform he yet remains human, a creature of time, place, circumstance, interests, predelictions, culture.[5]

The vital philosophical debates in historiography and the philosophy of history, within which Beard's remark is but an initial provocation, do not seem to have seeped into American mass communications history, however. Perhaps because it is less reducible to regularity, American mass communications history has taken a back seat to empiricist sociological research. Barnouw's pioneering attempt at a comprehensive history of American broadcasting stands virtually alone.

The historical model offered by traditional aesthetics is equally theoretically impoverished. Since it assumes that artists produce art and that potential artworks are to be evaluated according to historically transcendent standards, traditional aesthetic history regards its role as the chronological assessment of the lives and works of great artists and, thereby, the establishment of an eternal canon of "art."

Thus, oddly enough, the greater the work of art the less historical it is, and the more it transcends the boundaries of its own historical conditions of production and consumption. Because it values timelessness over historical specificity, traditional aesthetic history marginalizes both historical context and change. What we are left with as "history" in traditional aesthetics, as Droysen pointed out long ago, is little more than a *Sonntagsstrasse der Kunstgeschichte*—a Sunday afternoon stroll down the main boulevard of art, along which the reader pauses with the historian to peer into chronologically arranged art works as into so many decorated shop windows.[6]

Among reader-response theorists, Jauss has perhaps been the most historically oriented. Jauss insists that, as virtual semantic structures, literary works in and of themselves have no history except as they are received and responded to by successive waves of readers. Each new literary work is read against a historically specific horizon of expectations. "History of literature is a process of aesthetic reception and production that takes place in the realization of literary texts on the part of the receptive reader, the reflective critic, and the author in his continuing productivity."[7] Thus understanding the "history" of a particular work would entail a grasp of the text's use of previous aesthetic strategies and allusions, the horizon of expectations against which it was initially read, the articulated response the work engendered, its subsequent assimilation into or distancing from the reader's horizon, and textual changes brought about in other texts of the same form or genre by the resultant feedback process between readers, authors, and cultural institutions. Although Jauss is concerned with the connection between literary history and more general historical processes, in the end his model of literary history is largely insular and evolutionary. Furthermore, while Jauss attacks the view of literary history as the chronological assessment of a preordained body of great works, his own examples tend to be drawn from that same body of works whose status as art is unquestioned.[8]

The soap opera is and always has been a narrative text in service of an economic imperative, in a much more direct fashion than those works Jauss and other reader-response critics discuss. Thus, our consideration of the soap opera as historical phenomenon must proceed along two parallel tracks: an examination of the functions served by soap operas within the institution of American commercial broadcasting (including the changes in those functions over time) and (insofar as they are historically discernible) an examination of the origins and development of the soap opera as a textual system as received by succcessive generations of readers since the early 1930s. This chapter takes up the former of these tracks; the next considers the latter. It should be pointed out that while our examination of these two historical aspects will appear as parallel, in their historical relationship they cannot be separated out so neatly.

The general historiographic perspective from which this inquiry will be conducted is one based on *realism*, an ontological and epistemological position developed within the philosophy of science principally by Roy Bhaskar and Rom Harre. Although a fully developed position within the philosophy of science, realism has only begun to make itself felt in historical disciplines.[9] Extrapolating from basic statements of realist ontology and epistemology, we can construct a basic outline of realist historiography. A realist history would posit a historical past existing independently of the mind of the historian. Knowledge of this past comes through extant historical evidence, but in no sense does this evidence, or the "facts" of history to which it refers, speak for itself. Historical evidence forms the partial, mediated, yet indispensable record of the past, but in the realist view the historian's primary interest is not in this record or the chronicle it can be made to form but in the generative (causal) mechanisms that lie behind it. These generative mechanisms are multiple and interactive. Furthermore, they operate at a number of conceptual levels and with uneven force, so that historical events seldom provide illustrations of covering laws. The realist regards history as an open system, and, where history concerns human agency, an open social system. Thus Bhaskar finds all realist social science, including history, to be incomplete rather than definitive, epistemologically "open" rather than closed. The reassuring certainty that is the goal of empiricism is denied at every turn by the very nature of historical inquiry—if not by the nature of social systems in general.

## The Origins of Soap Opera Production

The principal generative mechanisms responsible for the soap opera's origin and perpetuation are easily discernible: as was noted in the last chapter, soap operas function within advertiser-supported broadcasting as advertising vehicles—to attract a particular audience at given times for the purpose of "selling" their attention to product manufacturers. Insofar as they share this function with soap operas, all instances of commercial broadcast programming can be "explained" by reference to their role in this economic system. But to leave the history of soap operas (or broadcasting) here would be the worst sort of reductive economism. We must account not only for the soap opera's general function as advertising vehicle but also for its particularities as a textual form. Why was the serial form employed in this fashion? Why did soap operas take on the character of asymptotic worlds? Why were they directed almost exclusively toward women? Why did they originate when they did? To answer these questions we must take a closer look at the generative mechanisms responsible for the soap opera. Here it is possible to see the initial development of the soap opera form and its dissemination over network radio as the conjunction of several distinct lines of causal force.[10]

### THE DEVELOPMENT OF NETWORK RADIO

American Telephone and Telegraph initiated the linking of geographically separated radio stations by telephone lines to form a network for the purpose of attracting national advertisers in 1923. Rather than use programming as an inducement for people to buy radio sets (as Westinghouse had done) or as an advertisement of other interests of the station owner (the call letters of the station owned by the *Chicago Tribune* stood for "*World's Greatest Newspaper*"), AT&T offered its Newark station, WEAF, and its monopolistic control of telephone long-lines to any corporate client that wanted to pay the "toll." After three years of industrial warfare between RCA, GE, Westinghouse, and AT&T over access to telephone lines and patent issues and three years of indecisiveness by various federal government agencies as to what, if any, power they had to intervene in the struggle, advertiser-based commercial network radio was firmly established by an agreement between the industrial parties to launch the National Broadcasting Company. The September 1926 newspaper ads announcing the formation of the network admitted that its principal interest in developing "quality" programming stemmed from the parent company's (RCA) desire to sell radio sets to every American family. The ads also implicitly acknowledged the more permanent basis upon which network broadcasting eventually would be established. Eager not to appear monopolistic, RCA generously offered other radio set manufacturers "the facilities of the National Broadcasting Company for the purpose of making known to the public their receiving sets . . . on the same terms as accorded to other clients." By 1928 NBC was operating two networks ("Blue" and "Red") and had been joined in the network broadcasting field by the Columbia Broadcasting System. Barnouw points out that, with the institution of advertiser-supported network radio, broadcasting became a servant of American industry to a degree unrealized in any other aspect of cultural production:

> Born of a military establishment, and still closely linked to it, it had now also acquired a special relationship to a wide spectrum of big business and its advertising agencies. No such constellation had ever planned and controlled a nation's popular culture. Most programs were being produced by advertising agencies, as an activity parallel to the planning and designing of billboards and magazine advertisements. The network, having "sold" a period, seemed to regard it as sponsor property, to be used as he designated. Sponsors were, in effect, being encouraged to take charge of the air.[11]

The parallel Barnouw suggests between radio and billboards as advertising media in the initial phase of network radio needs qualification. Most advertisers were slow in accepting network radio as an effective medium for the direct sale of products on a national basis. Wanting to be seen as serving "the interest of the listening public," NBC made certain that its first programming efforts were "high-brow" and sedate: classical music, historical dramas, adaptations of literary classics, and poetic recitations were standard fare. Advertisers sponsored much of this programming, but more with the aim of attaching the company name and image to such a prestigious endeavor than of selling the sponsor's product over the air. NBC forbade its sponsors to mention prices in their advertising messages until competition with CBS forced them to change this policy in 1932. There were also doubts as to how large the audience for any particular program really was. The first regular ratings service did not begin until 1930. Programs could not be broadcast simultaneously from coast to coast. While the number of radio sets in use grew enormously in the late 1920s, the 1930 census revealed that 60 percent of American families were still without radios.[12]

Ironically, the Great Depression contributed considerably to the growth of network radio and, as a result, to the development of radio as a direct-sale advertising vehicle. Most other entertainment industries were damaged by the economic contractions and dislocations of early 1930s. By 1931 RKO, Fox, and Warner Bros. were all operating in the red, and in 1933 movie box office receipts were but 40 percent of the already-sagging 1931 level. The recording industry was kept alive only by the use of records in juke boxes. Although the number of general-interest magazines in circulation nearly doubled between 1929 and 1933 (from 61 to 109), the advertising revenue generated from them was cut in half over the same period.[13] All of these entertainment industries depended upon direct and repeated consumer outlay. Once the initial investment was made in a radio receiver, however, the consumer could enjoy, in the words of *Broadcasting* magazine, "the least expensive form of entertainment ever made available to man." The expiration of key patents in the 1920s and economies of scale in production had reduced the cost of radio receivers by 1930 to the point that most Americans could afford one. Faced with a choice of making one expenditure for a radio receiver, with which one could then enjoy unlimited "free" programming, or of paying each week for a new record, magazine, or movie ticket, many Depression-era families chose the former. Between 1930 and 1932 Americans purchased 4.6 million radio receivers. In 1934, CBS estimated that 90.9 percent of all nonfarm families owned radios and the following year figured the aggregate audience for radio at 71 million persons out of a total population of 125 million.[14]

NETWORK PROGRAMMING: THE SERIAL FORM

In order for radio to expand its advertising role beyond that of corporate image-enhancer and to develop as a national mass-marketing medium for large corporations, advertisers needed to be assured that millions of Americans were listening to particular programs at particular times with habitual frequency, just as they knew that each new issue of a magazine would be read by its subscribers. Advertising agencies eagerly accepted the challenge of developing programming that listeners would tune to week in and week out, and local stations and networks quickly acquiesced. When NBC was launched in 1926, only a few programs were produced by agencies. By 1931 only a few network shows were not. Between commissions paid by the networks for sale of airtime and fees paid by sponsors for program production, an advertising agency could easily earn twenty-four hundred dollars per network program hour. The longer the show ran, the fewer staff-hours had to be devoted by the agency to developing new program ideas and securing talent, and, thus, the more profit the agency realized for each hour of programming produced.

Since audiences were larger and ad rates and commissions higher during evening hours, it is not surprising that prime time received the lion's share of programming attention during the first years of network radio. One model for attracting a large audience at the same time each week was offered by vaudeville and the movies: build audience interest and loyalty on the basis of stars. The demise of vaudeville in the late 1920s (in part a result of the introduction of sound motion pictures) left a large pool of stars and journeyman performers upon which radio could draw. By 1933, Eddie Cantor, Ed Wynn, Ken Murray, Al Jolson, Rudy Vallee, the Marx Brothers, Jack Benny, Fred Allen, and George Burns and Gracie Allen had all made the transition from vaudeville or the movies to radio. While the structuring of comedy and variety programs around already recognized stars succeeded in attracting large audiences, this strategy had an obvious disadvantage: the cost of the talent the audience had tuned in to hear. Performers who made thousands of dollars weekly in vaudeville or the movies expected salaries for radio work commensurate with their already established popularity.

By 1929 another programming model had been established, one which relied for its appeal upon audience interest in character and narrative rather than stars. Undoubtedly one program, *Amos and Andy*, was crucial in convincing advertisers that such a programming strategy would work. Developed for WGN in 1926 by two former minstrel performers, *Amos and Andy* was by 1929 a radio programming phenomenon. With an estimated weekly audience of forty million listeners, it provided its sponsor, Pepsodent toothpaste, with an advertising vehicle of hitherto unimagined proportions. *Amos and Andy* comic strips and phonograph records were "spun off" from the network program. Some contemporaneous commentators even went so far as to credit its overwhelming success for making radio a national advertising medium.[15] *Amos and Andy* also demonstrated the appeal of the serial radio form. The misadventures of two southern black men transplanted to the south side of Chicago (the show was written and acted by two white men), which formed the focus of the show, were continued through each "week-daily" episode. A breach-of-promise suit brought by Widow Parker against Andy Brown was drawn out for weeks. While some broadcasters feared that such narrative indeterminacy would frustrate listeners, it proved to have the opposite effect.

The success of *Amos and Andy* also helped to establish Chicago as a center for the production of radio drama. The variety-show format, dependent upon stars for its appeal, was developed in Los Angeles and New York. Proximity to movie or theatrical stars was much less of a factor in dramatic programming, however, which relied for audience appeal upon narrative rather than personality enticements. Advertising agencies and broadcasters found in the Chicago area a large pool of potential radio actors available at lower cost than on either coast.

Here and there, local stations also recognized the listener interest and loyalty to be secured through the serial format, particularly when applied to a "real-life" situation. In 1930 Kansas City station KMBC began running *Happy Hollow*, a nightly (except Sunday) "true-to-life portrayal of happenings in any small town in the United States." The leading denizen of Happy Hollow was Uncle Ezra, the town's mayor, principal shopkeeper, and station agent. He was frequently pitted against city slicker Harry Checkervest in comic repartee. Variety elements were introduced into the show via the mechanism of a twice-weekly town hall talent show. The show's writers were happy to oblige sponsors by placing their goods on the shelves of Uncle Ezra's store and having him extol their virtues as he sold them to the residents of Happy Hollow.

*Happy Hollow*, picked up by CBS in 1931 and broadcast throughout the Midwest, illustrated a basic radio marketing principle borne out by early empirical research. In 1931, Robert Elder of MIT surveyed 14,061 families in ten American cities to assess the effect of radio advertising on product preferences. He found that brand preference increased directly with the number of hours listened to radio each week, even controlling for family buying power. Furthermore, he concluded that the more frequently a program was on the air, the greater its power to establish and maintain preference for its advertised product. Taking Elder's research one step further, *Fortune* magazine urged the prospective radio advertiser to "go out and get himself a popular serial."[16]

## "DISCOVERING" DAYTIME RADIO

If broadcasters and sponsors could not be sure how many people listened to a particular program during prime time, they had very little idea of the prospects for daytime radio. Common sense and a few audience studies showed that most people who listened to radio did so between the hours of seven and ten in the evening and that since these hours are traditionally associated with leisure activities, the listening audience in prime time was an eager and receptive one. In 1930 no firm data existed on how many people were available to listen to radio before 6:00 P.M., who they were (except that they were female), whether or not they were disposed to listen to radio at all during the day, or if they would attend to advertisements broadcast during the day. Networks and local stations simply set their advertising rates at one-half that charged for prime time, figuring that, whatever the audience for daytime radio, it was at most one-half as large as that for prime time.

By 1932 there was some evidence that daytime's potential for advertising had been underestimated. A&P, the national grocery chain, had been an early radio advertiser, sponsoring a music program, *The A&P Gypsies*, since 1924. In 1930 the company used daytime radio for direct advertising through the sponsorship of several morning programs directed toward women at home. All of them featured cooking tips, food preparation ideas, and sample menus tied to products sold at A&P grocery stores. Even in the midst of the Depression, A&P's sales increased. In 1932 A&P attempted to test the extent of radio's power to "sell" particular products. Between May and November selected items were advertised only on radio and only on Monday programs. Sales for those items on Monday and Tuesday were then compared to their sales levels on other days. When the price of the item was not mentioned, sales increased 29 percent the days following its being advertised on radio; when price was announced, sales increased an astounding 173 percent. A&P was convinced of the efficacy of daytime programming and advertising.

When the manufacturer of Oxol, a liquid laundry bleach, introduced it in 1931, it decided to advertise exclusively on radio via *The Oxol Feature*, a fifteen-minute music and humor program carried by CBS at ten o'clock on weekday mornings. The question this strategy asked was, Would women listen while they worked in the home and would they pay attention to the ads? The campaign met with success, but the company wanted some further indication of audience attentiveness. Its advertising agency devised what came to be called a "mailhook": the offering of some sort of premium during a given radio program. In this case, listeners could receive a free rag doll by mailing in an Oxol label. More than seventy thousand requests were received. Once again, research data soon supported anecdotal evidence. In 1932 a study of nine hundred Pennsylvania women concluded that "the program sponsor should realize that the housewife in a majority of cases is the member of the family who has the most influence upon family purchases and is the one who spends the greatest amount of time in the home. She is, therefore, the member of the family most easily reached by radio broadcasts."[17]

INDUSTRIAL IMPERATIVES:
THE CASE OF PROCTER AND GAMBLE

The observations of this study were of greater relevance to some industries than others: soap, toiletry, and foodstuffs manufacturers all oriented their advertising and marketing strategies toward the female consumer, since women tended (and still do) to make most of the purchases for those categories of items. Thus, a further generative mechanism that needs to be considered in the origins of the soap opera arises from the position of those industries and their constituent companies in the early years of the Depression. The situation of one company, Procter and Gamble, is particularly illustrative, since by the late 1930s it had become the principal sponsor of radio soap operas.

From its mid-nineteenth-century beginnings as a Cincinnati chandlery, Procter and Gamble by the mid-1920s had grown into a major international corporation with a diversified product line of food products, household supplies, and toiletries. Gross sales in 1928 exceeded $202 million, with profits of $19 million. Procter and Gamble's success was based upon the mass production of consumer products that sold at relatively small unit prices and generated relatively low unit profits. The large corporate profits were secured through volume sales, and volume sales through heavy product advertising. In the mid-1920s Procter and Gamble decided to introduce new products in competition with those it already produced, reasoning that intracorporate competition kept management on its toes and, more important, that multiple products within a product line would keep total market share up and opportunities for market entry through innovation by other firms low. Thus, by 1929 Camay competed against Ivory, Oxydol against Duz, and Ivory Flakes against Chipso—all of them Procter and Gamble products. Different advertising agencies handled competing products, a strategy that provided a built-in test of relative advertising effectiveness and discouraged agency complacency.[18]

The idea of using the serial narrative form as bait to attract consumer attention to advertising messages was familiar to Procter and Gamble well before it contemplated using radio as a vehicle for those narratives. By 1921, the annual advertising budget for Ivory soap had already reached $1 million per year. For decades it had been Procter and Gamble's policy to advertise Ivory in a long list of general-interest magazines in full-page ads facing the first page of editorial content. Since the 1880s Ivory had been advertised as "pure," unadulterated soap, safe for all washing purposes from clothes and dishes to babies. These full-page magazine ads illustrated the purity and wholesomeness of Ivory through paintings depicting its use in idyllic, domestic settings. At the end of 1922, however, Procter and Gamble gave the Ivory account to another agency and charged it with the task of devising a new ad campaign for the product. Mark H. Wiseman of the Blackman Company suggested the creation of a comic-strip family to advertise Ivory in the Sunday rotogravure section of major newspapers. The Jollyco family—Mom, Dad, Sally (age sixteen), Bobby (age ten), and baby Teewee—was "tested" in New York, where sales of Ivory went up 25 percent in six months. By the end of 1923 newspaper readers across the country were following the domestic saga of the wholesome Jollycos, who, of course, used Ivory soap, and the meddling of the snobbish Mrs. Percival Billington Folderal, who used colored, perfumed soap. Readers even wrote to Procter and Gamble to suggest plot lines for the comic strip.

Procter and Gamble turned to radio advertising early in the 1920s. In 1923 Crisco sponsored the *Radio Homemakers' Club* on Monday nights over WEAF. Camay soap was the first Procter and Gamble product to be advertised on network radio. The company's brand of perfumed, colored toilet soap (but certainly not that used by Mrs. Percival Billington Folderal), Camay sponsored a Friday-morning *Radio Beauty School* over NBC in 1927.

Many companies responded to the Great Depression by cutting back on advertising budgets. For Procter and Gamble, however, advertising was central to its strategy for combatting the effect of economic constriction. Since its profitability was based upon volume sales, the company reasoned that in a period of reduced consumer buying power advertising efforts had to be increased if sales levels were to be maintained. Its advertising agencies no doubt noticed that daytime network radio rates were one-half those during prime time. Given the fact that Procter and Gamble's customers were overwhelmingly female, daytime radio seemed a logical and cost-effective advertising venue.

Between 1930 and 1932 the daytime programs sponsored by Procter and

Gamble were of the self-help and advice genre. Its initial daytime programming strategy was to run a different show in the same time slot each weekday. Chipso laundry powder sponsored *Ruth Turner's Washing Talks* one
day. The following day at the same time, audiences could hear Ivory's Mrs.
Reilly chat about baby care and fashion. The rest of the weekday slots featured Emily Post for Camay, Crisco's cooking show, *Sisters of the Skillet*,
and a monologist. Procter and Gamble stayed with this plan for two years.
By the end of 1930 Procter and Gamble had daytime programs being broadcast over a twenty-station hookup on the NBC Red network, over eleven
stations on NBC Blue, and over twenty-two stations on CBS. The first Procter
and Gamble program to be presented five days each week was *Mrs. Blake's
Radio Column*, an advice column of the air programmed in the time slot
immediately preceeding *Ruth Turner*, and the other programs. It went on
the air in 1931.

Procter and Gamble was not the only company with products in the
food, toiletry, or household supplies line to see the benefits of radio advertising in the early years of the Depression, nor was it the only company to
turn to the self-help genre as an advertising vehicle. The accompanying
chart indicates radio advertising budgets for selected companies in 1930
and 1931.

Radio Advertising Budgets, 1930 and 1931

| Company | 1930 | 1931 | Percentage Increase |
|---|---|---|---|
| Procter and Gamble | $255,168 | $499,261 | 96 |
| A&P | 345,318 | 914,606 | 163 |
| Kellogg | 34,275 | 118,343 | 245 |
| National Dairy Products | 5,121 | 123,104 | 2303 |
| Pacific Coast Borax | 25,799 | 145,074 | 473 |

By 1932 drugs and toiletries accounted for 20 percent of all radio-advertising
time sold. The largest single purchaser of radio time was the Pepsodent
Company, almost all of whose $1.7 million radio budget went for *Amos
and Andy*.[19]

The household-advice programs that many of these and other companies
sponsored were part of a larger programming trend. Barnouw points out

that the unprecedented social and economic pressures upon most American families caused by the Great Depression were eagerly capitalized upon by advertisers, who offered "free" radio solutions to listeners' every problem. Cries for help were answered by astrologers, numerologists, success experts, and palmists, provided, no doubt as a public service, by toothpaste and nail polish manufacturers. When in the early 1930s R. J. Reynolds Tobacco Company decided that women constituted an unexploited market for cigarettes, it devised a program of philosophy and inspirational verse, hosted by the ethereal-voiced Tony Wons, who reminded his female listeners at every opportunity of the pleasures of smoking Camels. In 1932 sales of Haley's M-O laxative more than doubled during the first months of its sponsorship of *The Voice of Experience*, which received upwards of twenty thousand letters of desperation each week.[20]

## *The First Soap Opera:* Painted Dreams

A Dayton schoolteacher turned radio actor, Irna Phillips, is usually credited with "inventing" the first soap opera, *Painted Dreams*, for WGN in 1930. Stedman notes that Phillips "was hired as an actress and did an extemporaneous talk program that was called *Thought for the Day*. Then the station asked her to use her writing talents. She did; and the result, as far as this writer could detemine, was the first daytime serial, *Painted Dreams*."[21] Because the historical import of a first is a retrodictive judgment of historians, contemporaneous accounts are frequently fragmentary—leaving plenty of room for historians to quibble years later over who *really* was the first to do something and what that person's motives *really* were. Phillips's "creation" of *Painted Dreams* is detailed in more that fifty-nine hundred pages of first-hand testimony, not because anyone was historically prescient but thanks to a copyright dispute between Phillips and WGN, initiated in 1932 and eventually adjudicated in 1941. The documentary evidence in the case demonstrates the convergence of the generative mechanisms discussed above in the genesis of the soap opera form and, for that reason, the futility of trying to assign the creation of the soap opera to the genius of a single individual.[22]

The court records show that in the spring of 1930 Henry Selinger, station manager of WGN, approached the advertising firm of Lord and Thomas with the idea of developing a daytime serial story that would be of special interest to women, and, hence, to manufacturers of products used in the home. He assigned a staff writer and actor to implement the idea in a series of experimental scripts for a serial entitled *The Sudds*, in hopes of attracting the sponsorship of the Super-Suds Company. When that company turned down the idea, the show was renamed *Good Luck Margie* and pitched—again unsuccessfully—to the Jelke Oleomargarine Company. In both versions the serial dealt with an Irish-American mother and her daughter and was set primarily in the mother's home.

In the midst of this process (May 1930), but initially quite apart from it, Irna Phillips became an employee of WGN. At first she read inspirational verse on WGN's amateur hour; then over the summer she was given several small acting roles, for which she was paid five or ten dollars each. During this time she constantly importuned Harry Gilman, assistant station manager, for a more permanent job as a staff writer or actor. In August she suggested to Selinger that she might be assigned to the "Sudds" project. Selinger asked Phillips to draft ten scripts for a daytime serial to involve "an Irish woman, her household, her daughter, and the daughter's friend." The program, now entitled *Painted Dreams*, was auditioned for several sponsors, but the as yet untried idea of a daytime serial generated little interest. In October, Selinger decided to launch *Painted Dreams* as a sustaining (nonsponsored) program, hoping that audience response would persuade a sponsor to take it on. Phillips was hired as its writer and one of its two regular actors, at a salary of fifty dollars per week. She played the roles of "Mother" Moynihan (named for Gilman's mother-in-law) and Sue Morton, the Moynihan's boarder. *Painted Dreams* premiered on 20 October 1930 and ran as a sustaining program daily except Sunday for a year.

During this year without a sponsor, Gilman, Selinger, and Phillips attempted to build a case for the show's popularity and advertising potential. Mailhooks were introduced into the narrative, encouraging fans to write letters to the station. In 1931, Phillips drafted a proposal to adapt the narrative of *Painted Dreams* "to the peculiar requirements of Montgomery Ward & Company, so that [its] value . . . will be that of a direct sales agent, rather than a mere agent of sustaining or creative good will." She argued that "any radio presentation which is sponsored, in order to be of utility to its sponsor, must actually sell merchandise; otherwise the object of radio advertising has failed." The accommodation of the "peculiar" needs of Montgomery Ward was to be accomplished through the marriage of either Irene Moynihan or Sue Morton: "It is then my plan to have an engagement, the wedding (in June), the trousseau, the furnishing of a home, actually occur via the air. This is the first step in developing the feature as a merchandising vehicle, and this plan opens an avenue to merchandize any article which may be sold by mail order or through the other retail outlets of Montgomery Ward & Company."[23] Montgomery Ward did not take on *Painted Dreams* as a "merchandising vehicle," but in October 1931 Mickleberry Products Company, a Chicago-based meatpacker, did. It sponsored the program until April 1932, when the dispute between Phillips and WGN over ownership of the show erupted.

Interestingly, the basis of the suit reveals that even in this embryonic stage of the development of the soap opera form, it was viewed as a set of structural principles that motored narrative and character development. In her initial chancery suit (1932) to restrain WGN from broadcasting *Painted Dreams* after her departure from the station's employ, Phillips had her attorneys argue that "she had never relinquished to defendants [WGN], by contract or otherwise, her author's property rights in her creation which consisted of the intangible common-law right of proprietorship—not in the *general or basic idea*—but in the *set-up*, the *scene*, and the *characters*, which she alone worked out and into which she had breathed her created brain conceptions [*sic*].[24] WGN found another sponsor for *Painted Dreams* and hired another writer-actress to take over from Phillips. Most of the original characters were written out and a new actress found to portray "Mother" Moynihan.

On 16 June 1932, Phillips returned to the air as writer and actress in *Today's Children* over WGN's chief competitor, WMAQ. Mother Moynihan became Mother Moran; Irene, her daughter, became Eileen; Sue Morton became Kay Norton. Even Mother Moynihan's dog Mike, who barked in protest at the excesses of his mistress's homespun philosophy, was transferred to *Today's Children* as Mickey, although this "spectral canine stooge," as WGN's attorneys called him, was no longer the voice of Phillips herself but was "done by a 'sound-effects man' using a mechanical barker—in deference either to the world trend toward mechanization or else to the increased artistic stature, dignity and opulence which plaintiff has now attained as Mother Moran."[25] Having learned her lesson from *Painted Dreams*, Phillips refused employment from WMAQ, preferring instead to act as the independent producer of *Today's Children* and bearing the entire costs of the program for four months of nonsponsored broadcasts.

In August, Phillips attempted the first mailhook for *Today's Children*.

The 3 August episode, in which Mother Moran's son celebrated his wedding anniversary, closed with the announcer saying:

> *Ann*: I'm sure all our friends join with me in wishing Dorothy and
> Terry many happy returns of the day. And now, I'm wondering
> bout that anniversary picture. I know I'd like to have one of them
> and perhaps some of our listeners would like one too. Pardon me
> just a moment. Oh, Mother Moran. . . .
>
> *Mother Moran*: Yes, Mr. Saks?
>
> *Ann*: Mother Moran, would you send a copy of this anniversary picture of yours to any of our friends in the audience who wanted one
> of them?
>
> *M.M.*: Why . . . Why . . . do you think anyone would be wantin' a
> picture of my Today's Children, Mr. Saks?
>
> *Ann*: Yes, I do, Mother Moran. I'm sure that many of your friends
> would like very much to have this picture.
>
> *M.M.*: Well, then, Mr. Saks . . . you tell them please, that I'll be
> happy to be sendin' this anniversary picture of my family to anyone that would be wantin' it.
>
> *Ann*: Thank you, Mother Moran, thank you very much. And now, if
> any of our audience would like one of these pictures of Mother
> Moran's Children, just write a note or a post card to Mother Moran, care of Station WMAQ, Chicago.

Phillips claimed that ten thousand requests were received for pictures of Mother Moran and her Today's Children.[26]

By November 1932, Phillips had secured General Foods as the sponsor for *Today's Children*. Insofar as her program's function as an advertising vehicle was concerned, Phillips was more royalist than the king. She immediately suggested ways in which Mother Moran and friends might more directly promote the sale of General Foods products, to which the company's advertising director responded:

> . . . I want to say that you can proceed further with this story without regard to the special plugging or working up to any merchandising offers on La France or Satina [both General Foods laundry products]. . . . The subject of commercial announcement is one that concerns me a lot. I would like to see everything done that would give
> them all the cutting edge that we can get into them, yet not interfere
> with the entertaining feature of the program itself.

When, in January 1933, General Foods was ready to test the appeal of *Today's Children*, Phillips proposed that the mailhook be even more directly tied to the story than was the picture offered in August:

> In our story, as it is now on the air, Terry Moran is a salesman for a wholesale hardware concern. I would develop this angle of the story to have Terry put in charge of the distribution of a new product—an inexpensive laundry accessory. I have in mind for this purpose, a wire coil spring, used to keep the ironing cord out of the way during ironing. Any inexpensive novelty of this sort would serve as well.
>
> Terry is told by his employer that on his success with this new product rests his job. Either he sells them, or out he goes. Terry brings one home to Mother Moran, who tries it out in the script, and finds it a great thing. During ten days or two weeks of buildup on this novelty in the daily episodes, Terry becomes increasingly worried over his results in outside selling of this item.
>
> Mother Moran takes it on herself to help Terry. She comes to the mike at the end of one episode and starts to appeal to her radio friends to help Terry. The announcer interrupts her to give her the good news that "La France" has just contracted to buy many thousands.[27]

It is unknown whether General Foods agreed to run Mother Moran's desperate appeal or, if it did, how many listeners responded.

Later in 1933, the Pillsbury Company took over sponsorship of *Today's Children* and arranged network broadcast of the program over NBC. It was with the network dissemination of the program that the true dimensions of the soap opera's appeal became apparent. After *Today's Children* had aired on NBC for a new months, Pillsbury offered a brochure outlining the history of Mother Moran and her problem-prone brood in return for a Pillsbury flour label. More than 250,000 labels were received in only a few weeks. "The amazing allegiance," wrote *Broadcasting*, "of hundreds of thousands of women not only to the members of the cast but to Pillsbury products is a constant source of wonderment even among those professional people who for years have been working with radio."[28]

## Procter and Gamble Turns to Soap Operas

At the same time that Pillsbury was discovering the "amazing allegiance" of listeners to soap operas, Procter and Gamble was independently confirming the advertising potential of the daytime serial. With increasing amounts of advertising needed to maintain sales levels and market shares of its products in the first years of the Depression, Procter and Gamble instituted an unparalleled program of market research to assure that its advertising budget was spent as efficiently as possible. Much of this research was aimed at pretesting new products and advertising campaigns before investing in full production. Marketing surveys also revealed that women at home during the day preferred to be entertained, rather than instructed, by the radio. Procter and Gamble saw the opportunity of creating favorable associations between entertaining programming heard while the listener performed household tasks and the Procter and Gamble products that could be used in their accomplishment. With these possibilities in mind, Procter and Gamble began experimenting with daytime dramatic programming for women in 1932.

The first Procter and Gamble programming venture, *The Puddle Family*, was a serial domestic comedy perhaps inspired indirectly by the Jollycos. Broadcast over WLW in Cincinnati in 1932, *The Puddle Family* had but a brief life as a vehicle for Oxydol. When in 1933 the Oxydol account was given to another advertising agency, an account executive there suggested a serialized radio drama that might incorporate elements of the self-help genre. *Ma Perkins*, the story of a self-reliant widow whose family and friends were constantly in need of her advice, went on WLW during the summer of 1933, and was much better received by Cincinnati listeners than had been *The Puddle Family*. By December daytime listeners along the NBC Blue network heard a baritone-voiced announcer intone:

> And here's Oxydol's own Ma Perkins again. The true-life story of a woman whose life is the same, whose surroundings are the same, whose problems are the same as those of thousands of other women in the world today. A woman who has spent all her life taking care of her home: washing and cooking and cleaning and raising her family. And now her husband's death has pitched her head-foremost into being the head of her family as well as the mother. And we'll hear her true-life story every day at this time, except Saturday and Sunday. Before we hear from Ma Perkins today, though, I want to tell

you about something else for a minute that will be of vital interest to every housewife listening; about a remarkable new laundry-soap discovery that . . .

Early in 1934, eager to measure the extent of *Ma Perkins*'s listenership and its geographical distribution, Procter and Gamble devised as a mail-hook the offer of a packet of flower seeds in exchange for ten cents and an Oxydol box top. More than one million requests were received. By computing the number of dimes received per geographic area, Procter and Gamble was able to arrive at a rough cost-per-thousand for its advertising messages. The flower seed experiment made it clear that serialized narratives offered during daytime hours to female listeners constituted the most effective advertising strategy for Procter and Gamble products ever devised.[29]

*Ma Perkins* was conceived and written by Frank and Anne Hummert, the husband-wife team responsible for nearly half of all daytime serials introduced between 1932 and 1937 and for seven of the first eleven. In 1927, Frank Hummert had left his job as an account executive with Lord and Thomas to join the Blackett-Sample agency. According to James Thurber, Frank Hummert was inspired to develop daytime serial programming after reading a serialized story in the Chicago *Daily News*. He hired its writer, Charles Robert Douglas Hardy Andrews, to do a serial for radio. Like its newspaper antecedent, *The Stolen Husband*, broadcast locally in Chicago in 1931, appears to have been a closed, serialized narrative. It was read by a single actor, who altered his voice for each character. It did not attract sponsorship. The Hummerts' first network daytime serial, also written by Andrews, was aired in October 1932. *Betty and Bob*, a narratively open story of a stenographer who marries her boss, was sponsored by General Mills for eight years. In the fall of 1933, *Betty and Bob* and *Ma Perkins* were joined on network radio by another Hummert soap, *The Romance of Helen Trent*, which ran continuously on radio until 1960.

The Hummerts were in an excellent position to capitalize on the first stages of the soap opera's popularity. Unlike Phillips, who before writing *Painted Dreams* had had only a few months' experience in commercial radio, Frank Hummert was already a successful advertising executive before he and Anne Hummert attempted a daytime serial. As an advertising executive, Frank Hummert knew that the key to success lay in servicing a number of accounts, rather than pouring all one's energies into a single project. Thus the Hummerts were the first soap writer-producers to employ dialogue writers.[30]

## Diffusion of the Soap Opera Form

Between 1933 and 1937 serial drama became a staple of daytime programming, and companies like Procter and Gamble, Pillsbury, American Home
Products, and General Foods came to rely more and more upon the soap
opera as their primary radio advertising vehicle. By the end of 1935 Procter
and Gamble was the largest user of network radio in the world and NBC's
most important client. On that network alone, Procter and Gamble sponsored 778 program hours in 1935—664 of which were daytime programs.
By 1937 its radio advertising expenditures were $4,456,525, with over 90
percent going to daytime programming. "Oxydol's Own *Ma Perkins*" was
joined in advertising Procter and Gamble products by *Home Sweet Home*
(1934), *Dreams Come True* (1934), *Song of the City* (1934), *The O'Neills*
(1935), *Pepper Young's Family* (1936), *The Guiding Light* (1937), *The
Couple Next Door* (1937), *Road of Life* (1937), and *Kitty Keene* (1937). At
CBS daytime advertising volume doubled between 1933 and 1935 and had
trebled by 1937.[31]

For sponsors, daytime advertising remained a bargain during these
years—rates continued to be set at one-half that during prime time, despite
indications that the daytime audience had been greatly underestimated. In
1934 CBS reported that among all income groups radios were in use in
more than half the homes with radios some time before 6:00 P.M. That
same year a *McCall's* magazine survey asked one thousand New Jersey
homemakers to name their "most essential household appliances." The results were:

|  |  |
|---|---|
| iron | 68.9% |
| radio | 64.4% |
| vacuum cleaner | 63.3% |
| refrigerator | 38.0% |

In 1938 CBS research concluded that the audience for daytime radio
might be as much as four times as large as that reported by the widely used
Crossley Ratings. The Crossley Ratings were based upon telephone interviews in thirty-three cities and gave an average day-part (fifteen-minute
period) listening figure for the week. Crossley placed the ratings for leading
daytime programs at 5 to 8 percent of the total number of households with
radios. However, telephone surveys in the 1930s were not very reliable. This
was particularly the case in surveys of radio listenership, since there were
26 million American households with radio in 1938 but only 11 million

residential telephones. Furthermore, by presenting only average weekly figures, the Crossley Ratings did not take into account the cumulative weekly audience for a program that was broadcast every weekday. By attaching an automatic recording device to radios in a sample of households, CBS found that a daytime program with a Crossley rating of 3 percent actually reached 12 percent of all radio homes during a given week.[32]

## The Soap Opera Boom

During the years in which soap operas went from being sporadic experiments to a permanent and vital feature of daytime commercial radio programming, few people except for those immediately involved in the phenomenon (broadcasters, advertisers, and, of course, the millions of women who listened each day) seem to have noticed. The term "soap opera" itself was not coined until the late 1930s. As Stedman points out, between 1932 and 1937 no research on daytime serials was published. Yet, thanks almost entirely to the success of *Ma Perkins* and its successors, daytime radio had developed faster during this period than any other form of advertising. In 1937 daytime advertisers spent $22 million, more that three times the amount spent in 1933. While its print advertising budget remained static, Procter and Gamble's radio expenditures increased from $2 million in 1935 to $4.5 million in 1937. Estimates of the number of households with radios that year ranged from 78 percent to 88 percent. Whatever the figure, *Broadcasting* claimed that nearly 60 percent of those radios were in use sometime each day before six o'clock in the evening.[33]

As the country began to recover from the Depression, Procter and Gamble, along with other soap companies, used radio not only in an attempt to hold its market share but also to introduce new products derived from synthetic detergents. Whether the product being sold was the old reliable Ivory or the new synthetic shampoo Drene, advertisements for it continued to be integrated into the soap opera world as tightly as possible. Writers like Irna Phillips kept uppermost in their minds the function of their stories as advertising vehicles. In 1934, Phillips proposed to several cosmetic companies a soap opera entitled *Masquerade*, in which a young, handsome painter realizes that while he possesses considerable talent, his work can be art only when he is able to discover the *real*, the *natural* that lies behind the masks of his subject. "The artist's search takes him from place to place,

## An Institutional History

from the lowest to the highest strata of society. His experiences bring him into association with women of all ages and all classes, and gradually he comes to recognize true values, a recognition that begins to manifest itself in his paintings." The program's title, character, and basic situation were all devised to relate to the propounded virtues of the cosmetic product advertised. Phillips wrote in her prospectus: "Sincerity, honesty, genuineness—true values. If the woman listener is made conscious of these standards in the story itself, how little effort it would take to make her conscious of these same standards in connection with the product advertised. Once you have gained her confidence, nothing will swerve her from her loyalty to the program." A 1933 proposal for *Office Girl* suggests as a frame for a serial drama the young heroine seated at her dressing table cleansing her face using Kleenex tissues, just prior to recording the day's events in her diary. "Thus," Phillips suggested, "the transition from commercial announcements to the story can be practically painless, and a great deal of actual selling can be done in the story itself."

In January 1937, Phillips introduced *The Guiding Light*, sponsored by Procter and Gamble's White Naptha Soap. The show's title referred to the example provided by its central character, Dr. John Ruthledge, minister of the nonsectarian church in the "melting-pot community of Five Points." After *The Guiding Light* had been on the air for a year, Procter and Gamble devised a novel mailhook in the form of a refrigerator giveaway—one in which Dr. Ruthledge himself took part. The script for the 16 May 1938 episode begins:

> Chords
> "The Guiding Light"
> Chords
> "Brought to you by the Makers of P and G White Naptha Soap—
>    largest selling bar soap in America today."
> Music. . . .

> *Dr. Ruthledge:* I suppose most of you kind people recognize my
> voice. If you don't, I would like to introduce myself. I'm Dr. John
> Ruthledge, a Minister in the Community of Five Points. Now, as
> you know, we have been telling our story of "The Guiding Light"
> to you for over a year. Still, in all this time, it has never been our
> good fortune to show you how much we appreciate your most
> thoughtful loyalty. You can well imagine, therefore, how happy we

are to tell you that with the program, today, you are to hear some news about which we are all genuinely excited . . . because it brings you such a splendid opportunity. Obviously, I can't go into all of the details, so I'm going to ask a gentleman I have come to admire, Fort Pearson, to tell you about this opportunity. Would you do that, Fort?

*Announcer:* Thank you, Dr. Ruthledge . . . and indeed I am happy to tell our thousands of loyal listeners about this thrilling opportunity we are offering. So listen carefully, please.

Everyday, for thirty days, the makers of P and G White Naptha Soap will give away TEN OF THE FINEST AUTOMATIC REFRIG-ERATORS MADE! Yes, ten beautiful new SERVEL ELECTROLUX REFRIGERATORS will be given away in the easiest contest ever! That's TEN REFRIGERATORS . . . EVERY DAY FOR THIRTY DAYS, beginning Friday, May 20, and continuing through July 1st—excepting Saturdays, Sundays, and holidays.[34]

Entrants were asked to finish the sentence "I like P and G White Naptha Soap because . . ." in twenty-five words or less and to attach five front panels from packages of White Naptha Soap.

According to Stedman, between 1937 and 1942 seventy-four new sponsored soap operas were introduced on network radio. By 1940 the sixty-four serials being broadcast each day constituted 92 percent of all sponsored daytime broadcast hours. The ten highest-rated daytime programs in 1940 were all soap operas, and between 1939 and 1943 only Kate Smith was able to break the serial's hold on the top-ten list.[35]

Ironically, the initial critical discourse on soaps in the early 1940s, as well as the firestorm of controversy generated by Dr. Louis Berg's denunciation of soap operas in 1942, came after the realization by advertisers and broadcasters that daytime listeners were being inundated by serial drama and after the total number of daytime quarter-hours devoted to serials was already in decline. Soap operas introduced after 1937 suffered a much higher mortality rate than those already established with listeners. Between 1941 and 1943, the total number of daytime serials declined by one-third, and only twenty-one new serials were introduced in the five years after 1942, compared with seventy-four debuts in the previous five-year period. In 1941, for the first time since *Painted Dreams* went on the air, more daytime serials were canceled than were added. This retrenchment was not, however, a product either of reduced listener interest or of pressure brought to bear upon broadcasters and advertisers by Dr. Berg and his fellow soap opera critics. By 1940, the number of daytime hours devoted to serial drama had reached the saturation point. In 1933 the soap fan had to scan the dial to search out *Today's Children* or *Ma Perkins*; less than a decade later her attention was being vied for nearly every quarter-hour period between breakfast and dinner by two or three competing serials. In 1943 NBC research found that while 53 percent of all households with radios tuned in serials during the day, more than one-third of these listeners felt there was a surfeit of serial fare.

Just as the soap opera had provided broadcasters with an instrument of innovation amidst the self-help and inspirational programming of the early network period, the superfluity of serials by the 1940s offered opportunities for innovation in nonserial formats. The NBC Blue network, in particular, regarded the domination of the daytime hours by soap operas as a chance for program differentiation. In 1943 it initiated a new programming form, the morning variety-talk show, with *Breakfast at Sardi's* and *Breakfast Club*—the precursors of *The Arthur Godfrey Show* and, ultimately, *Today* and *Good Morning, America*, as well as a host of local "breakfast" programs.[36]

Although *Breakfast Club* provided some competition for morning soap operas and *Kate Smith Speaks* became a ratings rival for afternoon serials during the war years, the spate of audience studies conducted during this period confirmed the continued popularity of soap operas among American women. And while a nonserial program might outdraw the soaps in its time slot, no alternative form of programming could match the serial in cost effectiveness. The production costs for *Kate Smith Speaks* amounted to $609.76 for each rating point it obtained. *Ma Perkins*, whose overall ratings were nearly as high, cost but $164.56 per point. On a weekly basis, *Kate Smith Speaks* required a production investment of $5,000; *Ma Perkins*, only $1,600. It is little wonder, then, that much of Procter and Gamble's $15 million radio budget in 1945 went for eleven soap operas, most of which were produced by its own production subsidiary, established in 1940. Even when wartime materials shortages brought the production of synthetic laundry products to a halt, Procter and Gamble continued to advertise Dreft on its soap operas—so important had soap operas become in maintaining product recognition among consumers.[37]

## The Transition to Television

In the years following the end of World War II, commercial radio was joined by a new advertiser-supported mass medium, which within a decade would supplant it as the primary leisure activity in America: television. The development of the television industry had been interrupted by the war, but by 1948 television sets were again being mass-produced, nearly one hundred television stations were on the air, and the regulatory door had been left open for advertising agencies and their clients to dominate American television as they had American radio. In the years of transition between one medium and another, radio soap operas continued to prosper; the competitive effects of daytime television would not be felt until 1951. Soap operas also held their own against nonserial radio programming. In 1948 the ten highest-rated daytime programs were all serials; *Arthur Godfrey* could manage but a twelfth-place showing. Of the top thirty shows, all but five were soap operas.[38]

The enormous potential of television as a medium of popular entertainment and mass advertising was quickly demonstrated. Large cities in the Northeast experienced declines in restaurant business, taxi receipts, library patronage, book sales, and sports attendance—all attributable to television. In 1950, Hazel Bishop, a cosmetics manufacturer with sales of fifty thousand dollars annually, began advertising exclusively on television. By 1952 revenues had reached $4.5 million. Perhaps the most striking indication of the nation's fascination with television was its effect upon the motion picture industry. Between 1946 and 1956 weekly movie attendance was cut in half, most of the reduction caused by television.[39]

Companies that had relied heavily upon radio advertising looked to television as a new means of reaching an expanding postwar population, whose pent-up buying power fueled a strong peacetime economy. Advertising was particularly important to Procter and Gamble in the late 1940s and early 1950s. The company needed a return on its investment in developing synthetic detergents, whose marketing had been halted by the war. A new synthetic laundry powder, Tide, was introduced in 1946, and a new synthetic dishwashing liquid, Joy, in 1948. Not only did these new products have to be established among their potential consumers, but name recognition had to be maintained in the face of competition from other companies which had also benefited from breakthroughs in "cleaning chemistry." No sooner had Tide hit supermarket shelves than Colgate-Palmolive countered with its synthetic detergent, Fab, and Lever Brothers with its Surf. Moreover, new companies, familiar with industrial chemistry but not with traditional soap manufacture, entered the consumer market. Between 1948 and 1952 the consumption of synthetic detergents in the United States doubled. Also Procter and Gamble expanded its product line in the postwar years, particularly in toiletry items likely to be purchased by women: Prell shampoo, Lilt home permanents, and Gleem and Crest toothpastes were all introduced during this period.[40]

Hence it is not surprising that by 1949 Procter and Gamble was a regular television advertiser, or that it produced the first network television soap opera, *The First Hundred Years*, in December 1950. The transition from radio serial to television serial was hardly unproblematic, however, and not everyone associated with radio soap operas viewed television as a new horizon. In a 1948 letter to Procter and Gamble executive William Ramsey, Irna Phillips expressed both her doubts about television serials and her fascination with the marketing possibilities they might afford.

> As you know, I have had very little interest in television from a daytime standpoint, and unless a technique could be evolved whereby the auditory could be followed without the constant attention to the visual as far as the home maker is concerned, I see no future for a number of years in televising the serial story. . . . The intriguing angle, of course, is the commercial angle where the product could be seen and used but not announced as much as it is announced today. In looking over *Today's Children*, which would be renamed *These Are Today's Children*, it seems to me that most of our action took place in the kitchen of Mother Moran. . . . It would depend entirely on the ingenuity of a writer to indirectly show the product and its use. Offhand I can see two girls washing out sheer hose in a hell of a dramatic scene. On the other hand, I can see making an announcer more than an announcer by becoming almost part of the cast. I'm thinking at the moment of *Point Sublime*, which had a short run on the Coast. It was sponsored by an insurance company, and the insurance salesman was part and parcel of the half-hour drama.[41]

For the first few years of full-scale television broadcasting, it was unclear whether daytime radio would be adversely affected at all. Again following the historical pattern set by the introduction of network radio, television broadcasters initially concentrated on prime-time programming, where the largest audience could be generated. It was not until the beginning of the 1951–52 television season that networks began to experiment with regular programming for daytime viewers. The first major network daytime programming efforts involved not soap operas but a television adaptation of the soaps' chief radio competition in the 1940s: the variety-talk show format. In the fall of 1950, NBC launched a television version of Kate Smith's radio program, calling it "the first daytime program of nighttime proportions." Its success prompted CBS to move Garry Moore and Arthur Godfrey from radio to daytime television and fledgling ABC to introduce the Frances Langford–Don Ameche Show on weekdays at noon. Through the 1951–52 season the most ambitious network daytime venture was NBC's *Today* show, which debuted on 1 November 1951 with Dave Garroway as host and with a production budget of twenty thousand dollars per week. Noting that network executives were unsure whether set owners could be persuaded to watch television in the early morning hours, *Newsweek* pointed out that *Today* "will thoughtfully remove any necessity for looking at the show continuously during the shaving and breakfast hours."[42]

The radio soap opera's success as an advertising vehicle was based upon its cost-effectiveness: huge numbers of listeners could be secured with very low production budgets. In the early days of television, not only was the number of potential daytime viewers small as compared with the radio audience, but production costs for a daily television serial proved to be two to three times that for a radio serial. Television required sets, props, and costumes, all of which radio left to the listener's imagination. The production apparatus for television was vastly more complex and, in the early days, uncertain. The production staff for *Ma Perkins* consisted merely of a director, announcer, actors, and perhaps a sound-effects technician. During its two-year run on television, *The First Hundred Years* required a crew of thirty, exclusive of actors. Because of rampant exploitation of radio actors in the 1930s, the American Federation of Radio Artists (AFRA), formed in 1938, fought for and by 1940 won a standard contract with the radio networks that set a minimum fee for actors (according to the length of the program in which he or she was to appear) *and* a maximum amount of rehearsal time per program. Radio soap producers could accommodate themselves to these time limits, but television serial producers could not. AFRA allotted two hours of rehearsal for a fifteen-minute radio drama; *The First Hundred Years* required four and one-half hours per fifteen-minute episode. Radio actors had no need to memorize their lines; television actors, obviously, did. Many observers, both inside and outside the broadcasting industry, believed television soap operas would never attract the audiences of radio serials for the simple reason that listening to radio soaps could be integrated into the performance of household chores in a way that watching television soaps could not. As Gilbert Seldes put it in 1953, "The daytime serial was perfectly adapted to the actual circumstances in which it was heard. And it seemed to us who were looking for a parallel in television that these devices were unsuitable."[43]

Thus the establishment of soap operas as regular television fare did not occur until television's ability to attract daytime audiences had been demonstrated and, concomitantly, when sponsors had reason to fear that the decline in listening that had affected prime-time radio (already apparent in 1950) would be felt by daytime radio as well. In conjunction with its overall expansion of daytime offerings for the 1951–52 season, CBS introduced three television serials in the fall of 1951: *Search for Tomorrow*, *Love of Life*, and an offbeat serial adaptation of the popular novel *The Egg and I*. The last was short-lived; the first two, however, proved to be extremely popular among daytime viewers and helped quickly to establish CBS's lead in the soap opera field.

On 30 June 1952 *The Guiding Light* became the first radio soap opera to make the transition to television, and the first to be broadcast over both media. Already the leading advertiser on network television ($12 million in 1951), Procter and Gamble had seen the first signs of ratings deterioration for its afternoon radio soaps during that season and decided it was time to test the television soap waters. But the company did not want to lose the 3 to 4 million radio fans of *The Guiding Light* in the process. The radio version continued to be broadcast at 1:45 P.M. in the East, and, as of 30 June 1952, the same episode could be *seen* on CBS television at 2:30. The same script (with some minor modifications; see appendix D) and actors were used for both versions, thus defraying some of the eight thousand dollars in weekly production costs for the televised version. By the end of 1953, some 3.5 million persons were watching *The Guiding Light* and only 2.6 million were listening. Simultaneous broadcasts were discontinued in 1956.[44]

It was not until the 1960–61 season that television serials completely supplanted their radio antecedents. Prime-time network radio succumbed to the competition from television within a few years, but, thanks in large measure to the loyalty of serial listeners, daytime network radio remained a viable national advertising medium for a decade following the initiation of regular television service. Between 1955 and 1960 soap operas were frequently the most popular shows on radio—prime time or daytime. In 1959 radio soap operas seemed to Stedman to be holding up well in a television-dominated media environment. Sixteen radio soap operas had survived. In 1957 CBS radio boasted that a single fifteen-minute serial broadcast five days per week could reach 6.4 million different listeners at a cost per thousand impressions of $.49.[45]

The prosperity Stedman observed was but a swansong, however. During the 1959–60 season CBS dropped three of its ten radio serials and NBC canceled its one remaining radio soap. ABC had discontinued its radio soaps the previous season. On 25 November 1960, Virginia Payne gave her 7,065th and final performance as Ma Perkins; the four remaining radio soap operas, *Mary Noble: Backstage Wife*, *Our Gal Sunday*, *Road of Life*, and *Ma Perkins*, all on CBS, were canceled. Three principal factors were responsible for the radio soap opera's final demise. First, many were still owned by their sponsors (including Procter and Gamble), who saw television soaps as a better advertising vehicle and abandoned radio soaps to "spot" advertising by other companies. By November 1960 only 25 percent of the advertising time was being sold. Second, as network radio deteriorated, local radio flourished. Station managers discovered they could make more from spinning records and selling airtime to local merchants than from running network programming. Thus by 1960 affiliates were pressuring networks to make more time available for local programming.[46] Third, the popularity of and audiences for television soap operas continued to grow. Between 1951 and 1959 thirty-five television soaps were introduced, and since then the number of soap operas running during any given year has never dropped below ten.

Since 1960 television soap operas have survived changes in network programming strategy, regulatory upheavals, innumerable network management regimes, cyclic economic fluctuations, and the entry of millions of American women into the paid work force. Part of the soap opera's success on television can be attributed to its "invisibility" to male opinion leaders, legislators, and regulators. Once the hysteria over soap operas in the early 1940s died down and the novelty of television soap operas wore off, they sank into a comfortable obscurity. As we have seen, until the 1970s few academics bothered studying them, few commentators wrote about them, and the trade press found the seasonal prime-time network crapshoot more exciting to cover than the much more static (albeit profitable) world of daytime programming.

One illustration of the soap opera's ability to survive by going unnoticed is the so-called quiz-show scandals of the early 1960s. During its first decade commercial television followed the pattern of network radio in turning programming control over to sponsors. This relationship was called into question by the revelation in 1960 that the Charles Revson Company, manufacturers of Revlon cosmetics, had "rigged" the outcome of its highly rated prime-time quiz show, *The $64,000 Question*, in order to make the program more exciting. Congressional investigations, lawsuits, and an FCC inquiry followed. Fearing increased regulation by the newly appointed "interventionist" FCC chairman, Newton Minnow, the networks took control of prime-time programming away from sponsors and their advertising agencies and created internal "standards and practices" divisions to assure that programming gave the appearance, at least, of serving the public interest. Since 1960 the networks have either produced prime-time programming themselves or secured it from independent producers. It has then been offered to advertisers, usually on a "participating" basis: several companies purchasing advertising time within the same program.

This major shift in programming practice affected every aspect of network programming *except* soap operas. In 1960 the four highest-rated television soap operas were owned by their principal sponsors: *As the World Turns*, *Search for Tomorrow*, and *Guiding Light* by Procter and Gamble and *Love of Life* by American Home Products. When in 1963 and 1964 NBC decided to challenge CBS's domination in the soap opera area, it did so by adding two sponsor-owned soaps: *The Doctors* (Colgate-Palmolive) and Irna Phillips's *Another World* (Procter and Gamble). A decade after the furor over sponsor involvement in network programming, Procter and Gamble owned six soap operas, and today its six soaps are the only regularly scheduled network programs owned by their sponsor.

The soap opera's longevity and remarkable resilience derive from its ability to serve the same economic function today that it first served nearly a half-century ago: it provides access to a huge audience of heavy consumers (women eighteen to forty-nine years of age) in a cost-effective manner. Networks have from time to time experimented with other programming forms, but no functional replacement for the soap opera has yet been discovered. As ABC executive Edwin Vane admitted in 1977, "Efforts to change the face of daytime have gone largely unrewarded." Game shows occasionally have produced higher overall ratings than soap operas, and they are cheaper to produce, but soap operas consistently draw more viewers in the target demographic group.[47]

The soap opera's narrative openness endows it with a unique ability to respond to social and demographic change. By the mid-1970s the portion of the soap opera audience that had begun watching *Search for Tomorrow* or *As the World Turns* in the early 1950s began to pass out of the demographic target range of eighteen to forty-nine years. To make matters worse for soap opera producers, the baby boom of the immediate postwar years 'had ended, and women had begun working outside the home in numbers unprecedented in peacetime. Soap opera ratings declined in 1977–78 as part of an overall drop in daytime HUT (households using television). Soap opera producers responded by introducing younger characters, injecting plot lines with social controversy, and making more female characters career oriented. In 1975 ABC's *General Hospital* could manage but an 8.2 rating and a 26 share. Two years later its figures were even worse, and the network considered cancellation. Gloria Monty was hired in 1978 in a last-ditch attempt to save the show. She fired some of the older actors, focused the narrative on two younger ones (Luke Spencer and Laura Baldwin), initiated a romance between them with a rape, and borrowed, admittedly, from the work of Alfred Hitchcock and Frank Capra. By 1980 *General Hospital* had become the highest-rated daytime program. Underlying Monty's strategy and that of other producers who followed her lead was the need to reorient soap operas toward younger viewers, not only to add viewers but also to establish soap opera viewing as a regular activity among women just entering their "prime" as consumers. When asked in 1977 if he was afraid the presentation of "liberated themes" might drive away older soap opera viewers, CBS executive Michael Ogiens responded, "I'd rather gamble on staying up to date. . . . These [older] women have daughters who watch too." By 1982 soap opera producers had succeeded in attracting more than 3 million college students as soap opera viewers, 70 percent of them women. In a brochure aimed at prospective soap opera advertisers, ABC noted that not only were college students "prime purchasers, particularly of leisure products," but, "equally important, many of these college students—by forming the serial viewing habit early—are likely to remain loyal viewers for years to come."[48]

There is little doubt, then, that the primary generative mechanisms responsible for the origination of the soap opera form and for its perpetuation over nearly fifty years can be located in the institutional requirements of American commercial broadcasting. Despite the obvious and important contributions to the soap opera form made by Irna Phillips, Frank and Anne Hummert, and, in the television era, Agnes Nixon, it is clear that the idea of presenting continuing stories focusing upon domestic concerns on daytime radio was the result of the conjunction of corporate desire to reach a particular audience (women eighteen to forty-nine) and broadcasters' need to fill the daytime hours with revenue-generating programming. The soap opera represents a form of cultural production that has been fully penetrated by capital since the moment of its conception, a form driven and sustained by corporate imperatives. From the beginning, writers and producers of soap operas have harbored no illusions about the sole criterion by which their work would ultimately be judged: could it secure and maintain an audience of soap or flour consumers at a low cost per thousand. The adversarial relationship we traditionally assume to exist between artistic and economic interests under capitalism simply does not obtain in the case of soap operas (nor, I would venture, in many other cases of contemporary cultural production).

# SIX

# Toward A History of Soap Opera Reception

Our historical account of the origins and development of the soap opera form would be incomplete without a consideration of the generative mechanisms governing the reception of soap operas as well as those responsible for their production. The key to the soap opera's success has obviously been its large, loyal, and dependable audience of listeners and viewers. We need to be able, however tentatively, to account for the soap opera's initial reception and for subsequent changes in its textual structure.

In all of popular culture studies few areas are more important and less developed than the history of the reception of cultural products. This is particularly the case with regard to American mass media. Where individual programs are dealt with historically at all, their "history" tends to end with their presentation to the public. How they were taken up by audience groups at a particular historical moment is reduced to their "success" or "failure" in terms of the ratings they produced, the longevity of their broadcast runs, or some assessment of their aesthetic or journalistic quality. Reception has been equated with raw numbers of viewers or listeners and with the "responses" of those in positions publicly to articulate them. These public pronouncements are of course worthy of study in and of themselves (as we saw in chapter 1) because of the "supervisory" nature of the discourses within which they are located, but the complex process of readers confronting popular fictional works in history is obviously much more than this.

Almost completely ignored in the history of American mass media have been changes over time in textual structure within individual programs and across genres and a consideration of how these changes might have conditioned the continuing reception of these texts. In part, this lack is a reflection of the transient nature of broadcast programming. In the 1930s and 1940s the vast majority of radio programming was live, and little of it was "saved" in the form of transcribed disks. Until the late 1950s all television programming that was not on film was also live and thus "lost" after its broadcast presentation. But there are more important reasons for the absence of historical textual analysis in American mass media research. The first has to do with the refusal by media historians to regard programming as textual systems. The second is the institutional perspective from which most media history is conducted: "broadcast" history in the United States is usually taken to mean the history of broadcasting companies and only marginally to mean the history of the insertion of the products of those companies within ongoing social processes. Hence, except where controversy erupts (as in the case of Dr. Berg's denunciation of soap operas), the enormous and enormously complex process of tens of millions of readers daily engaging with broadcast programming over the course of the last half-century flows along unnoticed.

When we consider the historical study of cultural products of a literary nature, we also find inattention to the reception of works. In this case, however, it is the persistence of the text and not its disappearance that is in part, at least, to blame. If one's chief goal as a literary historian is the identification of great works that transcend history, then how those works might have been received at a particular point in the past is a largely irrelevant issue. The call for the dethroning of the text as the primary object of literary history has been increasingly insistent among scholars working from a reader-response perspective, broadly defined. Jauss has proposed:

> A renewal of literary history demands the removal of the prejudices of historical objectivism and the grounding of the traditional aesthetics of production and representation in an aesthetics of reception and influence. The historicity of literature rests not on an organization of "literary facts" that is established *post festum*, but rather on the preceding experience of the literary work by its readers.[1]

Tony Bennett puts the case even more forcefully:

> I want to argue, then, that *texts* exist, but that "*the text*" . . . does not. . . . There is *no* text behind or beyond the diverse forms in which it is materially produced, the social relations in which it is inscribed and the interpretative horizons in which it is embedded such as could, *in principle*, limit the readings that might be generated in relation to it.[2]

Once we acknowledge that the relationships between readers and texts should form a major focus of historical inquiry in American mass media research, the question then becomes, How might such an inquiry be conducted? What, in effect, would we be studying? In sketching an answer to this question in this chapter, I can do no more than suggest some of the generative mechanisms, to use the terminology of realism, involved in the specific instance of the history of the relationship between soap opera text and reader. Furthermore, my aim is necessarily limited to specifying some of the conditions under which soap operas *might* have been received, rather than accounting for the reception of texts by actual readers.

In light of the discussion of relations between reader and text in chapter 4 and the consideration of the institutional functions served by soap operas in chapters 3 and 5, we might now recast those relations as an object of historical inquiry. As Stuart Hall and others have pointed out, the relationship between reader and broadcast text represents not only an engagement (of the reader with a fictive world) but also a confrontation—put in its starkest terms, a struggle for meaning.[3] From the institutional point of view, the reader comes to the viewing or listening experience as both a prize to be captured and a subject to be swayed. The text presented offers the reader a position that he or she is encouraged to take up—a position that represents the results of enormous effort, expense, and expertise. The reader's activation of the text is not determined by it, however. The distance between the position offered by the text and that actually occupied by the reader may be great or small. In the case of the soap opera, as well as other types of broadcast texts, this positionality may in fact change as the text is being read, since "reading time" is literally historical time. This does not mean, though, that the reader engages the text on his or her own terms. The power relations between reader and broadcast text are always asymmetrical. As Hall puts it, "Polysemy must not . . . be confused with pluralism. Connotative codes are *not* equal among themselves. Any society/culture tends, with varying degrees of closure, to impose its classifications of the social and cultural and political world. These constitute a *dominant cultural order*, though it is never univocal or uncontested.[4]

Any given reader's activation of a broadcast text will be in some sense idiosyncratic, but it will also be conditioned by the reader's position within society. It is this positionality, shared by groups of readers, that helps to determine the interpretative horizon against which a particular text will be read. As we shall see, in the case of soap operas the gender position of its primary readership has been central in setting the terms of its reception. In short, then, an initial understanding of the history of soap opera reception would entail:

1. grounding of the overall inquiry in the functions served by soap operas within the institutions that have produced them;
2. consideration of the strategies employed within the textual system of the soap opera that mark out a position for the reader and of changes in these strategies over time;
3. analysis of the social positions of soap opera audiences (insofar as this could be determined) and of changes in them over time;
4. in light of these positions, a reconstruction of the interpretative horizons against which soap operas have been read; and
5. examination of the articulated responses to soap operas, particularly within supervisory discourses that have conditioned the terms by which readers are likely to have engaged them.

This chapter will concentrate on points 2, 3, and 4—points 1 and 5 having been taken up in previous chapters. At the risk of being thought excessively timorous, I will again point out that doing justice to any one of these points would constitute an enormous undertaking—and one fraught with any number of theoretical and logistical difficulties. All I intend here is an initial mapping out of the terms by which such a historical inquiry might be conducted, and, in doing so, to bring together some of the lines of investigation begun in this book.

## Soap Opera Readership

Until the quite recent advent of marketing research even determining the likely community of readers for most texts at some point in the past was a major historical feat. Thanks to the soap opera's status as a national marketing device, however, we can specify with relative certainty the broad demographic and quantitative outlines of its initial community of readers. It was essential that broadcasters and sponsors knew (even if their methods of determination were approximate) what kind of person listened to soap operas and how many of them did so with what frequency. Combining this with our understanding that the initial economic impetus behind the development of the form was the need to use daytime broadcasting hours to reach female consumers, we can identify the soap opera's readership (as a historical construct) in the early 1930s, a readership which in turn suggests important aspects of the horizon of expectations against which *Painted Dreams*, *Today's Children*, and *Ma Perkins* were received.

As we saw in chapter 1, the feature that most distinguished the soap opera audience of the 1930s and 1940s was its gender, and while the proportion of the soap opera audience comprising men has increased considerably since the mid-1970s, women have always been the primary readers of soap operas. The studies of Summers, Herzog, Roper, and others during the heyday of soap opera audience analysis in the early 1940s showed that women of all ages, social groups, and locales listened to soap operas, although the "average" listener tended to be young (between eighteen and thirty-five) and working or middle class, and had little education beyond high school. We must be careful, however, not to equate soap opera listenership with this socioeconomic category alone (as researchers repeatedly have done since the 1940s); it seems likely that at least since the late 1930s half the adult female population of the United States could be considered soap opera "readers." And the tremendous and largely unanticipated volume of mail generated by premium offers as early as 1933 suggests that the form found a warm reception from large numbers of women almost immediately. In short, any description of the readership for the first soap operas must begin with its "femaleness," and, concomitantly, any attempt to reconstruct the horizon of expectations against which this community of readers received the first soaps must take into account the soap opera's status as a "woman's" form.

Ironically, the very size and scope of the soap opera audience enables us to extrapolate (albeit cautiously and with some qualification) certain basic social and economic features of soap opera readers from data on the female population of the United States as a whole in the early 1930s. We can safely say, for example, that few listeners to soap operas in the early 1930s would have been unaffected by the economic dislocations of the Great Depression. Between 1929 and 1932 national income was cut in half. At the Depression's lowest point 25 percent of the total work force was unemployed (12–15 million workers). Still, most women experienced unemployment not directly but as the wives, daughters, mothers, or sisters of the unemployed or underemployed. In 1930 women made up but 24.3 percent of the work force—a figure which rose but 1 percent during the decade. Most women who worked outside the home in the 1930s were young and unmarried, and they stopped working for pay when they did get married. Despite the economic pressures brought on by the Depression, the end of the decade found but 15 percent of all married women at work, a group which constituted but 35 percent of the total female work force. Even fewer married women with children worked; among women with children under the age of six in 1940 only 10 percent were employed outside the home.[5]

The scarcity of jobs was not the only reason most women worked as "homemakers" during the Depression; there was considerable public pressure to keep women, particularly married women, out of the paid work force. The prevailing view was that women worked merely to earn "pin money," while men worked to support families. Dozens of states attempted to pass laws barring married women from state jobs, and it is likely that most companies discriminated either explicitly or by practice against married women job seekers. A public opinion poll conducted in 1937 asked if a married woman should work if her husband were already employed; 82 percent felt she should not. Nearly half the respondents to a 1936 Gallup poll were opposed to a married woman working, even if the additional income were needed to support the family.[6]

The economic and ideological confinement of most women to their homes reinforced the notion, already deeply ingrained in American culture, of two separate social spheres defined by sex: the "outside world," which was the province of the male provider, and the home, toward which women were expected to orient their talents, energies, and desires. Robert and Helen Lynd, returning to Muncie, Indiana, in the mid-1930s to research a sequel to their landmark sociological study *Middletown*, found the social worlds of men and women to "constitute something akin to separate subcultures."[7] The nature and narrowness of women's confinement to the domestic sphere in the 1930s obviously varied considerably from household to household and among social, ethnic, religious, and economic groups. But it is accurate to say that during this period most women's lives centered upon the home, and most of their time was devoted to its maintenance and to serving the domestic needs of their families: cooking, cleaning, child raising, and shopping.

Women felt the impact of the Depression differently from men. For a woman there was no "unemployment," since regardless of whether she worked in a paying job or whether her husband had lost his, she was expected to continue her unpaid job as domestic servant. The Depression meant that most women had to make up for reduced family income with even harder work, greater personal sacrifice, and redoubled resourcefulness and ingenuity. As Eleanor Roosevelt characterized the effects of the

Depression on American women in 1933, "It means endless little economies and constant anxiety for fear of some catastrophe such as accident or illness which may completely swamp the family budget."

Historian Susan Ware has described the domestic economic situation of the "typical" American women in the 1930s. Most likely, her husband had managed to hold on to his job, although he had suffered a cut in pay; or if he had been made unemployed, the family's resources were sufficient to tide it over until another job was found. Her family's income was $1,100–1,200 per year ($2,500 per year placed the family in the upper 10 percent income bracket), 80 percent of which was turned over to her to spend on the family's needs. In the 1920s the same homemaker might have been able to afford the services of full-time or occasional domestic help, but the Depression precluded that luxury and returned nearly all the routine chores to the homemaker. The application of electric motors to household appliances (washing machines, refrigerators, vacuum cleaners, irons, and so forth) and the availability of canned or preprepared foods had made housework easier, but the typical woman still spent more than sixty hours per week cooking, cleaning, and washing. With the cost of housing and utilities relatively fixed, it fell to the homemaker to devise other ways of squeezing every bit of value from the household budget in order to cushion the inevitable fall in living standard caused by pay reductions or unemployment. Above all, she became a more perspicacious shopper. Many domestic tasks once performed in the home (butter churning, tailoring, canning, soap making) had long since been removed to the commercial arena, so that by the 1930s the choice faced by the typical homemaker in most cases was not whether to buy a good or produce it at home but whether to buy it or do without. The job of the typical woman in the 1930s was enormous but clearly defined: it was her task to "keep things going," to hold family and home together against the economic ravages of the Depression, to minimize the deterioration in living standards most families suffered. For all the talk of flappers and changing roles for women during the 1920s, what carried over into the 1930s was the division of family, social, and economic roles according to sex. As Ware puts it, "The man was the breadwinner and the woman ran the household. . . . In many ways the Depression actually reinforced and strengthened these traditional ideals."[8]

## The Soap Opera's Horizon of Expectations

In most cases repositioning a work within its context of reception involves understanding that text as a novel ordering of formal aspects already largely or entirely established by the text's genre or form. Even in the case of a text that creates a considerable aesthetic distance between itself and its horizon (Joyce's *Ulysses* or Manet's *Olympia*, for example), there is a pre-existent form (the novel, the nude) whose basic qualities the work can be seen to share—even if it shares them in order to subvert them. *Painted Dreams* and *Today's Children* represent not only new texts but initial examples of a new form as well. The horizon against which the soap opera was initially received, therefore, was constituted by other narrative forms, elements of which the soap opera appropriated. As was hinted in the previous chapter, the soap opera form is the result of a process of *bricolage*: the assemblage of bits and pieces of other forms into a new structure designed to meet certain narrative, cultural, and economic requirements. In order to arrive at a determination of those forms (the audience's prior experience of which conditioned their expectations about the soap opera), we must first identify, however roughly, the basic qualities which together marked the soap opera as a distinctive textual system. Or, put another way, What were the necessary and sufficient aesthetic elements the combination of which made any given text legible to its readers as a soap opera?

*Narratively, soap operas were marked by their absolute resistance to closure.* Early listeners were conditioned by the internal narrative structure of each episode and, in some cases, by introductory narration to expect the soap opera's diegesis to be asymptotic rather than determinant in nature. The announcer for *Ma Perkins* began each episode by saying, "And Here's Oxydol's own Ma Perkins again. The true-life story of a woman whose life is the same, whose surroundings are the same, whose problems are the same as those of thousands of other women in the world today. . . . And we'll hear her true-life story every day at this time. . . . And now we find Ma Perkins just where we left her yesterday."[9]

*As the* Ma Perkins *introduction indicates, soap operas were also marked by their contemporary setting and emphasis upon what we might call "domestic" concerns.* *Painted Dreams*, *Today's Children*, and *Ma Perkins* were all constructed around the relationship between a widowed mother and her children. Some later radio soap operas would concern themselves more with events in the "outside" world (*Mary Noble: Backstage Wife, The*

*Woman in White, Joyce Jordan, M.D.* among them), but even in these the overriding themes were those of home, family, parentage, and romance.

*Because of their status as vehicles for the advertising of consumer products, soap operas were from the beginning "didactic" in nature.* As we shall see, in some cases the didacticism was overtly moral, but in all cases the soap opera text, including its advertising messages, functioned to influence the listener in an economic sense.

*Soap operas were from their inception "woman's fictions," designed for and enjoyed by Depression-era American women, most of whom spent their weekdays at home, managing households and taking care of children.* The consequences of the implicit designation of soaps as "woman's stories" should not be underestimated. As works produced for and consumed by women, the soap opera form was not merely one distinguishable narrative structure among a number of others—even among those broadcast over radio. As earlier chapters have argued, the soap opera was regarded as a form marked by its difference from normative (read, "male") categories of art and narrative, as something apart from, not a part of, traditional narrative genres.

Some of these elements, singly or in various combinations, were to be found in a number of narrative forms at the time of the debut of the first soap operas. *Amos and Andy* would almost certainly have been an important, if indirect, intertext for the first soap opera listeners. It established serial fiction as a narrative form particularly well suited to the demands of commercial radio. Serialized fiction had also been a mainstay of magazines—particularly those oriented toward women—since the mid-nineteenth century. What *Amos and Andy* suggested was the possibility of a narrative with an indefinitely postponable termination. As such, it marked the first accommodation of narrative form to the imperatives of radio as a commercial medium. Presented within the covers of a book or across a number of magazine issues, the narrative fiction was a commodity to be purchased. To have expected the reader to purchase a narrative without an ending would have been like expecting him or her to purchase a shirt without buttons: the book or story's ending held the piece together and provided its ultimate logic and design. In radio, however, the *listener*, not the narrative, was the commodity being sold; thus, closure became an obstacle to be overcome in the attempt to establish regular, habitual listenership. *Amos and Andy* demonstrated that audiences would trade aesthetic investment in the one-time payoff of final narrative resolution for continuing gratification derived from setting, character interaction and development, and lower-level narrative closures built into the end of each episode.

The demands placed upon women by the Great Depression made them an eager audience for discourse on the home and family. Magazines and newspaper columns had offered domestic advice for decades, and it is not surprising that radio should have attempted to borrow this discourse for its own purposes. Cooking, recipe, and "household hint" programs were among the first "woman's" programming attempted by radio networks in the late 1920s. Unlike the domestic advice disseminated in magazines or newspapers, *Ruth Turner's Washing Talks* and *Sisters of the Skillet* could be "read" while the listener went about her housework. Furthermore, magazines and newspapers traditionally kept editorial matter and advertising matter separate (although in practice the distinction was often blurred)—recognition of the fact that revenue was derived both from multiple advertisers within a single issue and from direct sale of the text to the consumer. In radio the point was to make a definite connection between programming content and the sponsor of that content; thus listeners became accustomed to the intrusion of the sponsor's message into the diegesis of the program itself.

The domestic advice radio shows of the late 1920s and early 1930s also served to establish a quasi-fictional persona—the program's voice—who took on the role of "master" homemaker. The archetype in this regard is, of course, Betty Crocker, the personification of General Mills's projected corporate image, whose creation predates radio. Radio made Betty Crocker and her sisters into dramatic personae—aural representations of the ideal domestic consumer—and gave them the perfect rhetorical position from which to speak—that of the woman in the kitchen who during the course of a fifteen-minute program faced some of the same problems encountered by the listener at home: What do I fix my family for dinner? How can I make my food budget go further? How can I get one more year's wear out of a three-year-old dress coat? That the solution of these problems involved the use of Chipso, Crisco, Ivory flakes, or Campbell's soup came as no surprise to the listener. As we have seen, the problem for soap opera writers was as much How can domestic advice givers be totally fictionalized? as it was How can the sponsor's product be identified with program content?

The moral and social didacticism of soap operas will be discussed in some detail later on. For the moment we should recall from the previous chapter that cooking and recipe shows were not the only vehicles for advice and information carried by broadcasters during the early days of the Depression. All manner of experts answered listener problems over the air—from numerologists to ministers. Early soap operas fictionalized the real-life problems Depression-era women had to contend with, and presented Mother Moran, Mother Moynihan, and Ma Perkins as characters who combined the practical knowledge of Betty Crocker with the common-sensical armchair philosophy of *The Voice of Experience*.

## The Heritage of "Woman's Fiction": The Domestic Novel

While early soap operas drew upon the audience's familiarity with serial fiction, advice programs, and other types of popular discourse, the literary genre the soap opera resembles most closely was, ironically enough, one whose popularity had waned before the turn of the century. The "domestic novel," as it has been called, dominated fiction book publishing in the United States from the 1820s through the 1880s. Maria S. Cummins's *The Lamplighter* (1854) sold forty thousand copies in two months, prompting Nathaniel Hawthorne to complain that the works of "serious" writers could find no place in a literary marketplace controlled by "a D----d mob of scribbling women." The relationship of the soap opera to the domestic novel deserves to be considered in some detail, not only because the latter might have served as an obvious, if somewhat faded, intertextual reference point for soap opera readers but, also, perhaps more importantly, because the striking parallels between the two forms provide important insights into the reception of soap operas by their female readers in the 1930s.

Several writers have cited the domestic novel as an historical antecedent of the soap opera and have noted a number of superficial similarities in plot and theme between the two forms. As Cantor and Pingree point out, both were generally set in the present, concerned with domestic issues, and intended for a female audience. Among the twenty-five similarities Stedman finds are "strange diseases were common. . . . The stories frequently lacked humor . . . [and] few historical figures appeared." Modleski has noted deeper connections between the contemporary television soap opera and the domestic novel, particularly in their embodiment of "the fantasy of immortality."[10] The issue, however, is greater than the location of an interesting, albeit historically removed, precedent for soap opera "content" and audience composition. And while Modleski's recognition of similarities between the two forms is illuminating, hers is not meant as a historical argument. The role of the domestic novel in the horizon of expectations that greeted the radio soap opera in the early 1930s was an indirect one to be sure (few American women were reading *The Wide, Wide World* seventy-five years after its initial publication); however, its role was crucial in establishing the tradition of a "woman's narrative" into which the soap opera squarely fit.

The emergence and commercial ascendance of a distinctive "woman's fiction," as Nora Baym calls it, in the mid-nineteenth century has engendered considerable debate among scholars in literature and women's studies. There is even disagreement over what the genre should be called: the "sentimental novel," the "domestic novel," or, as Baym prefers, simply "woman's fiction." There is even more fundamental disagreement over the ideological position represented in these novels and by their authors. Some regard the pious, morally righteous image of the ideal woman that pervades the novels of Maria Cummins, Carolina Howard Gilman, Mary J. Holmes, Catharine Maria Sedgwick, E.D.E.N. Southworth, Susan Warner, and Mary Virginia Terhune as an implicit endorsement of the traditional view of women as dependent, inferior helpmates to men. Others argue that under the cover of innocuous moral tales, these authors constructed handbooks for feminist guerrilla warfare against male domination and, in the words of Helen Papashvily, advocated a response "so quietly ruthless, so subtly vicious that by comparison the ladies at Seneca appear angels of innocence." Taking a position somewhere between these two extremes, Baym suggests that these novels represent a "pragmatic feminism," which can be seen if their ideological stance is considered relative to nineteenth-century rather than mid-twentieth-century norms.[11]

Despite the fact that woman's fiction of the nineteenth century was didactic in nature, the relationship of its advocacy of a particular image of "feminine" virtue to some standard of feminist progressivism is, for my purposes at least, less important than the cultural and economic contradictions to which the image of the ideal woman was a response. Most of the scholars cited above are in agreement concerning these cultural and economic forces, which shaped both the production and consumption of woman's fiction. The era of the domestic novel (roughly 1820–80) is coterminus with the rise of industrialism in the United States and, concomitantly, with a period of profound "sociological transition" for American women. Increasingly during the nineteenth century, the economic locus of the American family shifted from the home to the industrial workplace. This shift resulted in some material improvement for women, particularly middle-class women, as domestic products were made available cheaply through mass production and distribution. But it also reduced the economic role of the woman from that of coprovider of the material needs of the family to that of dependent moral supporter of the male breadwinner. The industrial marketplace called for aggressiveness, individualism, risk taking, and competition, while the prevailing Protestant morality demanded a stable social structure, piety, and selflessness. The social bifurcation of home and workplace resulting from the pressures of industrialization was ideologically reinforced by what came to be known as the "separation of spheres." As Nancy Cott has put it,

> The wife's role in the home [in the mid-1800s]—not only maintaining her own virtue and gentility, but insuring her husband's comfort and her children's decency—became a crucial part of the rhetoric that championed the economic adventurer at the same time that it demanded social stability. Woman's "stationary place" supplies an element of anti-competitiveness and fixed morality, relieving the opportunism, greed, uncertainty, and impersonality that marked the dark side of the coin of Jacksonian "individualism."[12]

Women came to be regarded as moral and ethical agents charged with the responsibility of making the home a haven from the disturbing forces of the outside world and a place where children might be protected from the world's influence until they were able to assume their proper roles in this dichotomous social structure: boys in the sphere of commerce; girls in that of the home.

In what Baym defines as woman's fiction (those mid-nineteenth-century novels written and read by women that involve "the trials and triumph of a heroine who, beset with hardships, finds within herself the qualities of intelligence, will, resourcefulness, and courage sufficient to overcome them") the governing conventions of mid-nineteenth-century American culture were, via their removal from the real world and insertion in the fictional diegesis of the text, rendered subjects of scrutiny in and of themselves. The reader, guided of course by the author's interpretative directions, was left to determine why these particular conventions had been called to her attention and to sort out the relationship between their application in the fictive world of the text and their applicability in the real world. The conventions selected for inclusion in the woman's novel of the mid-nineteenth century were precisely those governing the bifurcation of American society into two spheres and, especially, the problematic role of women within that schema. As Carl Degler points out, the ideological assignment of women exclusively to the domestic sphere during the nascent industrial age repressively restricted her power and activities and, at the same time, endowed her with a unique moral platform from which to exert influence over family life. "Domesticity," he says, ". . . was an alternative to patriarchy, both in intention and in fact. By asserting a companionate role for women, it implicitly denied patriarchy."[13]

Given the centrality of sex roles in the social structure of any historical period and the enormous social upheaval caused by industrialization and its consequences, it is not surprising to find the position of these novels somewhat ambivalent, if not contradictory, with regard to the prescription of the woman's "place." The value system endorsed in woman's fiction of the period is clear enough: it is what Baym has called "domestic ideology." The home comes to stand for an entire value system, based upon liberal Protestant ideals of filial devotion, tolerance, charity, good works, forebearance, sacrifice, and self-effacement. The long-suffering, deferential heroines of the domestic novel are glorified as embodiments of this ideology and agents of its earthly realization. Deprived of their ability to act directly upon the world outside the home, the heroines of the novels act passively and indirectly, through example and influence. They are the victims of uncaring guardians, rapacious suitors, thoughtless and prodigal husbands and fathers, and the general vicissitudes of a hostile and selfish world. They respond with unfailing kindness, forgiveness, nurturing, and, once alone, torrents of tears. It is also clear that hundreds of thousands, if not millions, of women cried along with them, recognizing in the unabashedly exaggerated plights of these heroines a kernel of social truth.

What is not clear is the end served by this domestic ideology. In *The Feminization of American Culture*, Ann Douglas characterizes the stance of these novelists and the liberal Protestant ministers with whom they were frequently allied as nostalgic sentimentalism, a symbolic but ultimately useless protest against forces whose control over the protester had already been firmly secured. Its only positive function for Douglas was clearly to mark out the difference between a social world ordered upon selfless "feminine" principles, which these writers associated with the past, and the individualistic, Adam Smithian universe they saw around them.

It is to their credit that they indirectly acknowledged that the pursuit of these "masculine" goals meant damaging, perhaps losing, another good, one they increasingly included under the "feminine" ideal. Yet the fact remains that their regret was calculated not to interfere with their actions. . . . [Novelists and ministers] were in the position of contestants in a fixed fight: they had agreed to put on a convincing show, and to lose. The fakery involved was finally crippling for all concerned.

Baym argues that the ideological goal of these novels was not to offer sentimental solace to women for a world not even theirs to lose but rather to extend domestic ideology into the world at large. By making the family and home the center of the moral universe and by making the woman its divinely appointed guardian, domestic ideology "implied an unprecedented historical expansion of her influence, and a tremendous advance over her lot in a world dominated by money and market considerations, where she was defined as chattel or sexual toy."

Reading these novels, one can see that in a sense both Baym and Douglas are right: each simply approaches the novels' structuring contradiction from a different angle. Women are glorified in these works, not for their desirability as marriage partners or as fragile embodiments of an aesthetic ideal, as in the novels of the late eighteenth century, but for their moral and spiritual power. Supervision of the home is represented as an essential vocation and the homemaker as strong, resourceful, intelligent, and, above all, self-sacrificing. Men come across, for the most part, either as ineffectual or as agents of evil. As Mary Kelley points out, when the "ideal man" does appear, he is a male version of the feminine, domestic ideal: the minister or doctor devoted to advancing social welfare rather than his own fortune.

The contrast between the idealized world of the home and the real world of nineteenth-century America in these novels gives them a strong element of social protest that almost certainly would have been apparent to their female readers. The governing, male-constructed conventions of American society are introduced via abusive or negligent male characters so that these conventions can be seen in sharp contradistinction to those that *should* govern the domestic sphere and *might* govern the outside world if only. . . .

It is in the unanswerable conclusion to this sentence that Douglas and Kelley locate the ultimate pragmatic betrayal of the domestic novel. It is unanswerable because the very nature of the domestic ethos promoted in these novels also prevented the realization of that ethos outside of the restricted realm of the individual household. The instruments for social action sanctioned by domestic ideology were example and influence. As soon as women moved beyond them, they had been co-opted by the very values of individualism and aggressiveness they sought to combat. Women's ideological sphere could not be extended beyond the home, as Augusta Evans Wilson put it in one of her novels, "without rendering the throne unsteady, and subverting God's law of order. Woman reigned by divine right only at home." Kelley concludes that the domestic novel, which had begun as a utopian, if nostalgic, vision of what American society could become if domestic virtues were enshrined, had by the end of the 1880s been transformed into thinly disguised documents of bitter disillusionment. The Gilded Age and its laissez-faire materialism made a mockery of domestic ideology as an attainable model for American culture, and by the turn of the century the domestic novel had faded from the American scene.[14]

The legacies of this extraordinary publishing phenomenon were important and long-lasting, bridging the thirty-year gap between the demise of the domestic novel and the advent of the radio soap opera. The domestic novel established middle-class women as the primary consumers of literature in the United States. The increasing trend toward the production of consumer goods in factories rather than in the home gave the middle-class woman more leisure time, and the ideological connection between the domestic novel and Protestant theology helped to remove the last vestiges of the Puritan proscription of the reading of secular texts. Papashvily identifies Susan Warner's *The Wide, Wide World* as "one of the first real, full-length novels authority or conscience permitted many to enjoy." Domestic novels were not the only publications women read in the nineteenth century. By the end of the Civil War women constituted the primary readers of magazines as well. A number of the largest-circulation magazines in the United States were aimed exclusively toward women. In 1860 *Godey's Lady's Book*, then already past its prime, could still boast 150,000 subscribers, while *Harper's* claimed but 100,000. In addition to the major women's magazines of the 1880s and 1890s (*Ladies Home Journal, McCall's*) there were hundreds of so-called mail order journals, which carried serial fiction, household hints, and advertisements for products sold through the mail. *Comfort*, the largest of the mail-order publications, was begun in 1888. By 1894 it was being read in 1.3 million households, the largest circulation of any magazine in the world.[15]

The enormous success of the "woman's magazine" after the 1880s points to one of the principal ways in which the basic sexual contradiction in

American society represented in earlier decades by the doctrine of the two spheres manifested itself in the years following the demise of the domestic novel. Baym notes that during this period domestic ideology turned in upon itself, as discourse directed toward and, in many cases, written by women emphasized making the home a safe retreat from the outside world, rather than attempting to extend its influence into that world. The career of Mary Terhune, who under the pen name Marion Harland had written some of the most popular domestic novels of the 1850s and 1860s, is illustrative of this shift in emphasis. In 1871 she wrote a best-selling cookbook, *Common Sense in the Household*, the success of which launched the second phase of her career, that of domestic advisor. In 1901 she took over an advice column in the Philadelphia *North American*, which was soon nationally syndicated. Within two years she was receiving questions from women readers at the rate of one thousand per week about "everything from marmalade to matrimony." By the time she wrote her autobiography in 1910, she was much better known as a newspaper columnist than as the author of domestic novels. In *Marion Harland's Autobiography*, Terhune recounts a friend's gentle accusation that her cookbooks and domestic advice columns were not "literature." "No," she responded, ". . . but it is influence and that of the best kind."[16]

The domestic ideology of the early and mid nineteenth century implied that the expression of a woman's "true nature"—morally virtuous, passive, nurturing, self-sacrificing—resulted in the establishment of the ideal home environment. By the 1910s, however, women had been made to doubt that their innate "feminine" and maternal instincts were sufficient to make them good mothers. The Progressive Era's concern with childhood development and social conditioning gave rise to the notion of "educated motherhood": the belief that effective parenting (implicitly defined as the woman's vocation, not the man's) was not only the result of the exercise of instincts and common sense and of following mother's example but also and primarily the learning of management, psychological, and medical skills imparted by scientists, doctors, educators, and other "experts." The idea that managing a household and raising a family were difficult and complex tasks might have raised the self-esteem of the middle-class homemaker at the turn of the century and helped to rationalize her isolation from the world at large, but it also made her more dependent upon the discourse of "experts"—in women's magazines, cookbooks, and newspaper columns—if she was not to "fail" in her job as a woman.

As Sheila Rothman has noted, to the image of the ideal woman as virtuous moral agent and educated mother, the decade of the 1920s added
another dimension: that of the wifely companion to the upwardly-mobile
husband. The homemaker was expected efficiently to run the household, to
set the moral tone for the family, to care for and initiate the education of
children, *and* to remain an attractive romantic partner for her husband. In
the 1920s advice books and magazine articles counseled women on how to
"keep romance alive" in their marriages. *McCall's*, *Redbook*, and *Good
Housekeeping* featured advertisements for mouthwashes, deodorants, cosmetics, and lotions alongside those for food, baby clothes, and cleaning
products. Beauty parlors became commonplace, and by the time *Painted
Dreams* went on the air *Ladies Home Journal* was carrying more ads for
cosmetics than for food. "Clearly," says Rothman, "there was an untenable
quality about such a definition of a woman's roles—not only because her
wants and needs were consistently being defined in terms of the interests of
others but also because her own freedom within and without the family
was narrowly circumscribed." And yet the accretion of qualities associated
with the "ideal woman" continued (and continue). The core values of the
domestic ideology of the mid-nineteenth century survived, while others, in
many ways at odds with them, were nonetheless added as the complexities
of twentieth-century living placed new demands upon women.[17]

Certainly one of these core values of domestic ideology was that the appropriate mode of suasive behavior for a woman was influence. Men might
achieve success in the business world through the direct exercise of power
and authority, and, if necessary, physical force, but a lady could only effect
change gently, indirectly, through suggestion and moral appeal to a higher
authority. Ann Douglas sees more than a temporal coincidence in the rise
of commercial advertising at the same time (the 1870s and 1880s) that domestic ideology was at its most pervasive. Advertising adopted the rhetorical strategy of domestic ideology, influence, in the service of merchandising rather than theology.

> Influence, whether exerted by advertising or anything else, . . . is a
> technique adopted less to challenge than to seduce a competitive
> capitalist society too much in a hurry to get its tastes and values in
> any way but on the run, on the sly, and unawares. . . . Nor were the
> new advertising agencies unaware that their logical audience was
> feminine; they knew that, in some not altogether fanciful sense,

women would operate as the subconscious of capitalist culture which they must tap, that the feminine occupation of shopping would constitute the dream-life of the nation.

The translation of the moral didacticism of the domestic novel into the economic persuasion of the advertisement directed toward women might at first seem improbable. Certainly women, whether of the 1860s or the 1920s, recognized both the fictionalizing of values in the novel and the self-interest of the advertising pitch, as well as the difference in intent between the two forms. Both the domestic novel and the advertisement, however, spoke to the same basic question, How might a woman best fulfill her role in society? The domestic novel told her she might use her moral influence to return the home and family to the moral center of the social world. Advertisements suggested that being a successful homemaker, mother, and spouse required the purchase of certain mass-produced commodities.[18]

A final legacy of the domestic novel was the creation of an enormous literature that, obliquely or directly, fictively or nonfictively, concerned itself with and spoke to women as a distinct group within American society. Whether couched in terms of innocuous fiction or as "helpful" advice, this literature implicitly recognized the fact that, as Degler concludes, "women and the family . . . have been in unending tension for at least two centuries." I would agree with Modleski and others that as those most directly affected by this tension, and differently from the way men are affected, women have in some sense formed a subculture in American society, a subculture defined by sex and in relation to the dominant male culture and united by a common set of experiences and imposed values. The domestic novel represents the emergence of a vehicle of public literary expression for the American female subculture, the beginning of a discursive tradition continued in later fiction, women's magazines, and soap operas.

The identification of the entire female population of the United States as a single subculture admittedly borders on the stretching of the term beyond any real meaning—differences arising from class orientation, historical period, region, education, and politics do not somehow evaporate when women are considered as a group within American society. But the popularity of both the domestic novel and the soap opera across regions, educational and age groups, and class stratifications suggests that they dealt with concerns many different women identified as belonging to them and not to men. Papashvily reports Susan Warner's diary entry for 23 February 1859: "Got into the cooler little back room and rested with a charming little talk with Mrs. Hutton about her reading *The Wide, Wide World* in her kitchen to her black woman and Irish woman and two little children—all enchained." The irony, of course, in identifying the soap opera as the inheritor of a tradition of subcultural expression begun by the domestic novel is that culturally both forms of woman's fiction are defined by their exclusion from the mainstream of cultural production, while each quantitatively represents the dominant fictional narrative form of its day. The very size of the female subculture, along with its status as the primary consumer group in the United States since the mid-nineteenth century, predisposed its fictional expression toward accommodation with the status quo and toward commercial exploitation, while the exclusion of women from the centers of cultural power precluded the emergence of a fictional literature of revolt as anything more than a marginalized discourse.[19]

It would be simplistic to conclude that the domestic novel or the radio soap opera is merely an example of a patriarchal capitalist culture's ability to manipulate the tastes of women, or, conversely, to conclude that the popularity of either was based upon its audience's agreement with the strategies it presented. In the case of the domestic novel and the radio soap opera, as with other commercially produced fictions, actual decodings no doubt ranged (to use the categories provided by Stuart Hall) from dominant (fully taking up the position offered by the text), through negotiated (distanced to some degree from the proffered position), to oppositional (decoded within an alternative frame of reference).[20] However, both forms represent, above all else, the articulation of whole sets of concerns denigrated by or totally excluded from mainstream fictional discourse: home life, everyday social relations, family matters, the effect of external factors upon the home, and strategies for dealing with the multiple roles women were expected to adopt. Like the first readers of *The Wide, Wide World*, the first listeners to radio soap operas in the 1930s recognized in the narrative world of the soap opera a conceptual terrain at once familiar and, because of its removal from the real world, strange. That they were not deterred by impossibly idealized heroines, implausible plot twists, or, in the case of soap operas, the intrusion of product pitches should not be too surprising. Here, at least, was a narrative language that gave voice, however accented, to *their* concerns.

Thus one of the most important aspects of the horizon of expectations against which radio listeners positioned the first soap operas was the tradition of discourse that made them legible as "woman's fictions." As we have seen, soap operas were identified as such by both male and female readers.

To most men and to those women imbued with the values of the traditional aesthetics of "high art" the status of soap operas as women's fiction rendered them different, nonart, and, in the extreme reaction, potentially dangerous. To millions of other, predominantly female, listeners, this difference from mainstream narrative linked the soap opera to a tradition charged with significance for them but ignored or disdained by the former group. Early discourse on soap operas was shaped by the discursive hegemony exercised by a cultural elite (those with access to the instruments of public discourse) over a voiceless majority. The "male" response—when it finally came in the late 1930s—was public, individualized, and issued from a position of authority (magazine articles, editorials, scientific reports). The "woman's" response, when it was publicly articulated at all, came as answers to survey questions, depersonalized percentages, consignment to a demographic category.

Warner's novel *The Wide, Wide World* begins with the traumatic separation of the young heroine from her mother, as she is forced by financial difficulties to live with her aunt. As was typical of the handling of such scenes in the domestic novel, Warner pulls out all the emotional stops in encouraging the reader's sympathetic identification with the plight of the young girl. Baym comments, "These tears, which flow throughout the novel, have exasperated male critics, who repeatedly satirize its lachrymosity; for Warner, her characters, and her readers, the freedom to express grief is one of the few freedoms permitted women, though it must generally be indulged in private."[21] Baym's perceptive insight should serve as a reminder that in reconstructing the horizon of expectations for a historical text, the historian must take into account not only the public response engendered by the work but, particularly in the case of popular works, who is allowed to respond, in what ways, and from what positions. Furthermore, the historian must recognize that, in addition to the public response, there is that response "indulged in private," visible only as an absence and heard at the time only as an affirming silence.

## Changes in Textual Structure

Very few of the hundreds of thousands of hours of soap opera broadcasts were recorded and fewer still survive today. Media products are by their very nature transient, and only those thought to possess more than the usual aesthetic or economic value are preserved for any length of time. It was not until the "rediscovery" of the soap opera in the mid-1970s that networks and program owners began to submit individual soap opera episodes for copyright, in order to protect themselves against possible subsequent use of this material by others. Thus there are only a handful of recorded transcriptions of radio soap operas from the early 1930s or kinescopes of televised soap operas prior to the advent of video tape recording in the mid-1960s. Unless more recorded episodes are discovered, we must rely upon scripts to mark the major changes over time in the soap opera's textual structure.

On the admittedly imperfect basis of those surviving scripts it can be seen that the most striking change in soap opera form occurred with the advent of television. Obviously, the construction of the soap opera world as one to be heard *and* seen resulted in considerable textual reorientation, as was pointed out in the previous chapter. Television, however, also brought with it a less apparent but just as fundamental narrative transformation, one involving the nature of the soap opera's diegesis, its relationship to the reader, and the role of the narrator in that process. This discussion of both the textual structure of the radio soap opera in the 1930s and its transformation during the television era draws upon examples taken primarily from the work of Irna Phillips. Such a heavy reliance upon one author's work risks presenting as general tendencies what might have been idiosyncratic features, not to mention collapsing the considerable variety of soap operas into a single textual category. In their key textual features, however, soap operas produced by the Hummerts differed little from those written and produced by Phillips. Furthermore, the sheer number and success of Phillips's soaps supports their representativeness. Finally, thanks to the unique longevity of *Guiding Light* and its status as the only radio soap opera successfully to make the transition to television, we have an opportunity to trace textual changes in a specific text over nearly fifty years of continuous production and consumption.

## THE RADIO SOAP OPERA

Iser provides a useful schema for discussing the arrangement of normative perspectives within fictive texts and the positioning of the reader in relation to them. The world of the text is constructed through a system of perspectives provided by the narrator, characters, plot, and the "fictitious" reader. By "fictitious reader" (*fiktiver Leser*) Iser means the reader constructed by the author as the receiving agency of the narrative, an extreme example—

frequently cited—of which is the reader addressed in Sterne's *Tristram Shandy*: "How could you, Madam, be so inattentive in reading the last chapter? I told you in it, *That my mother was not a papist.*" These four perspectives "provide guidelines originating from different starting points . . . continually shading into each other and devised in such a way that they all converge on a general meeting place." This convergence of perspective occurs as the text is activated by the reader.

All four narrative perspectives (narrator, characters, plot, and fictionalized reader) embody norms, which may be ranked in a particular text, set in opposition to each other, or merely presented sequentially. In what Iser calls the counterbalancing text, a definite ordering of norms is established. In *Pilgrim's Progress*, for example, the hero represents the central perspective of the text. Minor characters represent invalid perspectives, which are more than counterbalanced by the affirmation of the positive qualities of the hero by the narrator and plot: those minor characters who most closely match the qualities of the hero continue with him longest on his journey, while those characters who violate these norms are punished. The emphasis in *Pilgrim's Progress* on man's continual search for salvation "counterbalances" the fatalistic Calvinist doctrine of predestination, thus restabilizing Protestant ideology. Counterbalancing is a strategy to be found mainly in didactic literature, where its function is "not to produce an aesthetic object that will rival the thought system of the social world, but to offer a *compensation* for specific deficiencies in specific thought systems."

Of the four types of perspective arrangement Iser enumerates,[22] counterbalance comes closest to describing the interaction of narrative perspectives in the soap opera. Implicit in this category of text is the mutual reinforcement of perspectives so that the hierarchy of norms is made clear. Where the soap opera differs from a text like *Pilgrim's Progress*, and to some degree challenges Iser's typology, however, is in its dual role as commodity (narrative to be consumed) and vehicle for the commodification of the reader. The didacticism of the soap opera text serves no specific ideological end *in and of itself* except insofar as it lays the groundwork for the *real* but displaced "message": that of the commercial sponsor. Given the soap opera's status as woman's fiction, we might read into it multiple "compensatory" functions: the very existence of the soap opera helps to compensate for the exclusion of domestic concerns in mainstream fiction; the glorification of its super-homemaker heroines counterbalances to some degree the ambiguous nature of women's roles in American society; the effective advice offered by those characters provides a restabilizing influence in the context of Depression-era uncertainties; the reassertion of the centrality of the family is counterposed to the threats marshaled against it; and so forth.

While these compensatory functions might all be at work, we must remember that the norms sitting atop the soap opera's perspectival hierarchy are those of the sponsor—a value system in which the ultimate deficiency is the reader's failure to purchase the advertised product. All radio and television narratives that serve as advertising vehicles evince two sets of norms: that of the "show" (the fictional diegesis) and that of the "message." At the very least they must not be contradictory; at best the former supports and encourages the reader's acceptance of the latter as valid. But the two must not appear to the reader to be identical; otherwise the "author's" (sponsor's) true intent is laid bare and the fictional narrative becomes nothing more than a parable in a marketing sermon. The message must be kept apart from but ultimately reassociated with the fictional world of the show. Thus, in a sense, the fictional text of the commercial media narrative acts as a counterbalance to the sponsor's text that punctuates and surrounds it: the former must supply a degree of indeterminacy to compensate for the absolute determinacy of the latter.

In the radio soap opera of the 1930s, we have a unique textual structure and arrangement of narrative perspectives. The mutability and openness of the soap opera's plot made it the weakest of the perspectives in terms of norm embodiment, yet its extreme indeterminacy sustained reader involvement, allowed for infinite textual regeneration, and enabled the soap opera to respond to external normative change. The network of character interaction, characteristic of the contemporary television soap opera, was present in its 1930s radio version, but only in embryonic form. Characters were frequently arranged in a definite hierarchy, presided over by a single character. This character might have acted as the protagonist of a plot line infrequently, but his or her values permeated the entire text and ultimately prevailed. The dominant voice (both narratively and physically) of the soap opera was that of the narrator. He (so far as I can determine, it has always been male) interpenetrated the world of the narrative and that of the commercial message, relating them yet keeping them distinct.

Having sketched the perspectival hierarchy of the radio soap opera of the 1930s, we can now examine in greater detail the interaction of character, narrator, and fictitious reader (or what I will call "narratee") in the text.

Modifying a schema of narration devised by Seymour Chatman, Shlomith Rimmon-Kenan suggests a model of narrative communication that, presented diagrammatically, would appear thusly:

$$\text{real} \longrightarrow \left( \begin{array}{c} \text{implied} \\ \text{author} \end{array} \right) \longrightarrow \text{narrator} \longrightarrow \text{narratee} \longrightarrow \left( \begin{array}{c} \text{implied} \\ \text{reader} \end{array} \right) \longrightarrow \begin{array}{c} \text{real} \\ \text{reader} \end{array}$$

Both the real author and the real or historical reader exist outside the text. The implied author is bracketed in Rimmon-Kenan's model because it is not an actual textual structure but a construct: the implicit norms governing the text as inferred by the reader and usually, at some level, referred back to the real author. Similarly, she would see the implied reader (perhaps model reader would be more precise here) as that potential reader envisioned by the author in the construction of the text. Where Chatman conceives of the narrator and narratee as optional textual structures (the teller and receiver of the story, respectively), Rimmon-Kenan regards them as constitutive elements of narrative communication. A tale presupposes a teller and someone to whom the tale is addressed. In every story we have not the presence or absence of narrator and narratee but variability in the manner in which their presence is called to our attention and to what degree. Narrative agency may be as assertive as the first-person narrators of the hard-boiled detective novel or as muted as the impersonal "force" that stitches together the dialogue in the novels of Ivy Compton-Burnett. The narratee may be specifically addressed and personified, as in Sterne's *Tristram Shandy*, or almost disdainfully ignored, as in the *nouveau roman*. At the risk of terminological confusion, I shall substitute "narratee" for Iser's "fictitious reader," since the former acknowledges the existence of an auditor for all narratives, whether their presence in the text is made explicit or not.[23] At a time when narrational presence was barely noticeable in elite literature and in most Hollywood films, the role of the narrator was strongly reasserted in the radio soap opera. Indeed, it is difficult to think of another twentieth-century fictional narrative form in which the narrator plays such a central and multifaceted role in the reader's understanding of the text.

A narrative text may contain multiple levels of narration and multiple narrative voices: characters who tell stories about characters who tell stories, ad infinitum. The narrator who precedes all others, who narrates from a position "above" the story, is its "extradiegetic" narrator. The voice commonly referred to as that of the "announcer" acted as the extradiegetic narrator of the soap opera text. The very nature of the radio medium's reliance upon a single channel of communication—sound—gives rise to a fundamental narrational difference between it and literature, on the one hand, and film and television, on the other. In a novel the extradiegetic narrator is the impersonal, quasi-omniscient agency through which we "know" the story. In Hollywood films and television it is the unquestioned but usually anonymous means by which we see and hear the story unfold before us. Only occasionally is extradiegetic narrative agency in the Hollywood film actually personified in the form of a narrational "voice-over" (Welles's *Magnificent Ambersons* is an example, and he, of course, was trained in radio drama). We notice the film story's "teller" only through an unmotivated camera movement, a verbal text on the screen ("Phoenix, Friday, December 12"), or other carefully regulated devices that call attention to the film's narrational, as opposed to dramatic, status. In radio narrative it is difficult *not* to personify extradiegetic narration since performing such simple narrational tasks as establishing locales and bridging spatial and temporal ellipses is difficult using sound effects and music alone. The novel can verbally describe; the film and television program can show; but radio sound effects and music can only refer metonymically or indexically to its diegetic world. In radio much more than any of the other media, the story depends upon a "teller." From the extant sources, it appears that all radio soap operas used an extradiegetic male narrational voice (the announcer) to tell, in part at least, the soap opera's story. His functions ranged from the obvious to the subtle, and his role in maintaining the perspectival hierarchy of the soap opera's narrative diegesis and in relating that diegesis to the nondiegetic portion of the soap opera text (the commercials) was vitally important.

One of the few functions of the extradiegetic radio soap opera narrator surviving on television soap operas today is that of signaling the resumption of the soap's narrative at the beginning of an episode and its suspension at the end of that episode. On some television soap operas this function has been taken over by a visual and musical signature (a slide of General Hospital with the legend *General Hospital* superimposed over it, for example), obviating the need for a personified narrational voice at all. Other soaps still use the male announcer, who intones, for example, "For the next full hour, *As the World Turns*" and, "Tune in again tomorrow for *As the World Turns*." The narrational introductions for radio soap operas ranged from the simple—"And now *Today's Children*—to the elaborate—*The Open Door*, a short-lived soap whose main character was Dean Erik Hansen of Vernon University, began each program with Hansen saying, "Come in, come in! The door is always open," followed by the announcer reciting,

> There is an Open Door
> To a Good Way of Life for all men,
> This Open Door is called brotherhood,
> And over its portal are these simple words:
> "I *am* my brother's keeper."[24]

Another function of the narrator now only vestigially present in the contemporary television soap opera is that of signaling the interruption of the narrative within each episode by the commercial "break," while linking the one to the other. Today, when an announcer is used for this purpose, his "voice" is distinct from both that of the narrative diegesis and that of the commercial messages: "We'll return to *One Life to Live* in a moment." In the radio soap opera the announcer's voice *was* that of the commercial message, as well as that of the extradiegetic narrator linking the two. The "links" effected by the announcer were frequently quite specific. The 20 December 1932 episode of *Today's Children* concluded with the announcer saying:

> December 20, and Bob and Fran are still friends. And today they both got new jobs they're very anxious to make good on. But after all, who doesn't want to make good on their job? To make good calls not only for work but for efficiency as well, and don't overlook the big part efficiency can play. Even in routine work like washing and ironing, it can make all the difference in the world. That's why so many women use Satina to get maximum results with minimum effort when ironing. And for washing they have discovered that La France has no equal. A quarter of a cupful used along with the regular laundry soap or soap flakes will make the most stubborn dirt disappear as if by magic. You just add the La France and go ahead with your washing in the regular way. But it takes so much less time. No hard rubbing is necessary. . . .

The relevance of the narrative of *Ma Perkins* to the program's commercial message on 13 December 1933 was clearly established by the announcer. "And so Ma Perkins has had a change of heart at last, realizes what mothers have found since the world began: that you can't run other people's affairs for 'em. You can't make 'em do what you think is best. You've just got to help 'em. And speaking of help, there's no household job that needs outside help more than washing clothes. . . ."[25]

## Toward a History

Because of the limitation of radio's representational resources to a single, aural mode, the announcer's narrational role vis-à-vis the soap's "story" itself began with the establishment of such basic diegetic features as setting and character identification, which in the novel or the film would be accomplished through description or presentation. The Tuesday, 4 July 1950, episode of *The Guiding Light* opened as follows:

> *Effect: Church bells. Under*
> Announcer: The Peal of church bells in the steeple of the Church of the Good Samaritan in Selby Flats—the peal of church bells calls the people of the melting pot community to a special service in commemoration of a Fourth of July one hundred and seventy-four years ago—when the pealing of another bell filled the heavens with its ringing cry of Liberty—Independence—Freedom.
> *Effect: Church bells up for a few seconds—fade out as shuffling footsteps of people entering the church are brought in. Hold under*
> Announcer: Dr. Keeler stands at the head of the church as men, women and children of his community enter to walk down the aisles and take their places.
> *Effect: Footsteps. Pause.*
> Announcer: Now, as the last pew is filled, he slowly mounts the steps into the pulpit—looks quietly at the congregation below him—and slowly begins to speak. . . .[26]

The announcer's narrational role went well beyond merely framing the soap opera story and relating it to the commercial message. He frequently intervened in the diegesis, mediating between characters and reader, and in doing so, firmly established the norms of the narrator's "voice" as those atop the soap's perspectival hierarchy. *The Guiding Light* might have been atypical in the frequency with which the narrator asserted himself and to what degree, but it does provide a good example of the nature and potential effect of extradiegetic soap opera narration in general. Perhaps nowhere is this narrational control more in evidence than in the 10 January 1950 episode of *The Guiding Light*. There the narrator not only normatively orients the reader toward one of the show's central characters and motivates that character's recollections but also orchestrates the reader's retensive reflections on the significance of past plot developments. The role of the narrator in this episode is extraordinary (the complete script is reprinted as an appendix); the opening sequence will suffice for the purpose of our present discussion.

*Music: under*

*Announcer:* This evening in the living room of a little house with a white picket fence on Elm Street in Selby Flats, the fireplace is ablaze with flame, but somehow it seems cold and cheerless to you, doesn't it, Ray Brandon? You sit with your tightly clenched hands pressed against your forehead—your thoughts are of Charlotte in a hospital where she has been confined because of her attempt to find forgetfulness, escape, in the twilight world of barbiturates, sleeping pills. . . . It's unbelievable, isn't it, Ray, what's happened to Charlotte . . . and what's happened to you. You're forced at this moment to recall the words of Dr. Mary Leland. . . .

*Music: Up and under*

*Mary: (Over filter)* Now of all times, Ray, you must give Charlotte all the understanding she needs and deserves. Ray, you've got to straighten out your own thinking a little before you can even begin to help Charlotte find her way back.

*Music: Up and under*

*Ray:* Apparently Mary feels that my thinking needs not just a little but a great deal of straightening out. She wouldn't even permit me to see Charlotte today. Somehow I got the idea that Charlotte must have made it very clear that she didn't want to see me.

*Mary: (Filter)* She's going thru mental and physical torment, Ray.

*Ray:* And so am I, so am I. But I've got to stop thinking of myself now. I've got to think as straight and as clearly as I ever have in my life.

*Music: Up and out.*

*Announcer:* But will you be capable, Ray, of seeing the past thru anything but a haze of bitterness? Will you be capable even now? We'll learn more about this shortly.

*Music: Out*

*Announcer:* Commercial[27]

The example above also indicates the narrator's power over characters' narrational perspective. The narrator's very description of a particular character could position him or her on a normative hierarchy, while, as in the above, the narrator's intervention could expose the normative basis for a character's actions. In the 7 May 1952 episode of *The Guiding Light* the announcer led into the first commercial by saying, "Well, Bill? What are you going to do about Bert? What are you going to tell her? I wouldn't want to be in your shoes, not for anything—because—well, we'll learn more about this in a moment."[28]

In many cases one character's perspective embodied the norms of the text as a whole: Mother Moynihan in *Painted Dreams*, Mother Moran in *Today's Children*, Ma Perkins in *Ma Perkins*, Dr. Jim Brent in *The Road of Life*, Papa David Solomon in *Life Can Be Beautiful*, and Dr. Allen in *Against the Storm*, among others. *The Guiding Light* was organized around a succession of ministers—Dr. Ruthledge, Dr. Matthews, Dr. Andrews, Dr. Keeler, and, finally, in the 1950s, Reverend Marsh—who were perhaps more closely identified with the normative stance of the programs than any other radio soap opera characters. The original plot of *The Guiding Light* concerned a widowed minister and his daughter moving to Five Points, "a melting pot district in one of America's cosmopolitan cities," where he becomes pastor of a nondenominational chapel. His helpful advice and selflessness soon make him a "guiding light" for the community. The ethos of *The Guiding Light*—charity, tolerance, self-sacrifice, forgiveness—derives from the same liberal Protestant theology that undergirds the nineteenth-century domestic novel and directly links the various ministers of that program to the "feminized" male protagonists of the older works. As he is confronted by one challenge to his values after another, the minister's reliance upon the values of "the guiding light" is tested and found warranted. An extended plot line or, as in the case above, a particularly recalcitrant character might call the minister's (and, hence, the show's) norms into question for some time, but the listener knows that ultimately those norms will prevail.

During the show's radio history (1937–56) a variety of devices were used to maintain an explicit connection between the character of the minister and the principles of "the guiding light." For a period in the 1940s the program opened with the minister delivering a prayer or homily, as in this episode from June 1947:

> *Dr. M [Matthews]:* Almighty God . . . help us to realize that it is not enough to be good merely for the sake of being good; not enough to do good to others, merely because of an abstract ideal of brotherhood. Help us to understand that goodness and brotherhood must be meaningless unless they are practiced in Your name and

thru Your light—the light which alone can show us the way and
the truth . . . the light which is our Guiding Light.
*Announcer:* Let us all join hearts in the sentiment expressed by
Dr. Charles Matthews, in his prayer for today.
*Music: Chords*
*Announcer:* And now, The Guiding Light. (*Pause*)

At least once each year, usually on the occasion of a holiday, *The Guiding Light's* narrative ground to a halt so that its current clerical character could deliver a sermon to his diegetic audience and to the show's radio listeners. The most famous of these was the "Seven Last Words" sermon delivered each Good Friday for the last ten years of *The Guiding Light* radio broadcasts. The final one, on 30 March 1956, had Reverend Marsh delivering his inspirational message via a nationwide radio hookup. Thus two characters living in New York are able to participate in the service in absentia.[29]

The privileged narrational status of the central soap opera figure is further indicated by that character's ability—apparently not enjoyed by lesser characters—to break through the invisible walls surrounding the diegetic universe of the soap opera narrative and acknowledge both narrator and audience explicitly. Two examples of this sort of diegetic extension were given in the previous chapter's discussion of "mailhooks": Dr. Ruthledge's direct address to both announcer and reader regarding the refrigerator giveaway and Mother Moran's being persuaded by the announcer to offer her listeners a photograph of her "Today's Children" family.[30]

The cumulative effect of the radio soap opera's intervening extradiegetic narrator, the direct linkage upon occasion of some diegetic element with the commercial message, and the clear normative hierarchy established by character stratification and maintained by both the privileged position of central characters and the interposition of the narrator was three-fold. First, it created a correspondence between the soap opera narrative diegesis and the commercial message through a sort of *mise en abyme* construction. Rimmon-Kenan gives as an example of *mise en abyme* Gide's *The Counterfeiters*, in which a character writes a novel that parallels in many respects the novel in which the character himself appears. In the case of radio soap operas the narrational perspective structure of the diegesis was made to mirror that of the commercial message. The announcer-narrator derived his authority from his narrational prescience and his mediating position between reader and text. His authority was reinforced by a pyramidal character structure, atop which was located, in many instances, a single character who embodied the implicit norms of the text. The narrator's power exceeded that of any single character, however. He controlled the flow of the story; his voice described the world in which all characters appeared; he knew and related the thoughts of characters and conditioned the reader's reception of those thoughts. His narrational authority was carried over from the diegesis to the commercial message, as was the normative force of the story, of which he was the guarantor.

Second, the radio soap opera's narrational system opened up its diegetic space. The boundaries of the radio soap opera universe were unspecified and could be stretched to overlap with the realm of the commercial message (through connections made between the two by the narrator) and with the world of the reader. Insofar as the sponsor was concerned, the optimum situation obtained at those times when all three arenas were simultaneously diegetically enveloped, as in the case of premium offers: the world of the soap opera narrative was allowed to spill over into that of the reader in the form of a tangible object (an anniversary picture, locket, ironing accessory, cake recipe, and so forth). The agency effecting this transubstantiation from fictive object to physical one was, of course, the sponsor. As in the case of Mother Moran and Dr. Ruthledge, characters were occasionally allowed to address their auditors directly; in doing so, they futher blurred the demarcation between the world of the story and that of the listener.

One of the most striking examples of the radio soap opera's diegetic elasticity is provided by the concluding episode of *Today's Children* in January 1938.[31] The script for this episode is included as an appendix. It begins with the announcer informing the listener that Mother Moran has gathered her children together for "a very important occasion in the Moran home," emblematic of which is the presence of one of Mother Moran's famous cakes (baked, of course, with Pillsbury's Sno Sheen Cake Flour). Mother Moran has assembled her clan to announce the marriage of two of her "children," Kay and Bob. But there is another reason for the gathering: it is "kind of a farewell party, too." Mother Moran explains:

> . . . Friends of Today's Chidren—for over five and a half years, you
> have been like neighbors to my family and to friends of my family.
> You have seen these Children of Today work out their problems, one
> by one—problems that sometimes were kinda hard ta work out. But

somehow, in some way, these children of mine now seem ta be on the right path, each one of them. Terry, Dorothy and their little family, are content and happy. Isn't that right?

The "children" agree that their problems have now been solved, thanks to "what we've learned from the teachings of a woman who has reared her family to manhood and to womanhood with an understanding and a sympathy that can't fail them, no matter what the future may hold." Mother Moran continues:

> Thank ya, Bob. Thank ya, my Today's Children—all of you. Eileen, who has finally worked out her problem—Katherine, Terry, Dorothy, Frances, Henry—it's with a great deal of pleasure that I can say that I feel that my work is over and I have indeed been repaid ta the fullest. And now, Friends of Today's Children, may I have the pleasure and the great happiness ta be the first one ta turn on my radio, just as you have yours turned on, ta hear another real life story. Will ya be turnin' on the radio, please, Frances?

Frances obliges, and Mother Moran *et fils* listens to the first episode of Pillsbury's new radio program, *The Woman in White.*

In 1943, Phillips revived *Today's Children* and in 1946 teamed it with *Guiding Light* and *Woman in White* as NBC's General Mills Hour. Not only were the three programs joined in the same programming block, but they were given interpenetrating diegeses: Dr. Jonathon McNeill of *The Guiding Light* visited patients at Municipal Hospital, the locale of *The Woman in White*, and discussed cases with Dr. Paul Burton of *Today's Children*. The announcer, Ed Prentiss, served as "meta-extradiegetic" narrator, introducing each program segment and linking all three together. In one of the early episodes of the General Mills Hour, Prentiss disingenuously announced his function as:

> merely to set the stage for the dramatic, deeply moving stories of folks so many of you have come to know as well as you do your own neighbors. I bridge the gap between yesterday and today, but beyond that I'm as much of a bystander and an observer as you are. I'm just as absorbed as you are in the way life unfolds in Five Points—at Municipal Hospital . . . just as concerned as you are with the vital problems of Today's Children. . . .

He then describes—presumably for new listeners—one of the characters in *The Guiding Light*, Tim Lawrence, a returned fighter pilot. "Want to meet Tim Lawrence?" Prentiss asks of the "fictitious" reader. He "calls Tim over," and discusses his problems with him. The exchange exposes Prentiss's power as narrator:

> *Ed:* I think I know what you mean, Tim.
>
> *Tim:* Yes, I guess you've been enough of an observer—a spectator, to know me pretty well.
>
> *Ed:* Well enough to be frank?
>
> *Tim:* By all means.
>
> *Ed:* You know, Tim—I don't mean to sound too objective but—a man like you, a man who didn't see happiness when it was right in his grasp—perhaps could have found real happiness with Nina Chadwick—a son you came to know too late—do you mind all this, Tim?
>
> *Tim:* I asked you to be frank.
>
> *Ed:* A man who not only failed to make a go of that first marriage, but who—well who flopped pretty miserably in his second . . . your marriage to Clare. Well, Tim—just what does a guy like you do with your life—where do you go from here?[32]

Third, the narrational structure of the radio soap opera attempted to fix the position of the reader as narratee. The perspectival hierarchy of the soap opera narrative and the univocal, direct-address style of the commercial messages both worked to locate the reader as the person for whose benefit the soap opera text was constructed and presented. Both sought to involve her directly as a participant in a textual and economic exchange. The reader was implicitly addressed by the narrator as he guided her through the diegetic terrain of individual episodes, pausing to comment upon actions and characters, directing her retention of past narrative segments, and giving protensive directions ("What has Sally got to hide? Tune in again tomorrow.") She is explicitly addressed on occasion both by the narrator and, as we have seen, less frequently by characters themselves. She was one-half of the "we" in "We'll learn more about this in a moment," and the "friend" addressed by Mother Moran. The acknowledgment of the reader as narratee reinforced her status as the object of the commercial message, in which the true didactic function of the soap opera was laid bare. She was here not only directly addressed but questioned ("What are you planning for dinner tonight?"), reminded ("Be sure to pick up a package of Satina the next time you go shopping"), importuned ("Why don't you bake Mother Moran's 'Happiness Cake' today?"), cajoled ("Doesn't your family deserve . . .?"), and ordered ("Do it today!")—all by the same voice that addressed her from his position as teller of the soap opera story. This attempted positioning by no means assured its desired effect: no doubt many soap opera listeners refused to accept the judgment of the narrator upon a character's actions just as they purchased brands of laundry starch other than that proffered by the announcer. Analysis of the perspectival hierarchy and diegetic elasticity of the radio soap opera, however, reveals the elaborateness with which the reader's *preferred* position was constructed and the text's investment in encouraging the reader to occupy it.

## THE TELEVISION SOAP OPERA

The advent of the television soap opera and the demise of its radio predecessor brought about considerable change in the form's narrative structure, particularly as regards its narrational agency. The nature of this change can be seen by examining scripts for *The Guiding Light*, the only radio soap opera successfully to be adapted for television. Despite its having been on the air for thirteen years (except for a brief hiatus in the mid-1940s when Irna Phillips's exclusive ownership of the show was challenged), *The Guiding Light* in 1950 continued to rely upon a strong extradiegetic narrator. In fact this period is one of frequent narrator intervention. Consider, for example, the opening of the 22 December 1950 episode:

> Announcer: Friends, I don't have to tell you with what great anticipation the Brandons have looked forward to bringing another child into their home. Well—today is the day. It has been my pleasure— I'm sorry you couldn't have been on hand to witness the preparations that have been going on in the little house with the white picket fence—preparations for Penny Brandon—an auburn-haired, blue-eyed little girl, almost a year old. Yes, I remember as you do, as the Brandons do, the room that was closed for so long—a boy's room— Chuckie's room. You wouldn't know that room today, because what Charlotte has done to it during the past few weeks—well, it's all girl, from its pale pink walls to its light maple furniture. It seems as tho Ray has been slightly premature, because right in the middle of that room is a small table, with two small chairs. One chair is empty,

the other—well, sitting in it in all her splendor is a great big doll, with auburn hair and blue eyes. The table is set with little dishes, plastic knives and forks. . . . Oh Ray, you're way ahead of yourself. Charlotte has been much more practical. She bought a playpen and in the playpen are delightful woolly toys (*Slight pause*). There is only one object in the room that is a reminder of another room, a boy's room—Chuckie's room. I don't have to tell you what that object is, because you know it's the music box. . . . Ray has just wound it up. The eyes of Penny, who is safely tucked in Charlotte's arms, widen as she hears the first strains of the music box that bridge the past with the present. (*Effect of music box*) We'll join the Brandons and Penny in a few moments.

The perceptibility of the narrator in *The Guiding Light* varies from episode to episode during the period 1950–52, but as late as May 1952 the announcer-narrator still comments upon the action: "Well, Bill? What are you going to do about Bert? What are you going to tell her? I wouldn't want to be in your shoes, not for anything—because—well, we'll learn more about this in a moment."

*The Guiding Light* became a television as well as a radio soap opera on 30 June 1952, and for the next four years each script was prepared for both media. With the transition to television the role of the announcer-narrator immediately diminished. The script for the 2 July 1952 episode called for the announcer to remark at the end of the first scene: "You realize, don't you, Meta, after Bruce leaves, how much truth there is in what he told you. And yet you feel that somewhere, somehow, there must be an answer for you and Joe, there has to be an answer. We'll learn more about this in a moment." In the margin of the script beside the announcer's lines has been written: "out for t.v.," and all the lines have been struck through with pencil, except for "We'll learn more about this in a moment."

Throughout the next four years of both radio and television broadcasts, the radio announcer retained a descriptive function while his interpretative and intervening functions quickly disappeared. The radio version of the 5 March 1956 episode opened with:

*Sound: Steeple clock chiming twelve, fade into bg.*

*Announcer: (Over the chimes)* Twelve o'clock. Midnight. Most of the people in the city of Los Angeles are asleep—most of the homes blanketed in darkness. But here and there the lights of living

rooms and bedrooms are burning as the early morning edition of
a newspaper is read. The account of an eleven year old boy named
Michael Bauer—missing since early this morning. On the front
page of the paper, beneath the headlines, is a charcoal sketch of
the young boy's face—the alert, rather sad eyes—the sensitive, unsmiling mouth. . . .
*Music: Up for a few notes and out.*
*Sound: Take the last of the chimes in distance.*

While the television version merely indicated:

For TV take a shot of a church steeple silhouetted against the night
sky. We hear the clock chiming twelve. Dissolve from steeple to
the Bauer living room. Bill's standing at the window. Papa is
seated, staring into space. Bert is seated on the couch, her head in
her hand.[33]

By 1956, except for the occasional need (as above) for radio description,
the announcer's narrational role had been reduced in both media versions
to merely that of introducing each episode ("And now *The Guiding Light*,
created by Irna Phillips") and signaling the interruption of the narrative by
the commercial message ("We'll learn more about this in a moment"). He
also provided the "voice" for the commercial messages, but, so far as I can
determine, no attempt was made to make events in the diegesis a pretext for
the product pitch, as was commonplace in radio soap operas.

In short, most of the basic narrational tasks performed by the radio announcer were obviated by the addition of a visual channel of information to
the soap opera form. Characters and settings no longer needed to be described to listeners. Long passages of narrational exposition could be
handled more economically by the visual specificity of a single shot. The
narrator's voice was no longer required to orient the reader's perspective
during an internal monologue or flashback, since this could be accomplished by the combination of visual and auditory devices. A close-up of a
character's face could induce protensive projection in the reader almost as
well as the narrator's commentary at the end of a scene or an entire episode
("Well, Bill? What are you going to do about Bert?"). In place of the personified voice of the radio soap opera's extradiegetic narrator the television
soap offered the largely unvoiced, "invisible" narrational agency of the
classical Hollywood narrative style.

The consequences of the shift from aural to audio-visual modes of representation and from personified to abstract extradiegetic narration entailed more than merely the addition of visual information and the corresponding diminution of the role of an announcer-narrator. The television soap opera's adoption of the classical Hollywood narrational system effectively sealed off its diegesis in an autonomous realm whose boundaries were much more fixed and inflexible than those of the radio soap opera. The reader as narratee, who had been explicitly addressed by the radio announcer, became the unacknowledged viewer of the television soap opera narrative. No longer would characters be called out of the diegesis and into the narrator's "space." The television soap opera viewer's gaze would never be returned by that of a character; the membrane separating their two spheres was made impermeable.

Ironically, the same forces that sealed off the television soap opera diegesis from the viewer also closed it off from its accompanying commercial messages. Irna Phillips's vision of the collapse of the commercial message and the televised soap opera story into one extended narrative advertisement never materialized. Instead, they became parallel but separate textual segments. For the first decade of television soaps, the announcer provided the voice for the commercial, thus maintaining some degree of linkage between the soap opera diegesis and advertisement. Because both commercials and "story" were broadcast live through the early 1960s, soap opera advertisements were limited to technically simple and rhetorically straightforward product pitches—a voice-over narrator extolling the virtues of Tide detergent while a model illustrated his points on a laundry-room set, for example. Anything much more elaborate was difficult to accommodate within the "real-time" restrictions of live television. With the advent of video tape as a recording and retransmission medium in the mid-1960s, however, advertisements could be prepared in advance and inserted into the program as it was broadcast. Soap opera commercials were prerecorded long before the narrative segments they surrounded were.

The use of video tape facilitated increased formal complexity of commercials and encouraged the incorporation of narrative elements within them. Sandy Flitterman has examined the relationship between soap opera "story" and advertisements from a semiotic perspective and has concluded that while the former is a technically and narratively impoverished form, the latter is "comparatively rich." Furthermore, she suggests, the "micronarrative" of the soap opera commercial message stabilizes the overall soap opera text by counterbalancing the soap opera narrative's absolute resistance to closure with "small oases of narrative closure, homogeneous and systematic units of unproblematized meaning."[34] Building upon Flitterman's insights, we might see the comparative formal complexity of the soap opera commercial as the investment of it with aspects of the diegetic flexibility and extradiegetic narrational authority formerly possessed by the radio soap opera but displaced in the transition to television. For example, one of the advertisements Flitterman discusses is a carefully constructed "testimonial" for Final Touch Fabric Softener, which begins with "Mrs. Kidwell" addressing the camera and saying, "I'll stop using it. Point blank." The offscreen narrator then responds, "We're teasing Mrs. Kidwell. We told her we're taking the whitener out of Final Touch Fabric Softener. Listen. . . ." An exchange between Mrs. Kidwell and the narrator follows in which she urges "him" to "Please leave it in." The form of this commercial message is so commonplace as to be unremarkable until one compares it with the classical Hollywood model of narrative construction of the television soap opera, on the one hand, and that of the radio soap opera, on the other. The implicit acknowledgment of the "narratee" in this commercial, the narrator's mediation of the "story," and the character's ability to address both narrator and narratee would all be anathematic to the narrative principles of the television soap opera, but are all accepted conventions of the radio soap opera.

A further consequence of the removal of a personified extradiegetic narrator in the television soap opera was the alteration of its perspectival hierarchy. No longer was there a "voice" to insure the continuing reassertion of the text's norms and to maintain the stratification of characters' perspectives. This is not to say that the soap opera ceased to privilege a set of ideological norms with the advent of television, but in the television soap the text's dominant perspective had to be internalized rather than imposed from "above" by the extradiegetic narrator. This was partially achieved—in television soaps as it was in the days of radio—by the plot itself, which ultimately "rewards" "positive" values over "negative" ones. Phillips commented directly upon the relationship of plot to the normative perspective of her programs in a 1942 letter to Procter and Gamble vice-president William Ramsey:

> Consciously or subconsciously I have attempted to hold to the philosophy of the Law of Compensation. Although it isn't always obvious at first, I believe the listener ultimately is aware of the fact that when a character is guilty of transgression, of evil doing in the sight of God and man, that character is punished in some way. . . . But

there must be rehabilitation, there must be hope—she cannot be forever condemned.[35]

The program's dominant values could also be embodied by central characters. Some early television soap operas continued to feature what came to be known in the business as "tent-pole" or "anchor" characters: usually older characters to whom others went for advice and guidance and whose own actions were in almost all respects exemplary. Papa Bauer, a character introduced on *The Guiding Light* in 1949, came to occupy that role when the story was transplanted to television. Phillips used similar characters as the moral center of the narrative when constructing subsequent television soap opera worlds: the Reverend Richard Dennis in *The Brighter Day* (1954), Grace Tyrell in *The Secret Storm* (1954), Grandpa Hughes in *As the World Turns* (1956), and Dr. Tom Horton in *Days of Our Lives* (1965). In other television soaps a younger and more active character was placed atop the character hierarchy—less perfect than the venerable Papa Bauers and Grace Tyrells, but clearly well intentioned and sympathetically depicted. Such a character formed the focus of *Search for Tomorrow* (Joanne Barron Tate—1951), *Love of Life* (Vanessa Dale—1951), *The Edge of Night* (Mike Karr—1956), and *The Doctors* (Dr. Matt Powers—1963).

Despite the internalization of norms by characters and the operation of a strong (if sometimes slowly enforced) moral code, the television soap opera's dominant normative perspective was rendered more ambiguous by the elimination of a clear, authoritative narrational voice. Concomitant with the demise of the announcer-narrator, another force was at work in the television soap opera to further disperse normative perspective: the multiplication of characters. Because of their length (only fifteen minutes per episode) and restriction to one channel of communication (sound), radio soap opera episodes seldom contained more than two scenes, and each scene rarely involved more than two or three characters. Thus the total population of a radio soap's diegetic universe at any given time was probably no more than a dozen characters or so. Although early television soap operas were also fifteen minutes in length, half-hour soaps were introduced in 1956. Producers soon discovered that viewers would watch longer episodes and realized that one half-hour program could be made for less than the cost of two fifteen-minute programs. All television soap operas introduced after 1956 were at least thirty minutes in length. In the 1970s a number of soaps expanded to a full hour. With visual as well as aural means of character representation and with the expansion of episode length, television soap operas were soon able to accommodate much larger communities of regularly-appearing characters. Rather than merely prolong one or two plot lines and focus upon a few characters, the television soap opera by the 1960s could simultaneously sustain three or four intersecting narrative lines involving dozens of characters. At last count, *The Guiding Light* "population" numbered nearly forty characters.

To assess the overall effect of the narrational changes in the soap opera brought about by its transferral to the television medium, we might return to Iser's typology of perspective arrangements. The removal of the extradiegetic voice and the dispersal of norms among characters in the television soap opera undermined its solidarity of perspectives and gave it some of the qualities of what Iser calls the "oppositional" arrangement of perspectives. Not nearly so determinant as the counterbalancing mode, the oppositional arrangement pits one set of norms, usually embodied by a character or group of characters, against another. The television soap opera stopped short of slipping into the oppositional category altogether, however, and remained (and remains) poised somewhere between the clear didacticism of the counterbalancing mode and what Iser calls the "reciprocal negation" of the oppositional text. "The negation consists in the fact that as each norm becomes thematic, it implicitly shuts out the others, which in their turn become thematic, thus undermining what went before. And so each norm takes its place in a context of negated and negating norms." The effect of this oppositional arrangement upon the reader, says Iser, is that he or she is encouraged to scrutinize the functions of these norms "in the system from which they have been removed"—that is, "real life."[36]

What prevents the television soap opera from being described as "oppositional" is that the result of the representation of competing norms is not mutual negation but ultimately reinforcement of some norms and rejection of others. In other words, the television soap opera does not tip its normative hand, as did its radio predecessor, but it does stack the deck. To change metaphors, its ideological "work" is carried out at a lower level (that of character and plot rather than narrational voice) and less obviously, but nevertheless some readings are clearly "preferred" over others.[37] In Iser's examples of the oppositional text (Smollett's *Humphrey Clinker* and Thackery's "novels without heroes"), characters are attitudinally static—they "are" their value systems. In the television soap opera, however, the opposition between perspectives can be made to dissolve as one character sheds an aberrant value system and is absorbed within the normative structure of the text as a whole: a "bad" character turns "good." The embodiment of "negative" values in a soap opera character (whether permanently, as in the case of resident villains and villainesses, or temporarily, as with the initially "bad" character who sees the light) might bring about the effect Iser sees of the oppositional perspective arrangement—the reader is brought to the point of examining the operation of the relevant norms in "real life"—but this examination is designed either to reassert the validity of the existing value system or to demonstrate that the threatening perspective only appears to be so and can be recuperated within the dominant value system.

In a sense, then, the removal of narrational power from the "top" in the television soap opera narrative and the dispersal of norms throughout the community of characters served to "open up" the soap opera text to the expression of a greater variety of perspectives while making more covert the overall normative perspective represented by the text. It is precisely this openness that has enabled the soap opera to give the appearance of normative daring without embracing anything other than normative values. A soap opera might deal with interracial marriage, abortion, incest, homosexuality, child abuse, or some other controversial issue, but any threatening values connected with those issues are attached to particular characters, who can be disposed of or attitudinally "defused." Perhaps the best example is provided by another Irna Phillips soap, *Love Is a Many Splendored Thing* (1967–73). Hoping to cash in on the popularity of the novel and film of the same name, Phillips initially based this soap upon a romance between a white American doctor and a Eurasian woman. Network executives succumbed to pressure from their affiliate stations, however, and ordered Phillips to drop the interracial plot line. Phillips resigned in protest, but the new writers simply "moved" the woman out of town and focused new plot lines on romantic relationships among younger (white) characters. Repositioning the normative center of the show onto safer ground took precedence over the intertextual connection that had provided the original impetus for the show.

One could argue, in fact, that the combination of the soap opera's decentered normative perspective with its narrative indeterminacy has been the key to its success in the television era. During the 1930s, although the pressures brought to bear upon American women by the Great Depression were enormous, the normatively acceptable responses to those pressures were greatly circumscribed. As Susan Ware puts it: "During the 1930s . . .

strong consensus shaped women's proper roles in society. This consensus, propagated by the media, religion, and other institutions of culture, guided men and women alike. Women had complete responsibility for the domestic sphere and played a critical role in holding families together against the disintegrating forces of the Depression."[38] On the eve of World War II, after a decade of economic dislocation, only 15 percent of married women worked outside the home, and the percentage of all women working was virtually the same as it had been in 1910. The social and moral didacticism of the radio soap opera contributed to and was reinforced by this cultural consensus. Its implicit endorsement of the doctrine of the two spheres, softened by the reassuring philosophy of liberal Protestantism, fulfilled the compensatory function Iser specifies for the counterbalancing text. Although World War II saw an additional six million women join the civilian labor force, the demands of the war effort merely increased pressures for social conformity. Despite the "alternative" image of "Rosie the Riveter," much of the government's effort to recruit women for the work force was aimed at persuading them to accept service jobs that had been regarded as "women's work" since the late nineteenth century.[39]

The postwar situation differed drastically. The proportion of women leaving the paid work force after World War II was much less than that after World War I. Also, more married women entered the job market in the 1940s than ever before. Whereas married women had constituted but one-third of female workers in 1940, by 1950 a majority of working women were married. By 1960, 30 percent of all married women in the United States were employed outside the home, and by 1975, 44 percent. In 1940 only 10 percent of women with children under the age of six held paying jobs; by 1975, 36.6 percent of them did. After the war women increasingly moved into new occupational areas—a trend accelerated in the 1960s and 1970s.

These economic changes were accompanied by the emergence of a new model for the American woman—what Sheila Rothman has called the "woman as person" model—according to which

> woman was not to be defined by her household role, by her responsibilities as wife or mother; she was in no way to be limited by any special gender characteristics. This new definition of womanhood emphasized the similarities between the sexes, not the differences. . . . In brief, woman as person was fully capable of defining and acting in her own best interest.[40]

As in the case of previous models of the "ideal" woman, however, that of woman as person did not supersede older images but for the most part was grafted onto them. Except in its most radical articulations, the "liberated woman" philosophy of the 1960s and 1970s called for women not to abandon their roles as nurturing parent, home manager, and companionate spouse but to add to these roles those associated with the upwardly mobile white-collar professional person. After examining women's employment patterns in the 1970s, Carl Degler concludes that the movement of women into the work force since World War II does not "signify a repudiation of the traditional primacy of the family in the lives of married women . . . [rather] it betokens a continuing involvement with the family, though that is now combined with work outside." This "outside" work, like the married woman's role "inside" the home, is usually subordinated to the needs of the family, so that the woman's position within the family structure is only marginally altered.[41]

The cultural consensus of the 1930s and early 1940s, which effectively marginalized images of the social role of women that could not be accommodated within the doctrine of the two spheres, has been fractured. And while many "voices"—ranging from the atavistic "Christian right" to exclusivist lesbian feminism—now offer philosophies and programs that speak to the position of women, the didacticism of the radio soap opera seems an inappropriate strategy for securing the interest of as many American women as possible. At times, the underlying normative perspective of the soap opera is exposed: family is to be valued over career; "feminine" fulfillment ultimately involves marriage and parenting; the social system is shown to be ultimately fair and just; virtue is ultimately rewarded and evil punished; and so forth. For the most part, though, the world of the soap opera does not express an ideological "message" (except in the broadest sense of supporting the socioeconomic status quo—an orientation shared by every other commercial television program) so much as it marks out a more general normative "territory."

At the center of this normative space are those values, attitudes, and behaviors believed by soap opera producers to be most dearly held by the "average" viewer. These norms form, for the most part, the unarticulated "givens" of the soap opera social structure. But there is also room within this "space" for the articulation of perspectives at some distance from these core values. The indeterminacy of the soap opera narrative allows for a sort of feedback mechanism, through which the fate of these perspectives can ultimately be decided. If network, sponsor, or viewer response indicates the perspective to be too far from the normative "center" and thus threatening or destabilizing, the character and plot line containing it can be dispensed with or the character made to dispose of it—as in the case of *Love Is a Many Splendored Thing*. Or the new perspective might be attached to a character on the margins of the soap's core value system and thus kept "at the edge" of the soap's normative territory. Finally, the new perspective might over time be absorbed within the dominant value system, as that system itself changed. As late as 1949, for example, Procter and Gamble strictly prescribed the manner by which divorce could be treated on its soaps.[42] Today, of course, nearly every soap opera character over the age of twenty-one has been divorced at least once.

Ironically, the underlying, inherently conservative value system of the soap opera is expressed most directly through the commercials, where there is no uncertainty regarding the position of women within the family, no question as to what her domain should be. As Flitterman puts it, "Daytime commercials affirm the centrality of the family and the important function of the woman as nurturing support system." Moreover, contemporary daytime commercials not only continue to define women within the domestic sphere (as they have since soap operas began in the 1930s) but they also reflect the accretion of "model qualities" added to this definition in the years since the end of World War II: woman as mother, nurse, cook, housekeeper, shopper, companionate spouse, *and* sex object, *and* competent professional person. Just as cosmetics commercials in the 1920s and 1930s showed women how to be attractive as well as efficient wives and mothers, advertisements today for frozen foods, time-saving appliances, no-iron clothes, fast-food restaurants, and other "convenience" products and services implicitly address the inflation of role expectations borne by women and explicitly propose "solutions" to this problem.

Counterposed to the perspectival determinacy of its commercial "messages," the perspectival openness of the contemporary soap opera diegesis enables it to accommodate a far greater range of "negotiated" readings than other, more normatively determinant forms of fictive narratives. Furthermore, this openness helps to account for the broadening of the soap opera audience in recent years to include more men, adolescents, and college students. Hall discusses negotiated decoding as an acknowledgment of "the legitimacy of the hegemonic definitions to make grand significations (abstract), while at a more restricted, situational (situated) level, it makes its own ground rules—it operates with exceptions to the rules."[43] In the soap opera the "grand significations" are seldom overt, and are detached from their usual regulatory functions by being fictionalized. At the same time, with a community of dozens of characters and a diegetic world that unfolds across hours of text each week for years on end, the soap opera generates a multiplicity of lower-level "situations" whose normative relationship to that abstract level might remain uncertain for months on end. Continuing this geographical metaphor, the soap opera's textual openness allows it to colonize new normative territory at little cost—in the process opening up spaces for new groups of readers. New characters and situations can be introduced in an attempt to attract new audience members, but since the new narrative strands are positioned alongside other, more "traditional" ones, there is little risk of alienating existing viewers.

Finally, the longer the soap opera can maintain the interest of a reader whose own value system is at some distance from that of the implicit central norms of the text, the more likely it is that that reader will tolerate aspects of the text she or he finds silly, uninteresting, or even insulting. Because of the paradigmatic complexity of the soap opera text and its syntagmatic indeterminacy, becoming a competent reader of it (competent in a minimal sense of achieving a threshold where the text becomes legible and reading it thus enjoyable) requires a unique investment of the reader's time and psychic energy. One might stop reading an uninteresting novel after a few chapters and not think too much of the time and money "wasted" in the reading activity to that point (unless, of course, the novel were purchased in hardcover and cost twenty-five dollars). Disengaging with a soap opera text after following the development of one of its plot lines for a while, on the other hand, might come after an investment of months of reading and after having accumulated a considerable amount of reading "capital," one's knowledge of the text. This investment is a curious one in which there is no ultimate narrative "pay-off"—as Modleski puts it, in the soap opera anticipation of an ending becomes an end in itself. The investment is more on the order of paying membership dues to an organization than of contributing to a pension fund: the longer one has been a member in good standing, the more there is to lose by dropping out of the club and the more one is willing to put up with aspects of affiliation that are disagreeable. The analogy of the "soap opera reader's club" is doubly apt for the considerable subaudience constituted by college student soap opera viewers. For them (as well as for some viewers who are not college students), watching soap operas is a social act as well as an engagement with a narrative text.

## Generative Mechanisms in Soap Opera History

As an object of historical inquiry, the soap opera represents the conjunction of a number of generative mechanisms, mechanisms that can be divided into two types: those that help to account for its origins and perpetuation within the institution of American commercial broadcastings and a related but separate set that help to account for the response it engendered among the audience at which it was and continues to be directed. These generative mechanisms might be thought of as lines of causal force, operating with unequal and changing determination upon the production and consumption of soap operas. The last two chapters have done no more than identify what appear (at this stage of the inquiry at least) to be the most important of those lines.

First, and most obviously, the soap opera is a creation of the particular institutional character of American commercial broadcasting. It did not emerge from some other context to be adapted by commercial broadcasting, but was from its inception one answer among many others posed to American broadcasting's central demand: How might a particular audience be most efficiently commodified? To say that the perseverance of the soap opera for half a century has been due in large measure to its success in responding to this demand may not be particularly startling (or intellectually exciting), but it is irrefutable. That the same generative mechanism can be seen in operation in any long-lived commercial broadcasting form is, given the structure of American broadcasting since the late 1920s, perhaps obvious, but it bears reiteration in each case. Just as clearly, however, the production and reception of each particular programming form represents a unique conjunction of generative mechanisms. The soap opera was among those forms devised to fill the need for daytime programming, and as the dimensions and demographic character of the audience for daytime programming became clearer in the early 1930s, the demand placed upon it shifted from that of "filling" airtime to capturing the largest possible share of the single most lucrative radio audience: women between the ages of eighteen and forty-nine.

As a programming form, the soap opera represents the coming together of a variety of textual features derived from other radio forms (the "advice" show, the "household-hints" program, the self-contained radio drama, and the dramatic and comic series), as well as from other popular media. Given the institutional demand for habitual listening, it is not surprising that the serial narrative form should have been applied to daytime as well as prime-time drama. The soap opera was relatively inexpensive to produce, did not rely upon expensive talent, and afforded abundant opportunities for renewal of narrative interest.

The linkage between the daytime serial drama and a particular segment of American big business was effected as a result of the demand within certain industries (foodstuffs, cosmetics, and household products) to keep the image of their product constantly before their target consumer audience (women) if corporate profits were to be generated on items with a small unit price and low unit profit. Daytime dramatic serials offered the added feature of limitless opportunities to relate the fictional realm of the "story" to the commercial message, and both to the situation of the reader-consumer. Again, it is worth pointing out in this regard that the soap opera did not develop "accidentally" but rather was the result of a search (conducted by local and network broadcasters, individual writers, and advertising agencies) for a programming form that "fit" the preexisting needs of big business. Thus, the force exercised by individual genius in the origins of the soap opera was slight, despite the roles played in its early development by such figures as Irna Phillips and the Hummerts. Many of the forces whose confluence was responsible for the origins of the soap opera are also responsible for its perpetuation over the years. The abiding structure of American broadcasting has assured the continuance of the same basic relationships between broadcasters, business interests, and audiences. Moreover, the flexibility of the soap opera form—its syntagmatic indeterminacy and ability to change to meet changing social circumstances—has also been a major factor in its survival and success within the institution of broadcasting.

But to say that the soap opera has "succeeded" because of institutional factors alone or even to note that this institutional success is predicated upon the soap opera's continuing ability to "appeal" to a large and loyal audience is to diminish the historical importance of the generative mechanisms deriving from the larger social formation and expressed through the decisions of tens of millions of American women to engage in the reading of soap operas. From the industry's standpoint, the audience's role in broadcast history has been to "choose" or "vote" for what programs it wishes to receive. The soap opera becomes a prime example of "giving the audience what it wants." As this chapter has sought to demonstrate, however, the generative mechanisms in broadcasting history represented by audience response are not nearly so simple or straightforward. The "choice" exercised by audiences must be regarded in light of the fundamentally unequal power relationships inherent in the structure of American commercial broadcasting. Audiences choose not necessarily what they want but from among what they are offered. That choice is conditioned by the institution's power to "speak" in favor of the choices they offer in any number of ways and the inability of audience members to register dissatisfaction through the same channels or with the same resources. The "choice" to become a viewer also involves an implicit willingness to take up a position vis-à-vis the institution of broadcasting whereby one is made into a commodity and into the subject of a suasive discourse. Thus the decision to become a soap opera reader made by millions of women over the decades since 1930 must be interpreted not as unmitigated affirmation (they "got what they wanted") but rather as the result of a much more complex negotiation between the audiences and the institution of broadcasting—a negotiation in which the latter definitely holds the advantage.

The mistake made by some researchers from the 1940s to the 1980s has been to assume that in this negotiation women viewers/listeners have been powerless—that their engagement with soap operas could be explained only as an involuntary compulsion ("addiction"), while the "choices" the rest of us make are just that: choices. This view is based upon two fundamental misrecognitions. The first is that asymmetrical power relations apply only where *women* are concerned, rather than obtain (although differentially expressed) throughout all relations between broadcasting and audience groups. The second is of the terms of engagement between women readers and soap opera texts. Like the domestic novel which preceded it, the soap opera has been received as a "woman's fiction," appropriating concerns and modes of address marginalized or excluded from mainstream fictional narratives. This status immediately rendered the soap opera alien to those whose primary frame of reference was provided by "normative" fictional discourse, but it also meant that the soap opera would be recognized as familiar by its primary audience. Despite the didactic structure of the radio soap opera, its immediate and widespread success in attracting the attention and engaging the imaginations of many American women (a further distinction it shares with the domestic novel) cannot be interpreted either as the unproblematic "reflection" in the text of the values of its readers or as the capitulation of those readers to the normative position the text "preferred" its readers to occupy.

Specifying the nature and range of the negotiation between soap opera readers and text at some point in the past is, of course, extremely difficult, but any consideration of what the historical success of the soap opera form means must acknowledge the ambiguous status of the soap opera as woman's fiction: regardless of the manner by which family, parentage, sex role expectations, romance, and emotional bonds were represented, they at least occupied positions high on the discursive agendas of soap opera texts. Women could "relate" to them, although the nature of the relationship was no doubt complex. As the soap opera has moved into the television age, it has adapted to a new medium and to new social conditions by diffusing its norms and "opening up" its textual structure. Perhaps more than any other textual system, the soap opera allows for reader negotiation and reader resistance to its normative perspective. The soap opera text has become so large and its features so malleable that it provides accommodation for a number of different audience groups: women working at home, women in the paid work force, college students, adolescents, retired men and women, and even a few male college teachers.

# Afterword

At this point it seems fitting to return to the metaphor used to describe the object of this study in the introduction: James Thurber's observation that "soapland" "is a country so vast and complicated that the lone explorer could not possibly hope to do it full justice." It might very well appear that, rather than arrive at some explanatory pinnacle from those heights the salient features of the soap opera terrain can now clearly be discerned, we have merely caught a few partial vistas, never climbing high enough above our object of investigation to take in the complete scene. Furthermore, we seem to have occupied ourselves as much with the accoutrements of exploration itself as with the specifics of the territory we have traversed. At the risk of belaboring this rather fragile metaphor, I would respond that both the circumambulatory path chosen and my concern for cartography in general arise from the complexity of the landscape, its uncharted character, and the recognition that soapland is but one of many terrains as yet relatively unexplored by the mass communications scholar. Hence it would be inappropriate (not to mention presumptuous) to end this study with a neat but ultimately facile set of conclusions about soap operas that pretends to resolve their many ambiguities and complexities.

My initial research on soap operas was propelled in large measure by what I saw as their uniqueness and the scholarly challenge represented by their peculiarities. What other modern narrative form, save perhaps the comic strip, is predicated upon the impossibility of closure? What other popular form is so dependent for its aesthetic effect upon a complex paradigmatic network? What other stories have ever been enjoyed by so many people at the same time over so long a period? What other form of broadcast programming has been so important a profit base for the past forty years? And yet, what other form of popular entertainment has been so consistently denigrated? These signal features of the soap opera and the incongruity of the public and scholarly disdain the form has provoked continue to fascinate and challenge. My interest in the soap opera now, however, resides as much in the fact that it brings into particularly sharp focus issues and problems related to the study of popular fictive narratives as a whole.

Having devoted a good deal of space to a consideration of what I perceive to be the inability of empiricist mass communications research as it is generally practiced in the United States to deal with these issues and problems, it is only fitting that I conclude by calling to the attention of the reader what I see as a major deficiency in the present undertaking (although the reader probably discerned it long ago). The application of critical methods drawn from the study of literature and film to soap operas has, I hope, reasserted the textuality of that form and effectively countered the view that soap operas are simple structures that mimic relations in the "real world." Similarly, by concentrating this critical exercise on the manner by which soap operas are engaged by their readers, I hope I have succeeded in refuting the notion that the text stands in its relationship to its audience as a stimulus automatically provoking an unproblematic response. Reader-response criticism acknowledges the active role assumed by the reader in the reading process and the polysemic nature of narrative texts.

That criticism and other models adapted from current critical practice can only go so far in accounting for *actual* responses of television readers, however. The "reader" constantly invoked in this examination of soap operas has been, for the most part, a theoretical construct—a position from which meaning *might* be constructed. My concern has been to lay out the conditions under which meaning might be produced and the constraints—textual, institutional, and social—upon that reading process. "Actual" readers have entered my discussion much more obliquely: as extrapolations from demographic and ratings data or from my own experience as a reader of soap operas. The implicit challenge is to relate these constructed reader positions to the experiences of actual soap opera readers. It is a challenge I fully admit to not having taken up.

While it does not reduce my accountability in the matter, it is perhaps worth noting that I am not the only one for whom specifying the relationship between reader/spectator and audience member, between textual engagement and the larger social formation, remains a methodological and conceptual puzzle. As Robert Holub has noted in his survey of German reader-response criticism, Iser and Jauss have been strongly criticized "for their lack of sociological grounding with respect to the reader." As a corrective, some scholars have attempted to study the responses of "real" readers. After considering the efforts of dozens of German scholars (both East and West) over a fifteen-year period, however, Holub concludes that "despite a variety of techniques and a great deal of statistical expertise, most contribute nothing to an understanding of the literary work and very little to knowledge about the readers of these works." Holub recognizes that studying actual readings of given texts could offer much to literary theory, but relating the former to the latter remains problematic. "Continuing on its present course," he warns, "empirical reception theory is bound to remain an isolated and ridiculed branch of literary endeavor." Similarly, Tony Bennett, surveying the current state of Marxist literary criticism, concludes: "Simply put, there are, as yet, no serious readership studies, a project which the literary left has culpably neglected." With specific reference to soap operas, Annette Kuhn poses as "the central issue" in the study of "gynocentric" forms of film and television "the question of the audience." But beyond recognizing that "spectator and audience are distinct concepts which cannot—as they frequently are—be reduced to one another," she offers little in the way of a method for relating the two.[1]

Still, it would be inaccurate, however, to say that nothing is being done from a nonempiricist perspective to attempt to integrate the responses of "real" readers into a theory of the relationships between audiences, texts, and cultural institutions. The work of the Centre for Contemporary Cultural Studies at the University of Birmingham, particularly that of Stuart Hall and David Morley, has been very important in suggesting how analyses of textual structure might be used in tandem with ethnomethodological audience investigations. In the most elaborate of the studies from this perspective, the two monographs on the British news program *Nationwide* and its reception by different audience groups, Morley poses the problem thusly:

> What is needed here is an approach which links differential interpretations back into the socio-economic structure of society, showing how members of different groups and classes, sharing different "cultural codes," will interpret a given message differently, not just at the personal idiosyncratic level, but in a way "systematically related" to their socio-economic position. In short we need to see how the different sub-cultural structures and formations within the audience, and the sharing of different cultural codes and competencies amongst different groups and classes "determine" the decoding of the message for different sections of the audience.[2]

Morley recognizes that the project outlined in this statement is enormously ambitious, at both the practical and the theoretical levels. He regards his own attempt to implement such an approach as only a "preliminary investigation" of "some of the ways in which social position and (sub)cultural frameworks may be related to individual readings." Not surprisingly, he sees one of his study's major shortcomings to be its inability to devise an adequate methodology: "In the absence of any method capable of satisfactorily meeting these difficulties, it seemed more useful to present the material in a descriptive format, in the hope that it would then be more 'open' to the reader's own hypotheses and interpretations where mine seem inadequate."[3]

Questions of the adequacy of Morley's approach to his particular object of study aside, it presents two difficulties as a model for the analysis of "real" reader responses to such texts as soap operas. The first is that the engagement of the readers studied with the text (two *Nationwide* programs) was produced as a result of the study: already constituted social affiliation groups were identified (trade union members, art students, teacher trainees, bank managers, and so forth—most groups involved in some sort of educational program) and then shown two episodes of *Nationwide*. Morley was able to demonstrate that different groups decoded the programs in different ways—differences related to the socioeconomic positions of the various groups. Whether or not the members of those groups actually watched *Nationwide* outside the context of the study was not considered. Thus, Morley found that some groups "imposed not so much an oppositional reading as a refusal to read at all." In the case of soap operas, however, the social act constituted *by* engaging the soap opera text is as important as the variations in decoding that, no doubt, would be produced by different groups of readers. The second difficulty is that while news programs such as *Nationwide* are not so straightforwardly referential as they pretend to be, their status as nonfiction texts renders the terms of the decoding operations applied to them significantly different from those used in constructing meaning from fictive narratives, such as soap operas. Our discussion of content analysis demonstrates the error of assuming that soap opera readers understand characters and situations as if they were people and situations in the "real world." If Morley certainly would not make this mistake, by choosing a nonfiction text he did obviate consideration of an entire level of methodological and conceptual problems that would be encountered in a similar study involving a fictive textual system.

In the United States, Janice Radway's recently published study of a group of romance novel readers should prove an important contribution to our understanding of the relationship between readers "who inhabit a particular social world" and the narrative texts they choose to engage and to the manner by which such relationships might be investigated. Radway brings to bear upon the act of romance reading developments in semiotics, reader-response criticism, Russian formalism, ethnographic anthropology, and feminist cultural analysis. In doing so, she attempts to resituate the cultural analysis of literature from "the text" to the activation of texts by particular groups of readers:

> To know, then, why people do what they do, read romances, for instance, it becomes necessary to discover the constructions they place on their behavior, the interpretations they make of their actions. A good cultural analysis of the romance ought to specify not only how the women understand the novels themselves but also how they comprehend the very act of picking up a book in the first place. The analytic focus must shift from the text itself, taken in isolation, to the complex social event of reading where a woman actively attributes sense to lexical signs in a silent process carried on in the context of her ordinary life.[4]

The analysis itself is limited to a small group of readers (forty-two women in Smithton, Pennsylvania), and some will find Radway's melding of literary, anthropological, and feminist approaches problematic, but her study will almost certainly serve as an important model for the joining of textual and audience analysis.

In the end, the admitted limitations of such studies as those by Morley and Radway and the tentative nature of their conceptual and methodological formulations bespeak the enormity and complexity of the questions they address: What is the extent of the determination of meaning exercised by the text itself? What forces condition the activations of texts within individual readers and among groups of readers? What levels of the reading process are accessible to empirical investigation and what methods are appropriate to that study? What is the role of the investigator vis-à-vis both the texts he or she wishes to study and the readers who consume those texts? What is the epistemological status of articulated responses of readers in understanding the relationships between reader, text, and institutions? The research paradigm upon which American mass communications study has been based for the past forty years is clearly inadequate to the tasks implied by these questions. The process of reconceptualizing these questions within alternative paradigms has in some senses only begun.

# Appendixes

*The following soap opera scripts are taken from the Irna Phillips Collection of the Wisconsin Historical Society. I have tried to preserve, insofar as is possible, the format from the original typescript documents. Thus, ellipsis points do not indicate editorial omissions, but are used in the scripts to signal pauses during a piece of dialogue.*

## APPENDIX A

### *Painted Dreams*
### Episode 25 (1931)

*(Kitchen. Irene and Sue arguing. Mrs. preparing breakfast.)*

*I:* I tell you, Sue, it won't work. I've never worn that shade of orchid in all my life. I'd look like a perfect washout. Besides, that's your very best special occasion dress. I wouldn't think of taking it.

*S:* Don't be silly. A wedding is a special occasion, isn't it? And as long as I won't need to wear it, you might just as well. If you're a bridesmaid, you've got to look the part, kid.

*I:* But I don't look good in that color. I'd look faded or something.

*S:* Cracked ice! You can't tell. You've never had it on. Gee, with gold slippers, and a gold turban hat, you'd be a whow! Wouldn't she, Mrs. Moynihan?

*Mrs.:* Won't you be wearing it Sue?

*S:* Why, no; there's no reasons for my dressing up. I'm not in the wedding party. And I think that it would be just right for Irene, if there were a few tucks taken in around the waist. Anyway, it would save her from buying a dress.

*I:* Well, who says that I don't want to buy a dress? It's about time I was getting a new formal, anyhow. I haven't got a rag that's fit to be seen.

*Mrs.:* Sure, now Irene, you'd rather be reasonable. What with the bank closed and all, I'm not so sure that I can be affordin' a new dress for you just yet. And if Sue isn't wearin' that lovely one of hers, well—if I were you, I'd wear it, since she's offered it to you.

*I:* Oh, Mom, you're getting to be a regular miser. This is the first time I have ever had a chance to be in a wedding, and I can't even have a new dress for it. Huh—I'll bet you'd make me wear a gingham apron to my own wedding.

*Mrs.:* Sure, an' your own weddin' is likely to be a long time off, as far as I can see. I'm hopin' to be able to provide somethin' nice for you by that time.

*I:* Oh gee whiz—then I don't get a new dress? What will Ellen think?

*S:* She won't think anything, if that's what you're worried about. She has never seen the dress. Come on, Irene; at least try it on and see.

*I:* Oh, gosh. What a break!

*Mrs.:* By the way, Irene, I just remembered somethin'. Sure, and it's not very nice either to be hearin' about a girl who has been raised in a good Christian home, I'm tellin' you that.

*I:* Go ahead and spill it. I can stand it, I suppose. What now?

*Mrs.:* Well, it's this; there's a lot of talk goin' on in the neighborhood about you and this Dick fellow, and sure, it's not so flattering to you. Not that I believe there is anything really wrong, myself; but people do talk alot about such things, and I won't have such talk goin' on any longer about a child of mine. Tis best that you make up your mind, once and for all, to have nothin' more to do with Dick.

*I:* Oh, yeah? Well, who slipped you that line-up on me and my business. I suppose it was your pet Sewing Circle? A bunch of cats, that's what they are. It's a wonder any of them ever got married. They should all be spending their time posing for holy pictures. Was it the Sewing Circle?

*Mrs.:* Well—'twas the Sewing Circle, but it's not as if they didn't have any grounds for it.

*I:* Say, listen here: the only grounds that they've got is in their coffee, if you ask me. Why should they bother about my business, anyway. What I do is my own affair, and nobody else's. I'm not asking for any advice.

*S:* Well, you have been coming home pretty late with Dick for the last few times, you know. And it's sure to get out—someone always is up with insomnia or a toothache, to see it. Maybe it would be best to lay off of Dick for a little while till things get settled down.

*I:* What? You too? Ye gods, can't you two ever let me alone. I'll see Dick, and go out with him just as much as I darn please. You can't stop me.

*S:* Suit yourself. It's not my funeral—even you can see that, I guess.

*I:* Then why go around looking like the Chief Mourner?

*S:* It doesn't really make a bit of difference. Forget it.

*I:* I would, if you'd only give me a chance.

*Mrs.:* Sure, and I'm not likely to be forgettin' it that quick—not with all the neighbors around to remind me of it. It's a bad thing, that it is! If you'd let this Dick alone there'd be no trouble about it at all.

*I:* Well, what do you want me to do? Sit around at home all the time and sing "Me and My Shadow"? I'm out for a good time, and I'll get it, too.

*S:* Suit yourself. But I think that you might consider all the trouble you are making for your mother. She is getting the worst of it, not you.

*I:* Oh, you're getting to be a regular goody-goody. Your name ought to be Saint Susan.

*(Doorbell rings violently. Someone pounds on the door.)*

*Mrs.:* The Lord have mercy on us! Who's makin' all that noise? It sounds like the end of the world was here.

*I:* I'll answer it.

*S:* No, let me. I'll do it. Just a minute there; don't break the door down. What do you want?

*Mrs.:* Who is it, Sue? *(calls from the kitchen)*

*S:* Just a minute—I'll find out. ——A warrant! What for? For Russell Moynihan. No,—he isn't here. I haven't even seen him. Oh, you can't go through the house. Honest he isn't here. Oh, please—don't do that. His mother doesn't know anything about it, and it would just kill her to find out that there was a warrant out for him.

*Mrs.:* What's all the arguin' about out there? What does he want, Sue?

*S:* Oh, it's nothing much, Mrs. Moynihan. It's just—it's—a man who is here to find out about the dog license for our pup. Irene, can you come here for a minute?

*I:* I'll be right there.

*S:* Hurry. It's important.

*I:* What's the matter? We have a license for our dog? What's all the noise about anyway?

*S:* Sh! not so loud. Your mother might hear. This man is a detective, and he has a warrant for your brother. They found out where his home was, and so he came out here to get him.

*I:* But—Russ isn't here. He hasn't even been near the house. Oh, gee— what are we going to do about it, Sue? Mom mustn't find out about it!

*S:* No—we can't let her. But this man wants to search the house for him.

*I:* Oh, he *can't* do that! Then Mom would see him. Besides Russ isn't here, so it wouldn't do any good. Can't you make him see that?

*S:* I'll try—you go back in the kitchen, and keep your mother from coming out here, and I'll see if I can get rid of him. Be sure you keep her out of here, at least till he's gone.

*I:* O.K.—but hurry. You know how Mom is when she makes up her mind to find out about anything.

*S:* Listen here, Mr.—Russell Moynihan isn't in this house. There's no use for you to go through it—you'd only scare his mother. Please go away, won't you? You're going to have the house watched? Well, go ahead—do it. You won't find him here. This is the last place to look for him. Only please don't let Mrs. Moynihan know about it, will you? (*Door closes*)

*Mrs.:* Well, is that dog-catcher gone?

*S:* Dog-catcher?! What—?

*Appendixes*

*I:* The dog catcher, you know, Sue. The one you were just talking to out there.

*S:* Oh—dog catcher. Yes, he's gone. I finally got rid of him.

*I:* Do you think he'll come back here again, Sue?

*Mrs.:* And why should he be comin' back, pray tell? Didn't you show him the license tags for our dog. I don't see why you should be arguin' so long with him, anyhow. It sounds funny to me—that it does.

APPENDIX B

## *Today's Children*
## Monday, January 3, 1938

*Opening Chords:*

*Theme:*

*Announcer: Today's Children*, presented by the Pillsbury Flour Mills Company, millers of Pillsbury's Best Flour, Sno Sheen Cake Flour, Pancake Flour, Pillsbury's Farina and Pillsbury's Wheat Bran.

*Theme up and out:*

*No commercial:*

*Announcer:* And now, *Today's Children*. On New Year's Eve, Katherine told Mother Moran that by the first of this week, she might ask a very special favor of her. What it was that Kay had in mind, we do not know. As we visit the home of Mother Moran this evening, we find gathered in her living room once again, her Today's Children. Altho' the family was together on New Year's Day, for some reason, Mother Moran has asked them to be with her this evening. It looks very much as though it were a very important occasion in the Moran home, for on the table in the living room, we see a large, beautifully frosted cake, and as we listen in, we hear. . . .

*Laughter—ad libs of* "Well, Mom, what's the idea?" "What's the occasion?" etc.

*Bobbie:* I want a piece of cake.

*MM:* Now children, I'd like ta have a little quiet in the room, if ya don't mind.

*Fran:* Why do we have to have our dessert in the living room?

*MM:* Well, it isn't exactly dessert that I'm servin. I don't know jest what ta be sayin.

*Terry:* Now, Mom. I've never known the time when you didn't know just what to say.

*MM:* Well, this is different. Katherine—

*Kay:* Yes, Mother Moran?

*MM:* Bob—

*Bob:* I'm right here.

*MM:* Children, on New Year's Eve, Katherine—well—she asked me if I wouldn't do somethin for her—a favor. I couldn't think what it was—I should have known but I didn't. If I had known at the time, I'd have said ta her, "Katherine, it isn't a favor you're askin—it's a privilege you're givin me." She wanted me ta ask ya all over there this evenin, so's I could tell ya that she and Bob are goin ta be married.

*Fran:* Kay!

*Kay:* That's right, Fran.

*Fran:* Oh, I'm so glad. And Bob—oh, I think it's wonderful!

*Henry:* I've been waiting a long time for just this to happen. Congratulations, Bob. I know that you and Katherine are going to be as happy as any two people can be.

*Bob:* I'm sure that we are, Henry.

*Terry:* Well, Kay, you know what I think—it's kind of hard for me to say it, but—well—I know that you're going to be really happy.

*Kay:* I know that I am, too.

*Dot:* Honestly, Kay. I'm so happy for you, I could almost cry. When are you going to be married?

*Kay:* Next week.

*Lucy:* Are you going with Bob to Pennsylvania, Katherine?

*Kay:* Yes, Lucy.

*MM:* I haven't been able ta tell Katherine how happy I am for her. I think maybe she knows and I think Bob knows, too.

*Bob:* Yes, Mother Moran, I do.

*Kay:* And so do I.

*Nancy:* Are you going to have a big wedding, Katherine?

*Kay:* No, Nancy, we're not.

*Junior:* You mean, we're not going to be invited.

*Kay:* There's just going to be Mother Moran, your mother and father, Uncle Terry and Aunt Dorothy.

*Lucy:* Oh, gee, Katherine—aren't you going to invite me?

*Kay:* Well, Lucy—

*Bob:* Maybe we can talk Kay into having you at the wedding.

*Lucy:* Well, if you can't, nobody can.

*Effect: laughing.*

*MM:* Well, children, now ya know the reason for the cake. It's a special— a very special cake and I'm goin ta say ta Katherine tonight—well, I guess maybe she knows.

*Kay:* Yes, Mother Moran, I do. But won't you say, as you have on so many occasions? It's something that I understand so very well today.

*MM:* "A cake ta bake, and a floor ta sweep. And a tired little babe ta sing ta sleep. What does a woman want more than this—A home, a man, and a child ta kiss." May you and Bob find the happiness that you both so richly deserve. This is not only an engagement party—it's—well, a kind of farewell party, too.

*Fran:* Yes, we know, Mom.

*MM:* I wonder, children, how many of our friends—friends that we've known for over five and a half years—how many of them will be able ta understand this farewell party.

*Henry:* Don't you think, Mother, that you owe all of these friends that you speak of some sort of an explanation so that they might better understand why this is, as you said, a sort of farewell party?

*Fran:* I think Henry's right, Mom.

*Terry:* So do I. Only I wouldn't call it a farewell party, if I were you, Mom.

*MM:* Well, maybe not. Friends of *Today's Children*—for over five and a half years, you have been like neighbors to my family. You have seen these Children of Today work out their problems, one by one—problems that sometimes were kinda hard ta work out. But somehow, in some way, these children of mine now seem ta be on the right path, each one of them. Terry, Dorothy and their little family, are content and happy. Isn't that right?

*Dot:* You know that it is, Mother, and no matter what problems we might have to face in the future, somehow I feel for the first time since Terry and I have been married, that we'd know how to meet them, because we've experienced a similar problem before and had solved it.

*MM:* That's what I mean, Dorothy. You're prepared for the future by what has happened ta you in the past. And you, Frances and Henry, and your little family—well—

*Henry:* Our little family, Mother—I think that Fran and I can say just as Dorothy has said, that anything that might happen to us in the future wouldn't be very much different from what has happened to us in the past. We've experienced sorrow—we've had our ups and downs—our trials—disappointments—and I believe that we know how to face anything that might happen to us in the coming years.

*MM:* Katherine—

*Kay:* Mother Moran, somehow I think that your friends should know that your wise teachings over the past five and a half years have given each of your Today's Children a foundation that nothing can destroy. You've shown us a road on which we know that our footing is sure. Don't you think I'm right, Bob?

*Bob:* I'm a comparative newcomer as one of Today's Children, but I too, would like to say to the friends of Today's Children that I feel sure that each one of us gathered here in the room this evening will be able to meet any situations thru what we've learned from the teachings of a woman who has reared her family to manhood and womanhood with an understanding and a sympathy that can't fail them, no matter what the future may hold.

*MM:* Thank ya, Bob. Thank ya, my Today's Children—all of you. Eileen, who has finally worked out her problem—Katherine, Terry, Dorothy, Frances, Henry—it's with a great deal of pleasure that I can say that I feel that my work is over and I have indeed been repaid ta the fullest. And now, Friends of Today's Children, may I have the pleasure and the great happiness ta be the first one ta turn on my radio jest as you have yours turned on, ta hear another real life story. Will ya be turnin on the radio, please Frances?

*Fran:* Sure, Mom.

*Effect: click of switch.*

*MM:* And now, children, not a word outta nay of ya while we listen ta Pillsbury's new radio program *The Woman in White.*

*Pause:*

*Announcer: The Woman in White*

*Theme music up and under:*

*Announcer:* "I expect to pass thru this life but once. If, therefore, there is any kindness I can show, or any good I can do to any fellow, let me do it now, for I shall not pass this way again."

*Music up and out:*

*Announcer:* A purple twilight descends on a large city hospital. The year is Nineteen and Thirty Eight. The hospital is built of gray granite, and is eight stories high. Here, for three years, young women clad in blue and white, have walked with humble steps that lead up the altar of service, involving the mysteries of life and death. This evening, many of these same women who have remained loyal to an ideal, are ready to face the world in a profession of service. Tonight, they stand before us as "women in white."

*Pause*

*Announcer:* In presenting to you the "Woman in White," the Pillsbury Flour Mills Company believes that it is bringing to you a type of entertainment which is unique, different and compelling—a story filled with problems that are as elemental and as important as life itself.

*Organ: (fade in) "Processional."*

*Announcer:* Come with us now to the auditorium of a large city hospital. The President of the Medical Staff is addressing the Nineteen Thirty Eight graduating class of nurses.

*Music out:*

*Dr: (fading)* However, it is quite a different problem to speak to nurses in a classroom, or at the bedside as I have done for many years, from attempting to say something worthwhile at a graduation exercise. It is heartwarming and inspiring to see a group of girls—young—at the threshold of life, who after a difficult and sometimes very trying course of training, have remained loyal to an ideal and persevered—are ready to face the world in a profession of service, anxious to heal the sick and maimed, relieve pain and suffering, comfort the dying, spread sunshine and warmth in the valley of tears and gloom. Could anything be nobler? Is it not a divine mission? The road to this stage of perfection is a long, hard and dangerous one, but you were willing to take it; one is forced to compliment and praise you. You have successfully completed the prescribed years of apprenticeship in our hospital. You are about to enter the hardest school of all—the school of Life. Here is where men and women are finally made or broken. "A talent is formed and developed in seclusion. A character only in the stream of life." *(pause)* This hospital has been, I believe, a good alma mater—a benevolent mother. In sending you forth, it trusts in your affection and loyalty and hopes that you will ever be a credit and an honor to your school. In closing, I wish you Godspeed, and may your lives be an eloquent testimonial to our best wishes.

*Chorus of women's voices singing with organ "The Perfect Day."*

*Song out*

*Voices of women giving nurses' pledge:* I solemnly pledge myself before God and in the presence of this assembly to pass my life in purity and to practice my profession faithfully. I will abstain from whatever is deleterious and mischievous, and will not take or knowingly administer any harmful drug. I will do all in my power to elevate the standard of my profession, and I will hold in confidence all personal matters committed to my keeping, and all family affairs coming to my knowledge in the practice of my calling. With loyalty will I endeavor to aid the physician in his work and devote myself to the welfare of those committed to my care.

*Organ fading up and under:*

*Karen:* After three long years, I, Karen Adams, have become a woman in white. Tonight I have dedicated myself to service—to service for others—

just as Florence Nightingale did many years ago. Will I be worthy of my white uniform? Will I be able to carry on the power for good, which I have felt for three years, can be carried on—the power for good that she brought into the world? Will I be able to help people, ease pain, bring new lives into the world, bring comfort to the dying? I only hope from the depths of my soul, that I will be worthy at all times of being the Woman in White.

*Announcer:* And so, we have met Karen Adams, the Woman in White. The Pillsbury Flour Mills Company hopes that you will find the Woman in White not only entertaining, but inspiring and helpful as well. What problems await Karen Adams on the threshold of the new adventure? Whom will she meet? We feel sure that adventure, romance, sorrow and happiness will all play a part in her experience as the Woman in White. Be sure to be with us tomorrow, when Karen Adams, the Woman in White, is confronted with a real problem—not as a nurse, but as a sister to the young and lovely Betty Adams, a student nurse, who finds herself in serious difficulty.

*No commercial:*

*Theme up and out:*

*Announcer:* The Woman in White has come to you as a presentation of the Pillsbury Flour Mills Company and will again be heard tomorrow morning this same time.

APPENDIX C

## *The Guiding Light*
## Tuesday, January 10, 1950

*Music: under*

*Announcer:* This evening in the living room of a little house with a white picket fence on Elm Street in Selby Flats, the fireplace is ablaze with flame, but somehow it seems cold and cheerless to you, doesn't it Ray Brandon? You sit with your tightly clenched hands pressed against your forehead—your thoughts are of Charlotte in a hospital where she has been confined because of her attempt to find forgetfulness, escape, in the twilight world of barbiturates, sleeping pills . . . It's unbelievable, isn't it, Ray, what's happened to Charlotte . . . and what's happened to you. You're forced at this moment to recall the words of Dr. Mary Leland. . . .

*Music: up and under*

*Mary: (over filter)* Now of all times, Ray, you must give Charlotte all the understanding she needs and deserves. Ray, you've got to straighten out your own thinking a little before you can even begin to help Charlotte find her way back.

*Music: up and under*

*Ray:* Apparently Mary feels that my thinking needs not just a little but a great deal of straightening out. She wouldn't even permit me to see Charlotte today. Somehow I got the idea that Charlotte must have made it very clear that she didn't want to see me.

*Mary: (filter)* She's going thru mental and physical torment, Ray.

*Ray:* And so am I, so am I. But I've got to stop thinking of myself now. I've got to think as straight and as clearly as I ever have in my life.

*Music: up and out*

*Announcer:* But will you be capable, Ray, of seeing the past thru anything but a haze of bitterness? Will you be capable even now? We'll learn more about this shortly.

*Music: out*

*Announcer: Commercial*

*Music: under*

*Announcer:* You sit alone, Ray Brandon, in a house haunted by memories of the greatest happiness and yet the deepest misery that you've known. But you're not thinking of happiness now, are you—the days in which you made this house ready for Charlotte with your own hands—the days thru which the laughter of an adopted son gave you new warmth and depth to your love for a woman. You're forcing yourself to remember the dead, lifeless weeks and months that followed the return of that child to its real mother, Meta Bauer . . . an act of renunciation for which you've never really forgiven Charlotte. For the first time, now, you force open the stubborn gates of your own selfishness, attempt to look into Charlotte's heart as it must have been in those lonely, empty days.

*Music: up and under*

*Char: (slightly on echo chamber)* We still have each other, Ray. Isn't that all that really counts? You and me—our love for each other, that's something no one can take away, nothing can change. *(falteringly)* Isn't it, Ray?

*Music: up and under*

*Announcer:* Yes, Charlotte was trying to reach you in those days, trying to break thru the veil of bitterness with which you'd enshrouded yourself. She'd forced a smile to her lips as she'd ignored your sullen moods, your harsh indifference to her. She knew how you missed a little boy, but she clung desperately to the thought that you still loved her. Remember how she begged you to take her on that trip you insisted on making alone?

*Music: up and under*

*Char: (echo chamber)* But Ray, please—I—I've got my suitcases all packed. I know you'll be busy but I won't be any trouble. I—I just don't want to be here alone. Please take me with you.

*Music: up and under*

*Announcer:* But you left her alone, didn't you, and then when her mind went back to Chuckie, when she tried to think of constructive ways in which she could help Meta with the future of that child, do you remember what you said?

*Ray: (echo chamber)* You had no right, Charlotte, sending the nursery things over to Meta's without consulting me, you had no right even talking to Meta.

*Announcer:* Yes, that's what you said, Ray. You didn't even seem to be aware of what dismantling that nursery must have meant to Charlotte. And even in such a little thing as her expressing satisfaction over the fact that Dr. Ross Bolinger lived just upstairs of Chuckie and Meta. . . .

*Music: up and under*

*Char: (echo chamber)* Well I was thinking—it's kind of nice, a good feeling, to know that someone who knew Chuckie a little bit—well, I mean, if Chuckie should ever get sick—

*Ray: (echo chamber)* Look Charlotte, it's out of our hands now. Just remember that.

*Char: (echo chamber)* But Ray——

*Ray: (echo chamber)* Charlotte, I don't want to talk about it! It's over and done with as far as I'm concerned. A closed book.

*Music: up and under*

*Announcer:* And still Charlotte kept trying to mend things between you.

*Music: up and under*

*Char: (echo chamber)* Our nursery doesn't have to be empty forever, Ray. Maybe in time, maybe later on—

*Ray: (echo chamber)* Charlotte, I'll never consider adopting another youngster. There'll be no children in our life from now on. That's why it's pointless to keep this house. An apartment in town closer to my work will make much more sense.

*Char: (echo chamber)* Give up this house—our—our beautiful garden, leave a neighborhood that's almost a part of us? Ray!

*Music: up and under*

*Announcer:* But you insisted, didn't you, Ray, upon tearing your lives away from this house. Forcing Charlotte into a pattern that she never wanted, for which she was never made. Even so she tried to believe in your love.

*Music: up and under*

*Char: (echo)* Sure, I know we've lost our way—we're kind of feeling our way thru the darkness. I'm trying so hard to see a light, just a faint glimmer of—well, a guiding light. But there's something you haven't said for a long time—the only thing that can put us on the right road again. You know what I'm talking about, don't you, Ray?

*Ray: (echo)* No, Charlotte—I don't.

*Char: (echo)* Love. You haven't said "I—I still love you."

*Music: up and under*

*Announcer:* You didn't say it even then, Ray. No, you and Charlotte kept living under the same roof, a man and wife—but strangers to each other. No wonder Dr. Mary Leland spoke to you as she did.

*Mary: (over filter)* What have you done to that girl—crucified her. You've done a very cruel thing, Ray. And now you wonder why she's shut you out of her life.

*Music: sting it*

*Char: (filter)* You can't take love, a woman's feelings, Ray, tear them apart like you would a piece of cloth and try to put the pieces together again. The pieces never fit quite the same.

*Music: up and under*

*Announcer:* Yes, it's no wonder, Ray Brandon, that your wife rejected your half-hearted protestations of love when they finally did come. Actions speak louder than words, Ray, and the tenderness was missing, wasn't it? And then, when Charlotte's nervous system had given way, when you remained blind to the fact that she was finding escape in self-medication, how else did you think she'd react to your magnanimous suggestions that you return to this house?

*Music: sting it*

*Char: (filter) (violently)* I said forget it, Ray. I don't care what you do with the house in Selby Flats. I don't want any part of it, not any part of it!

*Music: up and under*

*Announcer:* And now she's lying in a hospital after you forced her to return to this house, this wife who stood by you thru that difficult period in your life when you fought to clear yourself of a crime you didn't commit, a prison sentence you didn't deserve, a battle to build a legal career for yourself, a wife who believed in you, gave you encouragement, loved you with every fibre of her being, a wife who was ready to forgive you anything, everything, as long as you loved her. Do you wonder, Ray, why the words of Dr. Mary Leland and the words of Sid Harper, a man who really understands Charlotte, keep pounding in your brain?

*Music: building under—rapid tempo*

*Sid: (filter)* When there was no longer a child in your home Charlotte needed you more than during your whole married life together. And what did you do—you turned your back on her.

*Mary: (filter)* You've crucified that girl, Ray.

*Sid: (filter)* You're a stupid fool, Brandon.

*Mary: (filter)* You've rejected her as a woman.

*Sid: (filter)* Stupid fool.

*Mary: (filter)* She's lost complete confidence.

*Sid: (filter)* Fool. . . .

*Mary: (filter)* You've been cruel . . .

*Sid: (filter)* You fool, you stupid fool.

*Music: up in payoff*

*Ray: (on mike) (brokenly)* I have been to blame—it has been my fault. A chance—yes . . . I've got to have another chance to make everything right again.

*Music: up into bridge*

*Announcer: (tease)* Meta Bauer learns of Charlotte's hospitalization in the next dramatic episode of *The Guiding Light* brought to you by the New Duz.

## APPENDIX D

### *The Guiding Light*
### Monday, March 5, 1956

*Telop: (The Guiding Light)*

*Organ: theme*

*Announcer:* And now *The Guiding Light* created by Irna Phillips.

*Organ: out*

\* \* \* \* \* \* \* \* \* \* \* \* \* \* \* \* \* \* \* \* \* \* \* \* \* \* \* \* \* \* \* \* \* \* \* \* \* \* \*

*For radio:*

*Sound: steeple clock chiming twelve, fade into bg.*

*Announcer: (over the chimes)* Twelve o'clock. Midnight. Most of the people of the city of Los Angeles are asleep—most of the homes blanketed in darkness. But here and there the lights of living rooms and bedrooms are burning as the early morning edition of a newspaper is read. The account of an eleven year old boy named Michael Bauer—missing since early this morning. On the front page of the paper, beneath the headlines, is a charcoal sketch of the young boy's face—the alert, rather sad eyes—the sensitive, unsmiling mouth. . . .

*Music: up for a few notes and out.*

*Sound: take the last of the chimes in distance*

\* \* \* \* \* \* \* \* \* \* \* \* \* \* \* \* \* \* \* \* \* \* \* \* \* \* \* \* \* \* \* \* \* \* \* \* \* \* \*

*For TV take a shot of a church steeple silhouetted against the night sky. We hear the clock chiming twelve. Dissolve from steeple to the Bauer living room. Bill's standing at the window. Papa is seated, staring into space. Bert is seated on the couch, her head in her hand.*

*Bill:* Midnight

*Papa:* Ya.

*Bill: (looks at him)* You must be tired, Papa.

*Papa:* Nein, but—*(for TV he motions toward Bertha) (for radio: Bertha)*

*Bill: (for radio: Yeah) (for TV Bill just walks over to her, puts his hand on her shoulder)* Bert? . . . Honey?

*Bert: (looks up)* Yes?

*Bill:* You're exhausted.

*Bert:* No, I'm not.

*Bill:* Sweetheart—. Why don't you go upstairs.

*Bert:* I don't want to go upstairs. Mother'll hear Billy.

*Bill:* I'm not thinking of Billy . . .

*Papa:* You need to get some sleep, Bertha.

*Bert: (She couldn't possibly sleep)* Oh, Papa Bauer—

*Papa:* Meta, she left some of those little pills for you, nicht wahr?

*Bill:* Yeah, she did, Papa. I'll get you a glass of water, honey—*(he starts toward kitchen)*

*Bert:* No.

*Bill:* But, Bert—

*Papa:* They will make you sleep, liebling.

*Bert:* I don't want to sleep.

*Bill:* You can't just—

*Bert:* I don't see you going to bed.

*Bill:* But *you've* got to get some rest, you're at the point where—

*Bert:* Just leave me alone.

*Papa:* You ain't doing nobody no good like this, Bertha.

*Bill:* That's right, honey, you're just wearing yourself out and—

*Bert: (gets up)* What's the matter with you two? You think I could go upstairs and lie down knowing that Michael might be—*(She breaks. Just one sob, and sits down)*

*Bill: (goes over to her)* Okay, sweetheart, okay. *(sits down beside her)*

*Bert: (leans against him)* What's happening to him, Bill? What's happened to him?

*Bill:* Honey, I'm sure nothing's really happened to him—

*Bert:* Past midnight—he's been gone since before breakfast and you say—

*Bill:* I mean—wherever he is, I'm sure he's okay.

*Papa:* Ya, Bertha, Willie is right.

*Bert:* Then why haven't we heard anything? Why haven't they found him? He wouldn't stay out this late on purpose, he'd come home!

*Bill:* Well now, you don't know that, sweetheart.

*Bert:* I know Michael—I know my son. Oh, I'll never forgive myself never!

*Papa:* Bertha, it ain't your fault. How was you to know—

*Bert:* I should have known, I should have known when he wasn't at school—*(clutches him)* Bill, I'm so scared, I'm so—

*Sound: phone rings*
*This makes them all jump. And they all start for the phone.*

*Bert: (gives an audible gasp)* Let me—

*Bill:* No, I'll get it, Bert. I'll get it.

*For radio: receiver up*

*Bill:* Hello?

*Mr. Baker: (for TV take Mr. Baker in their living room) (for radio, cross fade to him live)* Mr. Bauer?

*Bill: (filter for radio)* Yes?

*Mr. Baker:* This is Henry Baker. Jock's father.

*Bill:* Oh, —yes, Mr. Baker?

*Mr. Baker:* I'm just calling to—well, I just wondered if you'd heard anything?

*Bill:* No—not yet.

*Mr. Baker:* We—saw the paper.

*Bill:* Yeah, we—we thought it might be a good idea. I mean any—

*Mr. Baker:* Sure, I understand. I—don't suppose there's anything we can do?

*Bill:* Thanks, I don't think so.

*Mr. Baker:* Well—I won't tie up your phone . . . If you do hear anything—

*Bill:* We'll let you know. Thanks for calling, Mr. Baker.

*Mr. Baker:* Goodnight, Mr. Bauer.

*For radio: receiver replaced.*

*As Mr. Baker hangs up, we move back to take in more of the room and we see Jock standing in the doorway in his pajamas and robe. Mr. Baker gets up slowly, turns and then sees Jock.*

*Mr. Baker:* Jock . . .

*Jock:* Did they hear yet, Dad?

*Mr. Baker:* No, son.

*Jock:* What did Mr. Bauer say?

*Mr. Baker:* Nothing else he could say. Don't you think it's pretty late for you to be up?

*Jock:* Yes, sir.

*Mr. Baker:* Well, then—

*Jock:* But I—I wanted to—

*Mr. Baker:* You wanted what, son?

*Jock: (A beat. He looks down, then looks squarely at his dad)* I want to tell you something Dad. *And take it out on Jock's face.*

*Music: Note. Sustain under.*

*Announcer:* We'll learn more about this in a moment.

*Music: out*

*Announcer: Commercial*

*Same scene, no lapse in time*

*Mr. Baker:* Well let's sit down, Jock. *(He sits)*

*Jock: (comes over and sits down)* Dad, you—you don't think I know where Mike is?

*Mr. Baker:* Of course not, son.

*Jock:* Detective Burgess—

*Mr. Baker:* He had to ask you a lot of questions, Jock—that's his job. But I'm sure the police know you were telling the truth—I'm sure Mr. Bauer knows that too.

*Jock:* Yeah *(a beat)* I know everybody thinks it's kind of funny that I went around with Mike—I mean, being as he was a few years younger'n me.

*Mr. Baker:* I think you explained that very satisfactorily, son. You walked to school with him and he watched you play basketball . . .

*Jock:* It was more than that, Dad.

*Mr. Baker:* How do you mean?

*Jock:* Well, I do go around with an older gang, but—I don't know, I sort of felt sorry for the kid.

*Mr. Baker:* Sorry for him?

*Jock:* Yeah.

*Mr. Baker:* Why?

*Jock:* Well, he thought I was real great. I mean, you know how little kids are sometimes . . .

*Mr. Baker:* He's not that little, Jock—eleven years old.

*Jock:* He seemed little to me—and I was pretty big to him.

*Mr. Baker:* What do you mean, *were* pretty big?

*Jock:* Well, that's—that's just what I mean.

*Mr. Baker:* But you make it sound as tho—

*Jock:* What?

*Mr. Baker:* Nothing, son, go ahead.

*Jock:* Well, kids like Mike, they look up to fellows who are good in athletics. . . .

*Mr. Baker:* Yes, that's normal.

*Jock:* I never told you that—well, once in a while Mike used to come back to the house with me after school—watch me practice. . . .

*Mr. Baker:* You hadn't mentioned it to me, but I heard you tell Detective Burgess about it. You said he used to watch you shoot baskets and you'd let him shoot a few.

*Jock:* But I meant I didn't tell you—well, one day his grandmother came over to get him.

*Mr. Baker:* His grandmother?

*Jock:* Yeah, and boy, did she ever lay him out—really laid him out—said he had no business being over here playing with a boy so much older than he was. She said a few things to me too—asked me why I didn't play with boys my own size, my own age.

*Mr. Baker:* Oh? What did you say?

*Jock:* Nothing. What should I have said?

*Mr. Baker:* Well—nothing.

*Jock:* It was Mike really got the bawling out—and *I mean* that poor kid got it.

*Mr. Baker:* Uh-hmm?

*Jock:* When I saw him the next day, he was still mad, really burned up, in a funny way, you know?

*Mr. Baker:* No, I don't.

*Jock:* I couldn't figure out what the detective thinks exactly—

*Mr. Baker:* He doesn't think anything except—after all, the boy's been missing since early morning and it's past midnight. Detective Burgess was just trying to get all the information he could.

*Jock: (a beat)* I think he ran away.

*Mr. Baker:* What?

*Jock:* I think Mike ran away.

*Mr. Baker:* Why do you think that, Jock?

*Jock:* Well, in the first place, he's got this baby brother, see, and from what he's told me—I guess his grandmother plays favorites a lot. Everything the baby does is swell—everything Mike does is wrong.

*Mr. Baker:* Oh?

*Jock:* And his mother—she's real swell and all, but she sort of agrees with everything Mike's grandmother says, you see?

*Mr. Baker:* Yes . . . but I still don't know why you'd think Mike ran away.

*Jock:* 'Cause that's what he told me.

*Mr. Baker:* He—. What do you mean, son?

*Jock:* He said if his grandmother didn't let up on him, someday he'd run away.

*Mr. Baker:* Jock, you're sure he told you that?

*Jock:* Sure I'm sure.

*Mr. Baker:* Why didn't you tell this to—

*Jock:* He made me promise I wouldn't, Dad.

*Mr. Baker:* But, Jock—

*Jock:* Yeah, Dad, but I gave Mike my word—

*Mr. Baker:* Son, the boy's been missing for—

*Jock:* I know, and after the detective talked the way he did—you didn't hear him talking to me the second time he came over?

*Mr. Baker:* No, he said he wanted to talk with you alone.

*Jock:* He kept telling me the way Mike's parents felt—and I knew you were kind of worried too, thinking that—well, I don't know what you thought exactly—

*Mr. Baker:* I was only thinking of how I'd feel if I were in Mr. Bauer's place, how your mother and I would both feel if something happened to you.

*Jock:* Yeah, Detective Burgess said that too. I know he ran away, I'm sure of it, Dad.

*Mr. Baker:* Did he tell you yesterday that he was going to—

*Jock:* Oh no, but he said it to me a couple of times.

*Mr. Baker:* Did he ever say where he might go, or—?

*Jock: (shakes his head)* He just said he'd run away. Said if she didn't leave him alone, he'd run away.

*Mr. Baker:* His grandmother?

*Jock:* Yeah. I didn't know he really meant it at the time, I mean, I thought he was just talking, the way kids do. I didn't think he'd really do it.

*Mr. Baker:* Well, son, I think we'd better call the police right now.

*Jock:* Dad—

*Mr. Baker:* What, Jock?

*Jock:* Well, if Mike—I mean I did promise him . . .

*Mr. Baker:* Look, Jock. Mike's gone. And I *did* hear you promise Detective Burgess you'd cooperate in every way you could.

*Jock:* Yeah, I—I said I would.

*Mr. Baker:* I just wish you'd have told him all this when he was here.

*Jock:* Yeah, I—I wish I had too. It isn't too late now, is it, Dad. It isn't too late?

*Mr. Baker:* Well, let's hope not, son.

*Sound: receiver up, number dialed.*

*Music: in to bridge.*

# *Notes*

## INTRODUCTION

1. Raymond William Stedman, "A History of the Broadcasting of Daytime Serial Dramas in the United States," Ph.D. diss., University of Southern California, 1959, pp. 73, 116; "Soap Operas: Men Are Tuning In," *New York Times*, 21 Feb. 1979, Sect. 3, p. 1; *Newsweek*, 28 Sept. 1981, p. 60; "They're Watching," Brochure, ABC-Television Social Research Unit, 1982.

2. James Thurber, *The Beast in Me and Other Animals* (New York: Harcourt, Brace, 1948) p. x.

3. George Comstock, "The Legacy of the Past," *Journal of Communication* 33 (Summer 1983): 42–50. See also in this same issue Lee Thayer, "On 'Doing' Research and 'Explaining' Things," pp. 80–91; and Gerald Miller, "Taking Stock of a Discipline," pp. 31–49. This special issue of *Journal of Communication*, devoted to "ferment in the field," provides a particularly good overview of the range of research positions occupied by most American media researchers and some of the (unfortunately more obvious) points of difference between them and their European counterparts.

4. Jonathan Culler, *The Pursuit of Signs* (London: Routledge and Kegan Paul, 1981), p. 5.

5. In using the terms "reader" and "text" rather than "viewer" and "message" or "program," I am obviously indicating my preference for the terminology of contemporary literary and cinema studies over that in common usage among American media researchers. This choice is also motivated by my desire to highlight something which is too frequently ignored in American media research: soap operas and, indeed, the preponderance of programming carried by the commercial broadcasting networks, are *narrative* and *fictional* in nature. The term "reader" enables us to refer to the role anyone assumes when he or she engages a fictional narrative (whether that narrative is encountered via radio, television, the movies, or literature). The term "text," which indicates the formal system of relationships encountered by the reader, is particularly appropriate when discussing soap operas, since the world of the soap opera transcends any individual episode.

6. Thomas Kuhn, *The Structure of Scientific Revolutions*, 2nd ed. (Chicago: University of Chicago Press, 1969), p. 202.

## CHAPTER 1

1. The notion of the "always-already-read" text and the "always-already-predisposed" reader are taken up in, among other works, Tony Bennett, "Text and Social Process: the Case of James Bond," *Screen Education* 41 (1982): 3–14; his "Marxism and Popular Fiction,"

*Literature and History* 7 (1981): 138–65; and Fredric Jameson, *The Political Unconscious* (Ithaca: Cornell University Press, 1981). The notion of discursive encrustation Bennett takes from an interview with Pierre Macherey in *Red Letters* 5 (1977).

2. "Among New Words," *American Speech* 20 (1945): 145. The earliest citation listed in the above article is 1939: *Newsweek*, 13 Nov. 1939, p. 44.

3. E. Carswell and R. Rommelveit, *Social Contexts of Messages* (London: Academic Press, 1971), pp. 9–10. Their work is related to the study of television by David Morley, *The "Nationwide" Audience* (London: British Film Institute, 1980), pp. 156–57.

4. "Daylight and Drama—Salesmen for Flour," *Broadcasting*, 1 March 1935, p. 12.

5. Katherine Best, "Literature of the Air," *Saturday Review of Literature*, 20 April 1940, p. 12; Whitfield Cook, "Be Sure to Listen In," *American Mercury*, March 1940, pp. 318–19.

6. As literary theorist Pierre Macherey has put it: "Either all around or in its wake the explicit requires the implicit: for in order to say anything, there are things *which must not be said.* . . . There is not even the slightest hint of the absence of what it does not, perhaps cannot, say: the disavowal . . . extends even to the act that banished the forbidden term; its absence is unacknowledged" (*A Theory of Literary Production*, p. 85).

7. Michel Foucault, *The Order of Things: An Archaeology of the Human Sciences* (New York: Vintage Books, Random, 1973), p. xiv.

8. Joseph Margolis, *The Language of Art and Art Criticism* (Detroit: Wayne State University Press, 1965), pp. 37–47.

9. Dennis Porter, "Soap Time: Thoughts on a Commodity Art Form," in Horace Newcomb, ed., *Television: The Critical View*, 3rd ed., (New York: Oxford University Press, 1982), p. 89.

10. Marya Mannes, "Massive Detergence," *Reporter*, 6 July 1961, p. 39.

11. René Huyghe, *Les Puissances de l'image, bilan d'une psychologie de l'art* (Paris: Flammarion, 1965), p. 105, quoted in Nicos Hadjinicolaou, *Art History and Class Struggle* (London: Pluto Press, 1978), p. 21; M. Collins and Olive L. Riley, *Art Appreciation for Junior and Senior High Schools* (New York: Harcourt, Brace, 1937), p. 150.

12. Tony Bennett, "Marxism and Popular Fiction," p. 160. Illustrative of Bennett's view that "the critic, as the interpreter of meaning, requires an author as a necessary fiction" is the influence exercised by the *auteur theory* over academic film criticism in the 1960s and 1970s. Auteurism ordered the entire critical and historical enterprise of film around the discovery of artists (film directors) whose visions transcended the depersonalizing constraints of the Hollywood studio system. A body of work by a particular director was analyzed in order to uncover the artistic world view that tied all the films together and marked them as "authored." Even Peter Wollen, hardly an aesthetically naive critic, could write in 1969 that only the qualities of a film that could be ascribed to its inferred author were critically legible. "Everything irrelevant to this, everything non-pertinent, is considered logically secondary, contingent, to be discarded" (*Signs and Meaning in the Cinema*, 3rd ed. [Bloomington: University of Indiana Press, 1972], p. 105).

13. "The Hummert's Super Soaps," *Newsweek*, 10 Jan. 1944, pp. 79–80; Best, "Literature of the Air," pp. 11–16; "Soap Opera," *Fortune*, March 1946, pp. 119–24, 146–48, 151–52; Merrill Dennison, "Soap Opera," *Harper's*, April 1940, pp. 498–505. See also, "Are Soap Operas Only Suds?" *New York Times Magazine*, 28 March 1943, pp. 19, 36.

14. Mark Harris, "Easy Does It Not," in *The Living Novel*, Granville Hicks, ed. (New York: Macmillan, 1957), pp. 113–16. Quoted in Wayne C. Booth, *The Rhetoric of Fiction* (Chicago: University of Chicago Press, 1961), p. 90.

15. For a discussion of "figure in the carpet" criticism see Wolfgang Iser, *The Act of Reading: A Theory of Aesthetic Response* (Baltimore: Johns Hopkins University Press, 1978), p. 4. For an example of a primer that "teaches" one how to appreciate art, see Laurence Buermeyer's widely reprinted monograph, "The Aesthetic Experience" (Merion, Pa.: Barnes Foundation Press, 1924).

16. Dwight MacDonald, "A Theory of Mass Culture," *Diogenes* 3 (Summer 1953), pp. 10–17; Ernest van den Haag, "Of Happiness and Despair We Have No Measure," in *Mass Media and Mass Society*, ed. Alan Casty (New York: Holt, Rinehart, and Winston, 1968), pp. 5–11. In her very useful study of popular feminine narrative forms, including the soap opera, Tania Modleski addresses the distinction between high art and mass art which pervades the cultural criticism of the Frankfurt School (Adorno, Horkheimer, Marcuse). See *Loving With a Vengeance: Mass-Produced Fantasies for Women* (Hamden, Conn.: Archon Books, 1982), pp. 26–27.

17. Jose Ortega y Gasset, *The Revolt of the Masses* (London: George Allen and Unwin, 1932), p. 68. MacDonald, "A Theory of Mass Culture"; van den Haag, "Of Happiness and Despair We Have No Measure."

18. The following discussion is based on Paul Lazarsfeld, "An Episode in the History of Social Research: A Memoir," in Donald Fleming and Bernard Bailyn, eds. *The Intellectual Migration: Europe and America, 1930–1960* (Cambridge: Harvard University Press, 1969), pp. 270–337. The Beville study was published as "Social Stratification of the Radio Audience" (Princeton: Princeton Radio Research Project, 1939). It later appeared as "The ABCD's of Radio Audiences," *Public Opinion Quarterly* 4 (1940): 195–206. See also Stedman, "A History of the Broadcasting of Daytime Serial Dramas in the United States," pp. 148–51.

19. Louis Berg, quoted in Thurber, *The Beast in Me and Other Animals*, pp. 251–52, and in Max Wylie, "Dusting Off Dr. Berg," *Printer's Ink* 202 (12 Feb. 1943): 44.

20. Todd Gitlin, "Media Sociology: The Dominant Paradigm," *Theory and Society* 6 (1978): 209–10. See also Elihu Katz and Paul Lazarsfeld, *Personal Influence: The Part Played by People in the Flow of Mass Communications* (New York: Free Press, 1955), pp. 16–17.

21. Herta Herzog, "What Do We Really Know about Daytime Serial Listeners?" *Radio Research 1942–43* (New York: Duell, Sloan, and Pearce, 1944), pp. 6–8.

22. "Broadcast Serial Audience Not Typed," *Broadcasting*, 26 April 1943; Stedman, p. 193.

23. Stedman, pp. 185–89, 197. The research was published in 1945 as a brochure by CBS entitled "Radio's Daytime Serial." Paul Lazarsfeld and Harry Field, *The People Look at Radio* (Chapel Hill: University of North Carolina Press, 1946), pp. 49–53.

24. Dennison, p. 505

25. Charles Siepmann, *Radio's Second Chance* (Boston: Little, Brown, 1946), pp. 58–59.

26. Max Wylie, "Washboard Weepers," *Harper's*, Nov. 1942, p. 635.

27. W. Lloyd Warner and William E. Henry, "The Radio Day Time Serial: A Symbolic Analysis," *Genetic Psychology Monographs* 37 (1948): 3–71.

## CHAPTER 2

1. Natan Katzman, "Television Soap Operas: What's Been Going on Anyway?" *Public Opinion Quarterly* 36 (1972): 200–212; Patricia Tegler, "The Daytime Serial: A Bibliography of

Scholarly Writings, 1943–1981," *Journal of Popular Culture* 16 (Winter 1982), also in Mary Cassata and Thomas Skill, *Life on Daytime Television: Tuning-In American Serial Drama* (Norwood, N.J.: Ablex, 1983), pp. 187–96.

2. Everett M. Rogers, "The Empirical and the Critical Schools of Communication Research," *Communication Yearbook* 5 (1982): 126.

3. David Willer and Judith Willer, *Systematic Empiricism: Critique of a Pseudo-Science* (Englewood Cliffs, N.J.: Prentice-Hall, 1973), p. 1. It should be pointed out that while the empiricist tradition in American mass communications research descends in a straight line from the work of Lazarsfeld's Bureau for Applied Social Research, Lazarsfeld himself seems to have been more conscious of the philosophical dimensions of social research than many of those who unquestioningly followed his methodological lead. Trained in psychological theory and research in Vienna, Lazarsfeld's move toward American-style sociology was in part a reaction against what he saw as the unnecessary theoreticism of European psychological and sociological thought. Once in the United States, however, he also rejected the "radical behaviorism" of those for whom number gathering was an end unto itself. "It would have been unacceptable," he recalled in 1969, "just to report that X per cent of people did or thought this or that about some topic. The task was to combine diverse findings into a small number of 'integrated constructs.'" In 1937 he even assembled a group of prominent psychoanalysts to ask them if the insights of Freudian psychology might be helpful in understanding relationships between radio programming and listeners.

It is also interesting to note that the arguments against the brand of empiricist "administrative" research fostered by Lazarsfeld raised today within American mass communications research are direct echoes of those posed by Theodor Adorno in the late 1930s. In 1937 Lazarsfeld invited Adorno, whose work was associated with the Frankfurt School, to become director of the music division of the radio research project at Columbia. Lazarsfeld seems to have been convinced that the research orientation of the Frankfurt School, influenced as it was by Freudian and Marxist theories, was not necessarily incompatible either with American sociology or the requirements of a research institute funded in large measure by the broadcasting industry itself. The three-year association was not a happy one. Lazarsfeld expected Adorno to be able to "test" his ideas through the administration of survey questionnaires. The difficulty for Adorno was that, in his words, "something specifically musical impeded my progress from theoretical considerations to empiricism—namely the difficulty of verbalizing what music subjectively arouses in the listener, the utter obscurity of what we call 'musical experience.'" Adorno was also told that his research could not call into question the viability of the structure of commercial broadcasting—the terms of the initial Rockefeller grant funding the radio research project specified that research was to be conducted "within the limits of the commercial radio system prevailing in the United States." This implied, said Adorno, "that the system itself, its cultural and sociological consequences and its social and economic presuppositions were not to be analyzed." Finally the combination of the bureau's empiricist research slant and its "administrative" imperatives proved too much for Adorno: "When I was confronted with the demand to 'measure culture,' I reflected that culture might be precisely that condition that excludes a mentality capable of measuring it. . . . The task of translating my reflections into research terms was equivalent to squaring the circle." The charges leveled against "mainstream" American mass communications research by what are called "critical" scholars are, more than forty years later, almost exactly the same. See Paul Lazarsfeld, "An Episode in the History of Social Research: A Memoir," in

Donald Fleming and Bernard Bailyn, eds., *The Intellectual Migration: Europe and America, 1930–1960* (Cambridge: Harvard University Press, 1969), pp. 270–337; and, in the same volume, Theodor Adorno, "Scientific Experiences of a European Scholar in America," pp. 338–70. On contemporary critical studies in mass communications research, see the several articles from that perspective included in the "Ferment in the Field" issue of *Journal of Communication* (vol. 33, Summer 1983), including William H. Melody and Robin E. Mansell, "The Debate over Critical vs. Administrative Research: Circularity or Challenge," pp. 103–16; Dallas W. Smythe and Tran Van Dinh, "On Critical and Administrative Research: A New Critical Analysis," pp. 117–27; Timothy R. Haight, "The Critical Researcher's Dilemma," pp. 226–37; Jennifer Daryl Slack and Martin Allor, "The Political and Epistemological Constituents of Critical Communication Research," pp. 208–18; and James W. Carey, "The Origins of the Radical Discourse on Cultural Studies in the United States," pp. 311–13.

4. As David Willer and Judith Willer put it, "After centuries of study involving an incalculable number of hours of mental labor, social phenomena still cannot be explained and predicted" (p. 6). My discussion of empiricism is based upon Willer and Willer; Russell Keat and John Urry, *Social Theory as Science* (London: Routledge and Kegan Paul, 1975), pp. 4–44; Richard Bernstein, *The Restructuring of Social and Political Thought* (New York: Harcourt, Brace Jovanovich, 1976), pp. 1–54; and Terry Lovell, *Pictures of Reality* (London: British Film Institute, 1980), pp. 10–19.

5. Bernstein (p. 6) calls this view of explanation a "primitive myth":

It is also frequently believed that when and if we collect enough data and discover correlations that hold among these data, then we will be in a position to arrive at those higher empirical generalizations that constitute genuine science. Even those who are dimly aware that there is more to science than collecting data and formulating empirical generalizations based upon data, are nevertheless convinced that this is a proper way of preparing the terrain for more advanced theories. This is a primitive myth because—even though it is widely held[—] . . . it is completely fallacious. It would be difficult to name any philosopher who ever held such a simplistic conception of the nature of science. . . . Further, despite the wide and sometimes sharp disagreement among contemporary philosophers about the nature and role of theory in the sciences, there is a rational consensus that it does not simply consist of empirical generalizations based on the collection or observation of facts.

6. Rogers, among others, distinguishes between "empirical" (rather than empiricist) and "critical" schools of communication research. This imprecision merely serves to confuse an already complicated set of issues. "Certain members of the critical school," he admits, "resent the nomenclature (of an empirical and a critical school) because they claim, quite correctly, that they often use empirical data in their critical analysis" (p. 126). The philosophical distinction between *empiricist* and *nonempiricist* orientations becomes further muddled when it is reduced to an ideological dichotomy: "Most critical scholars explicitly identify themselves with leftist political ideologies, while most empirical scholars claim they are objective social scientists and work to avoid any connection with a political ideology" (p. 135). This political alignment does tend to hold for mass communications research; however, there is no necessary connection between an antiempiricist philosophy and a Marxist political position. Such reduction allows Rogers to view a genuinely philosophical distinction as a simple misperception caused by the fact that "most critical scholars do not include many (if any) empirical scholars in their personal friendship networks; similarly,

the empirical scholars lack much personal contact of a professional nature with critical scholars" (p. 137).

7. Gerald Miller, "Taking Stock of a Discipline," *Journal of Communications* 33 (Summer 1983): 34.

8. As has been noted, the hypodermic theory of the relationship between media messages and audiences lost favor among academics in the 1940s and 1950s. It was replaced by more subtle formulations of media effects, chief among them Lazarsfeld and Katz's "personal influence" emphasis, functionalism or, as it is sometimes called, a "uses-and-gratifications" orientation, and the "agenda-setting" model of media influence—all of which downplayed the direct impact of media on behavior and attitudes.

Recently, however, some scholars have reasserted the power of the media to inflence viewers' outlooks on the world. Rather than claim short-term changes in attitudes and behaviors as a result of television viewing, the cultivation paradigm developed by George Gerbner, Larry Gross, and their colleagues at the University of Pennsylvania alleges that viewing contributes to the individual's overall conception of social reality. In general, the heavier the viewing over a greater period of time, the more overlap there is found to be between television's "picture of the world" and that inside the viewer's head.

Cultivation studies usually consist of two parts: a quantitative analysis of salient aspects of television's depiction of social reality is compared to the statistical incidence of those aspects in real life (in order to demonstrate a divergence between the television world and the actual "real life" situation of the viewer), and an audience survey is conducted in which viewers and nonviewers are asked to estimate the frequency with which the selected factors occur. The sample is then divided into groups according to the "amount" of television consumption and their mean responses are compared to see if differences between them are likely to have occurred as a result of chance (the test of the null hypothesis). In the more recent studies by Gerbner et al., other, possibly confounding factors (age, sex, income, education, and so forth) are also controlled for in an attempt to insure that connections between the amount of television viewing and the impact of the cultivation effect are not spurious. The findings of this type of research, widely published over a fifteen-year period, have prompted considerable controversy, primarily over methodological issues and the inability of some subsequent studies to replicate the group's findings.

This is not the place, nor am I the person, to untangle the intricacies of this essentially methodological dispute. What we should ask here is, How do the underlying assumptions of empiricism affect the production of "knowledge" about soap operas within this particular analytical framework? In "Soap Opera Viewing: The Cultivation Effect," Nancy L. Buerkel-Rothfuss and Sandra Mayes ask, "What types of effects could we reasonably expect from repeated exposure to soap opera content?" On the basis of work by Gerbner et al., they predict that heavy viewers of soap operas "would exaggerate the prevalence of soap opera 'problems' in the real world." They reason that "heavy exposure to any systematically distorted view of the world will result in similarly distorted viewer perceptions." On the basis of their study they are prepared to conclude that "there appears to be an important relationship between what a person watches on daytime serials and what he or she believes to be true about those aspects of the 'real world' which tend to be portrayed with exaggerated frequency on soap operas" ("Soap Opera Viewing: The Cultivation Effect," *Journal of Communication* 31 [Summer 1981]: 108–15.)

As their subjects the investigators chose 290 students in an introductory communications class at the University of Kentucky. They were asked questions about their viewing of soap operas, as well as their grade-point average, class standing, age, and "self-concept." Seventy-one percent of the sample claimed to watch at least one episode of a soap opera each week; the range of viewing during a "typical" week for the entire sample being from 0 to 37 episodes. The students were then asked to estimate the number of females in the general population who were doctors, lawyers, housewives, involved in extra-marital affairs, divorced, mothers of illegitimate children, mentally disturbed, and happily married. Similar questions were asked regarding males in the general population. Simple correlations were then computed between exposure to soap operas and the "real world" estimates given by the students. These showed that "increased exposure to soap operas is positively associated" with higher estimates of the relative frequency of most categories in the "real world." These correlations were found to be "statistically significant" at various levels. The significance of the correlations was upheld even when age, sex, grade point average, class, and self-concept were controlled for simultaneously. The sample was divided into viewer and nonviewer groups and the mean responses compared. They were found to be significantly different in most respects. Buerkel-Rothfuss and Mayes concluded from this that "strong indications of significant differences between viewers and nonviewers with regard to 'real world' perceptions of professionals and problems suggest that this extension of the cultivation hypothesis has empirical support."

These conclusions about the long-term effects of soap opera viewing upon the general viewer need to be examined in light of the process used to derive them. The first problem is methodological rather than theoretical. What has been "observed" are differences in the responses to questions asked of two nonrandomly selected and nonrandomly assigned groups of college students—one group that watched at least one episode of a soap opera each week and another that did not—and that overall the more a member of the survey group watched soap operas the higher his or her estimations of the relative frequency of certain occurrences tended to be. A sample is only a group chosen to represent a larger group: in this case, college students taking introductory communications courses at a large university. Since the sample was not selected randomly, however, it is uncertain how representative these 290 students were of even that limited population. Obviously, only a small percentage of the total soap opera viewing population is composed of college students, a smaller proportion is constituted by students at large universities, and a smaller proportion still by those students taking introductory communications courses at large universities. Thus whatever generalizations can be extended to the population of this study cannot be further extended to include all soap opera viewers.

But if the differences between viewers and nonviewers were found to be statistically significant even when possible confounding factors were controlled, does this necessarily mean that any differences found must be associated with the independent variable in the study: soap opera viewing? This is the conclusion pointed to in the study, but it does not necessarily follow from the data or from their analysis. The test of significance upon which the conclusions rest is a test of *data* not a test of *association*. All that it indicates is that differences found were not likely to have been the result of chance—that the null hypothesis can be more or less (depending upon the level of significance) ruled out. The test of significance says nothing about associations that are *not* random. As Willer and Willer put it, "Any inference made of an association between variables in such an experiment cannot result from the test of the null hypothesis itself but must come from elsewhere, principally from the intent of the experimenter in designing his experiment and consequently determining his controls." Of course Buerkel-Rothfuss and Mayes claimed to have eliminated the possibility that other factors were responsible for the differences by running what are called partial order correlations (the "controlling" of several possibly confounding dependent variables simultaneously through multivariate statistical analysis), but the problem here is that this procedure presumes that the researchers have identified and isolated all other potential associations and *by default* have identified the "real" association. As Willer and Willer object, "[Partial order analysis] . . . turns the procedure of finding an objective real association into a completely *subjective* process. The result is one subjectively selected association sorted out from an objectively unlimited universe. The number of associations found is thus limited only by the number of researchers." In keeping with the framework of the cultivation effect within which this study was conducted, it could well be, for example, that belief in a "distorted" view of the world is associated with heavy television viewing in general and not with soap opera viewing alone. But since it was one of a myriad of possible associations not controlled for, the study cannot address this possibility. (See Willer and Willer, pp. 52–53, 83; Russell Keat, "Positivism and Statistics in Social Science," in John Irvine, Ian Miles, and Jeff Evans, eds., *Demystifying Social Statistics* [London: Pluto Books, 1979], pp. 75–86; and, in the same volume, Liz Atkins and David Jarrett, "The Significance of 'Significance Tests,'" pp. 87–110.)

Let us, however, assume for the sake of argument that the "association" found between soap opera viewing and exaggerated estimations of some aspects of the real world is not an artifact of some other connection—that, despite the fact that such an extrapolation is unwarranted by the Buerkel-Rothfuss–Mayes study, we accept their finding of some cultivation effect among soap opera viewers in general. What have we learned about this relationship? We have been told nothing concerning whether all viewers are affected to the same degree or in the same ways. The statistically significant correlations found between amount of viewing and category estimations say nothing about which viewers of which soap operas who watch with what frequency are affected in what ways. The "significance" could be the result of extremely heavy viewers reporting grossly exaggerated estimations. There is no way within the methodological or philosophical framework of the study to account for several anomalous findings. No significant differences were found between viewers and nonviewers in their estimations of the proportions of men and women who have had affairs, who are happily married, or who are blue-collar workers. If there is, as the researchers claim, "an important relationship between what a person watches on daytime serials and what he or she believes to be true about those aspects of the 'real world' which tend to be portrayed with exaggerated frequency on soap operas," why would this distortion affect some parts of viewers' world views and not other, equally exaggerated parts?

The aim here is not to make this study bear the burden of an entire philosophical position, but it does reveal the discrepancy between what the empiricist philosophy claims to be able to explain and what such studies are in fact able to demonstrate. Even if all the methodological questions raised by this study were satisfied, its findings, expressed as empirical generalizations derived from observed regularities, could not go much further in accounting for what goes on between a soap opera and its viewers or how, to what degree, and in what ways the world of the soap opera is assimilated into or separated off from the rest of their lives.

A good introduction to functionalism is Jay G. Blumler and Elihu Katz, eds. *The Uses of*

*Mass Communication* (Beverly Hills, Ca.: Sage, 1974). Although, as Adorno pointed out some years ago, functionalist research (what he called "motivation analysis") helped to move audience studies away from the stimulus-response model and opened up the possibilities of a polysemic text "used" variously by various audience groups, it fails to take into account the degree to which responses are "determined by the so-called cultural climate and over and above this through structural factors in society" ("Scientific Experiences of a European Scholar in America," p. 345). The limitations of functionalism are also discussed by David Morley in *The "Nationwide" Audience* (London: British Film Institute, 1980), pp. 4–6. Soap opera audience research from the functionalist perspective includes Ronald J. Compesi, "Gratifications of Daytime Television Serial Viewers: An Analysis of Fans of the Program *All My Children*," Ph.D. dissertation, University of Oregon, 1976; and Sally Johnstone and Robert C. Allen, "Functional Analysis of Soap Opera Viewing: A Comparison of Two Populations," paper presented at the Conference on Communication and Culture, University of Pennsylvania, 1981. The research for the latter paper was conducted during 1979 and 1980 as an initial attempt to specify differences among subaudiences for soap operas, particularly "college" and noncollege groups. The limitations of the approach employed now seem much more glaring to me than they did six years ago. The key work on agenda setting is Maxwell McCombs and Donald L. Shaw, "The Agenda-Setting Function of the Mass Media," *Public Opinion Quarterly* 36 (1972): 176–87.

Todd Gitlin discusses what he sees as the profoundly ideological implications of the "low effects" shift in "Media Sociology: The Dominant Paradigm," *Theory and Society* 6 (1978): 205–253.

See, among others, the following "profiles" of the Cultural Indicators team's analyses, published in *Journal of Communication:* "Living with Television: The Violence Profile," 26, no. 2 (Spring 1976): 173–99; "TV Violence Profile #8: the Highlights," 27, no. 2 (Spring 1977): 171–80; "Cultural Indicators: Violence Profile #9," 28, no. 3 (Summer 1978): 207; "The Demonstration of Power: Violence Profile #10," 29, no. 3 (Summer 1979): 177–96; "The Mainstreaming of America: Violence Profile #11," 30, no. 3 (Summer 1980): 19–29.

For the debate over the "Cultivation Effect," see Thomas E. Coffin and Sam Tuchman, "A Question of Validity: Some Comments on 'Apples, Oranges, and the Kitchen Sink,'" *Journal of Broadcasting* 17, no. 1 (1972–73): 31–33; Anthony N. Doob and Glenn E. MacDonald, "Television Viewing and Fear of Victimization: Is the Relationship Causal?" *Journal of Personality and Social Psychology* 37, no. 2 (1979): 170–79; Michael Eleey, George Gerbner, and Nancy Signorielli, "Validity Indeed!" *Journal of Broadcasting* 17, no. 1 (1972–73): 34–35; David Blank, "The Gerbner Violence Profile," *Journal of Broadcasting* 21, no. 3 (1977): 273–79; and the exchanges between Gerbner, et al., and Paul Hirsch in *Communication Research* 8 (1981): 3–96.

9. Bernard Berelson, *Content Analysis in Communication Research* (Glencoe, Ill.: Free Press, 1952), p. 18.

10. Mary Cassata, Thomas Skill, and Samuel O. Boadu, "Life and Death in the Daytime Television Serial: A Content Analysis," pp. 47–69; Thomas Skill and Mary Cassata, "Soap Opera Women: An Audience View," pp. 23–36; Michelle Lynn Rodina, Mary Cassata, and Thomas Skill, "Placing a 'Lid' on Television Serial Drama: An Analysis of the Lifestyles, Interpersonal Management Skills, and Demography of Daytime's Fictional Population," pp. 3–22; all in Mary Cassata and Thomas Skill, *Life on Daytime Television: Tuning-In American Serial Drama* (Norwood, N.J.: Ablex, 1983).

A second scholarly book on soap operas was published in 1983: Muriel G. Cantor and Suzanne Pingree, *The Soap Opera* (Beverly Hills: Sage, 1983). Unlike the Cassata and Skill work it is almost entirely a summary of previously published research; like the former, however, it manages to pass along a conception of the soap opera audience as "them": "It is widely accepted that the members of the soap opera audience are intellectually limited and watch soap operas because they are socially isolated, lonely, and/or emotionally deprived" (p. 127).

11. Rodina, Cassata, and Skill, "Placing a 'Lid' on Television Serial Drama," p. 5.

12. Lee Thayer, "On 'Doing' Research and 'Explaining' Things," *Journal of Communication* 33 (1983): 89.

13. David Hackett Fischer, *Historians' Fallacies* (New York: Harper and Row, 1970), pp. 90–91; Abraham Kaplan, *The Conduct of Inquiry* (New York: Harper and Row, 1968), p. 11.

14. George Comstock, "The Legacy of the Past," *Journal of Communication* 33 (1983): 47.

15. Thayer, p. 84.

16. Russell Keat, "Positivism and Statistics in Social Science," in John Irvine, Ian Miles, and Jeff Evans, eds. *Demystifying Social Statistics* (London: Pluto Books, 1979), pp. 80–81. See also Richard Bernstein, *The Restructuring of Social and Political Thought*, p. 10.


## CHAPTER 3

1. Les Brown, *Television: The Business behind the Box* (New York: Harcourt, Brace, Jovanovich, 1971), pp. 15–16.

2. Janet Staiger, "The Hollywood Mode of Production: The Construction of Divided Labor in the Film Industry," Ph.D. Dissertation, University of Wisconsin, 1981, pp. 1–24.

3. The following discussion of soap opera production is based upon interviews with a number of producers, writers, and actors, conducted between February 1981 and September 1983. It is supplemented by information taken from Harding LeMay, *Eight Years in Another World* (New York: Atheneum, 1981); Dan Wakefield, *All Her Children* (New York: Avon Books, 1976); and Muriel Cantor and Suzanne Pingree, *The Soap Opera* (Beverly Hills, Cal.: Sage, 1983).

4. Cassata and Skill's *Life on Daytime Television* contains an interview with Robert Short, for twenty years Procter and Gamble's manager of daytime programs.

5. Cantor and Pingree, p. 58.

6. Taken from David Sirota, "An Ethnomethodological Study of Soap Opera Writing," Ph.D. dissertation, Ohio State University, 1976, pp. 165–67.

7. Ibid., p. 43.

8. Interview with Nancy Franklin, 4 Feb. 1982.

9. Interview with Charita Bauer, 11 Dec. 1982.


## CHAPTER 4

1. For example, in an essay on television aesthetics Fred Schroeder sees the serial form as central, yet he omits discussion of the soap opera—despite its being the most fully realized

embodiment of the serial narrative ever produced in any medium. In his *TV: The Most Popular Art*, Horace Newcomb comes as close as any traditional critic to opening a space within the aesthetic field for soap operas, but it winds up being a very small and ill-defined space indeed. Newcomb lists intimacy and continuity as distinguishing characteristics of television art. "Television is at its best," he says, "when it offers us faces, reactions, explorations of emotions registered by human beings." Soap operas, he admits, do fulfill this criterion of intimacy to some degree. But as an illustration of how exploitation of television's intimacy has resulted in "moments of great symbolic power," Newcomb offers not a soap opera but a BBC adaptation of *The Golden Bowl*. He devalues the prime-time series because it offers no opportunity for sustained and developing characterizations: "There is no sense of continuous involvement with these characters. They have no memory. They cannot change in response to events that occur within a weekly installment, and consequently they have no history." Again, Newcomb sees soap operas overcoming this problem, but he calls them "distorted by their own stereotypical views." It is yet another BBC serialized adaptation of an accepted literary classic that Newcomb holds up as a model of "a new work of art." See Fred Schroeder, "Video Aesthetics and Serial Art," in Horace Newcomb, ed., *Television: The Critical View*, 2nd ed. (New York: Oxford University Press, 1979), pp. 407–19; Horace Newcomb, *TV: The Most Popular Art* (New York: Anchor, 1974), pp. 248–55.

2. Tzvetan Todorov, *Introduction to Poetics* (Minneapolis: University of Minnesota Press, 1981), p. 6. Jonathan Culler counterposes the poetic programmatic with that of traditional criticism:

> In this critical climate [that dominated by the precepts of New Criticism] it is therefore important . . . to take up a tendentious position and maintain that while the experience of literature may be an experience of interpreting work, in fact the interpretation of individual works is only tangentially related to the understanding of literature. To engage in the study of literature is not to produce yet another interpretation of *King Lear* but to advance one's understanding of the conventions and operations of an institution, a mode of discourse. *The Pursuit of Signs* [London: Routledge and Kegan Paul, 1981], p. 5.)

3. Theodor W. Adorno, "Scientific Experiences of a European Scholar in America," in Donald Fleming and Bernard Bailyn, eds., *The Intellectual Migration: Europe and America, 1930–1960* (Cambridge: Harvard University Press, 1969), p. 344. In the "Ferment in the Field" issue of *Journal of Communication* (Summer 1983) not one of the thirty-five essays explicitly addresses the need for textual analysis of mass media programming.

4. Jonathan Culler, "Prolegomena to a Theory of Reading," in Susan Suleiman and Inge Crossman, eds., *The Reader in the Text: Essays in Audience and Interpretation* (Princeton: Princeton University Press, 1980), p. 49.

5. As Suleiman and Crossman note, audience-oriented or reader-response criticism "is not one field but many, not a single widely trodden path but a multiplicity of crisscrossing, often divergent tracks that cover a vast area of the critical landscape in a pattern whose complexity dismays the brave and confounds the faint of heart." See their "Introduction: Varieties of Audience-Oriented Criticism," in *The Reader in the Text*, pp. 3–45.

On reader-response criticism (in addition to Suleiman and Crossman) see Jane P. Tompkins, ed., *Reader-Response Criticism: From Formalism to Post-Structuralism* (Baltimore: Johns Hopkins University Press, 1980); Robert Holub, *Reception Theory* (London: Methuen, 1984); and Steven Mailloux, *Interpretive Conventions: The Reader in the Study of American Literature* (Ithaca: Cornell University Press, 1982).

The key English translations of Wolfgang Iser are *The Implied Reader: Patterns of Communication in Prose Fiction from Bunyan to Beckett* (Baltimore: Johns Hopkins University Press, 1974) and *The Act of Reading: A Theory of Aesthetic Reception* (Baltimore: Johns Hopkins University Press, 1978). Those of Hans Robert Jauss are *Toward an Aesthetic of Reception* (Minneapolis: University of Minnesota Press, 1982) and *Aesthetic Experience and Literary Hermeneutics* (Minneapolis: University of Minnesota Press, 1982).

6. Iser, *The Act of Reading*, p. 18.

7. This discussion of the classical Hollywood narrative style is based upon David Bordwell, Janet Staiger, and Kristin Thompson, *The Classical Hollywood Cinema: Film Style and Mode of Production to 1960* (London: Routledge and Kegan Paul, forthcoming). I am grateful to the authors for allowing me advance access to their manuscript.

8. One exception to this generalization is the lighting in *The Young and the Restless*, in which the background is left in shadow. The function of this lighting strategy, however, is not to call attention to itself but to draw the eye away from the set and toward the characters.

9. The soap opera is by no means the only popular narrative form to evince an elaborate paradigmatic structure. See, for example, Charles F. Altman, "The American Film Musical: Paradigmatic Structure and Mediatory Function," *Wide Angle* 2 (1978): 10–17; and Jane Feuer, "The Self-Reflexive Musical and the Myth of Entertainment," *Quarterly Review of Film Studies* 2 (1977): 313–26.

10. Shlomith Rimmon-Kenan, *Narrative Fiction: Contemporary Poetics* (London: Methuen, 1983), p. 51.

11. Iser, *The Act of Reading*, p. 109.

12. Ibid., pp. 109–12.

13. Quoted by Iser, p. 66.

14. Ibid., pp. 190–91. See also, Iser, "Indeterminacy and the Reader's Response in Prose Fiction," in J. Hillis Miller, ed., *Aspects of Narrative* (New York: Columbia University Press, 1971), pp. 1–45.

15. Sandy Flitterman, "The *Real* Soap Operas: TV Commercials," in E. Ann Kaplan, ed. *Regarding Television* (Frederick, Md.: University Publications of America, 1983), pp. 84–96.

16. Umberto Eco, *The Role of the Reader: Explorations in the Semiotics of Texts* (Bloomington: Indiana University Press, 1979), pp. 1–11.

17. Ellen Seiter, "The Role of the Woman Reader: Eco's Narrative Theory and Soap Operas," *Tabloid* 6 (1981). See also in *Regarding Television*, Robert C. Allen, "On Reading Soap Operas: A Semiotic Primer," pp. 97–108.

18. Richard Dyer, *Stars* (London: British Film Institute, 1979).

19. Sari Thomas, "The Relationship between Daytime Serials and Their Viewers," Ph.D. dissertation, University of Pennsylvania, 1977.

20. See Holub, pp. 96–101.

21. Tania Modleski, *Loving with a Vengeance* (Hamden, Conn.: Archon Books, 1982), p. 87. All subsequent references are to this book's chapter on soap operas, "The Search for Tomorrow in Today's Soap Operas," pp. 85–109.

22. See, for example, Laura Mulvey's influential essay, "Visual Pleasure and Narrative Cinema," *Screen* 16 (Autumn 1975): 6–18; reprinted in Karyn Kay and Gerald Pearcy, eds., *Women and the Cinema* (New York: Dutton, 1977), pp. 412–28.

23. Julia Kristeva, "Women's Time," *Signs* 7 (1981): 16.

## CHAPTER 5

1. Eric Barnouw, *Tube of Plenty: The Evolution of American Television* (New York: Oxford University Press, 1975), pp. 72–73, 249–50.

2. Raymond William Stedman, "A History of the Broadcasting of Daytime Serial Dramas in the United States," Ph.D. dissertation, University of Southern California, 1959. Cantor and Pingree base their discussion of the historical development of soap operas largely on Stedman.

3. Hayden White, *Metahistory: The Historical Imagination in Nineteenth Century Europe* (Baltimore: Johns Hopkins University Press, 1973).

4. See Carl Hempel's "Reasons and Covering Laws in Historical Explanation" in Patrick Gardiner, ed., *The Philosophy of History* (Oxford: Oxford University Press, 1974), pp. 90–105; William Aydelotte, *Quantification in History* (Reading, Mass: Addison-Wesley, 1971).

5. Charles Beard, "That Noble Dream," in Fritz Stern, ed., *The Varieties of History* (New York: Meridian Books, 1956), p. 324.

6. Droysen is quoted in Jauss, *Toward an Aesthetic of Reception*, p. 63. In the same work, see also chapter 1, "Literary History as a Challenge to Literary Theory." Traditional art history is critiqued from a Marxist perspective in Nicos Hadjinicolaou, *Art History and Class Struggle* (London: Pluto Books, 1979).

7. Jauss, *Toward an Aesthetic of Reception*, p. 21.

8. Robert Holub, *Reception Theory* (London: Methuen, 1984), pp. 66–69.

9. The most fully developed consideration of the implications of realism for historical study is Gregor McLennan, *Marxism and the Methodologies of History* (London: Verso Books, 1981). See, in particular, chapters 2 and 4. As McLennan points out, "A systematic realism is only now coming onto the agenda in historiographic thinking" (p. 66).

Some note, however brief, of the basic assumptions of realism as a philosophy of science should be made here. Like empiricism, realism takes as its goal the explanation of a world, whether scientific or historical, that exists independently of the investigator. Explanatory theories must be assessed ultimately by reference to the "real" world. However, realism departs from empiricism over the nature of that reality and its explanation. As we have seen, to the empiricist explaining a phenomenon entails its subsumption under a covering law of absolute regularity. Realism regards this kind of explanation as limited in two important respects. First, empiricism oversimplifies reality by reducing it to a one-dimensional realm of observable phenomena. Second, it conflates an expression of regularity with explanation of what causes regularity. To the realist, the level of observable phenomena is but one of a multilayered structure. The regularity the empiricist observes in events is but the *effect* of processes and mechanisms at work in other layers of reality. Explanation for the realist consists of describing not only the observable layer of reality but the working of the generative mechanisms that produced observable events. What the scientist or historian studies, then, are these structures or generative mechanisms, which produce the "flux" of observable phenomena.

Theory plays a key role in this process. Since the mechanisms that underlie empirical phenomena are themselves directly unobservable, they can be constituted only by and through theory. Whereas empiricism regards theory as the largely unwarranted intrusion of subjectivity in the scientific process or, at best, merely second-level generalization, realism sees it as an indispensable component of scientific explanation. Realists, here in agreement with the more epistemologically skeptical position of conventionalism, regard the process of theory building, and, indeed, the entire scientific process, as inevitably conditioned by "conventions" of culture, ideology, language, and the investigatory mechanism itself. Unlike conventionalism, however, realism does not resign itself to a coherence theory of truth, which holds that one theory cannot be more empirically valid than another, only more logical, elegant, or useful. For the realist, a theory must be these things, but ultimately it must also be tested by its correspondence to the real.

Recognizing the impact of culture, ideology, and discourse upon inquiry while holding fast to a correspondence theory of truth relies upon the distinction between meaning and referent. Scientists or historians working from fundamentally different perspectives may seem to constitute the world in such radically different ways that their findings are incommensurable. This does not mean, however, as some conventionalists would hold, that because they take aspects of the empirical world to *mean* different things, the empirical world *is* only what they take it to mean. The real cannot be reduced to discourse, nor can we know it outside of discourse. The real exists beyond discourse even if it is known within discourses. Without this key distinction between meaning and referent, scientific inquiry is reduced to a pointlessly relativistic game and scientists themselves to mere sophists.

On realism see Roy Bhaskar, *A Realist Theory of Science* (Atlantic Highlands, N.J.: Humanities Press, 1978), p. 47. See also Rom Harre, *Philosophies of Science* (Oxford: Oxford University Press, 1972); Terry Lovell, *Pictures of Reality* (London: British Film Institute, 1980); Ted Benton, *Philosophical Foundations of the Three Sociologies* (London: Routledge and Kegan Paul, 1977); and Russell Keat and John Urry, *Social Theory as Science* (London: Routledge and Kegan Paul, 1975). The conventionalist position is outlined in Lovell. Perhaps the most influential among American conventionalist thinkers has been Thomas Kuhn, particularly his *Structure of Scientific Revolutions* (Chicago: University of Chicago Press, 1970). On the mediating power of language, see Rosalind Coward and John Ellis, *Language and Materialism* (London: Routledge and Kegan Paul, 1979). Contemporary film theory has been greatly influenced by conventionalism, particularly through the work of Louis Althusser, Jacques Lacan, and Jacques Derrida.

10. Unless otherwise noted, information on the history of soap operas and the broadcasting industry in this chapter is taken from Barnouw, Stedman, and Thurber.

11. Barnouw, pp. 56–57.

12. *Broadcasting*, 1 Dec. 1931, p. 7; 15 July 1935, p. 19.

13. For the effects of the Depression on the film industry, see Garth Jowett, *Film: The Democratic Art* (Boston: Little, Brown, 1976). Figures on magazine revenues are taken from Publisher's Information Bureau.

14. *Broadcasting*, 15 Oct. 1931, p. 15; 1 Dec. 1931, p. 7.; 1 April 1932, p. 6; 1 Dec. 1934, p. 7.

15. Barnouw, pp. 226–30; *Broadcasting*, 15 April 1932, p. 13.

16. *Broadcasting*, 15 Mar. 1932, p. 9; 1 Nov. 1931, p. 11, 32; 15 Sept. 1932, p. 15.

17. *Broadcasting*, 15 July 1935, p. 19; 15 April 1933, p. 9; 15 April 1932, p. 7.

18. Unless otherwise noted, information on Procter and Gamble is taken from Alfred Lief, *It Floats* (New York: Reinhart, 1958).

19. *Broadcasting*, 15 April 1932, p. 13.

20. Eric Barnouw, *A Tower in Babel* (New York: Oxford University Press, 1966), pp. 240–42.

21. Stedman, p. 71. Similar accounts are contained in Cantor and Pingreee (p. 43), and Robert LaGuardia, *Ma Perkins to Mary Hartman: The Illustrated History of Soap Operas* (New York: Ballantine, 1977), p. 11.

22. *Irna Phillips* vs. *WGN, Inc.*, Petition for Leave to Appeal, Supreme Court of Illinois, February Term, 1941.

23. Proposal contained in file marked "Painted Dreams—1931," Irna Phillips Collection, Wisconsin State Historical Society, Madison, Wisconsin. Hereafter cited as Phillips Collection.

24. *Irna Phillips* vs. *WGN, Inc.*, Petition for Leave to Appeal, p. 10.

25. *Irna Phillips* vs. *WGN, Inc.*, Answer to Petition for Leave to Appeal, Supreme Court of Illinois, February Term, 1941, p. 36.

26. Audition script for *Today's Children*, 24 Oct. 1932, Phillips Collection. At this time, NBC believed such mailhook responses to represent 1–3 percent of the program's total audience (*Irna Phillips* vs. *WGN, Inc.*, Answer to Petition for Leave to Apppeal, p. 28).

27. Letter, C. H. Gager to Irna Phillips, 17 Nov. 1932; "Suggested Tie-In for 'La France'; and 'Satina' with the Story of *Today's Children*," handwritten draft proposal; letter, Irna Phillips to C. H. Gager, 4 Jan. 1933, all in Phillips Collection.

28. *Broadcasting*, 1 March 1935, p. 12.

29. Lief, pp. 176–78.

30. Stedman, pp. 73–86.

31. *Broadcasting*, 1 Oct. 1934, p. 22; 15 June 1936, p. 20; 15 Feb. 1938, p. 40; 1 May 1939, p. 30; 15 May 1938, p. 34.

32. *Broadcasting*, 1 Dec. 1934, p. 11; 15 Mar. 1935; 15 Mar. 1938, p. 34.

33. *Broadcasting*, 15 May 1938, p. 34; Lief, p. 180; *Broadcasting*, 1 Jan. 1938, p. 20; 1 May 1937, p. 11.

34. Proposal for *Masquerade* (1935); proposal for *Office Girl* (1933); script for *The Guiding Light*, 16 May 1938, all in Phillips Collection.

35. Stedman, pp. 155–56; *Broadcasting*, 13 Jan. 1941, p. 19; 18 Jan. 1941, p. 11; *Broadcasting Yearbook*, 1943, p. 48.

36. George Wiley, "End of an Era: The Daytime Radio Serial," *Journal of Broadcasting 5* (Spring 1961): 97–115; *Broadcasting*, 24 May 1943, p. 44.

37. *Billboard*, 18 Dec. 1943, p. 8; *Broadcasting Yearbook*, 1943; Lief, p. 228.

38. Stedman, pp. 205–7.

39. Barnouw, *Tube of Plenty*, p. 114; Fredric Stuart, "The Effects of Television on the Motion Picture Industry," in Gorham Kindem, ed., *The American Movie Industry* (Carbondale, Ill.: Southern Illinois University Press, 1982), pp. 257–307.

40. Lief, pp. 246–56.

41. Letter, Irna Phillips to William Ramsey, 7 Sept. 1948, Phillips Collection. The direct use of the sponsor's product in dramatic programming that Phillips envisioned did not come to pass. Section 317 of the Communications Act of 1934 required the separation of commercial messages from the programming in which they were imbedded. While, as Phillips indicates, this mandate was frequently violated on radio, broadcasters were wary of flouting the law on television in so flagrant a fashion. So far as I can determine, television soap operas have avoided the diegetic representation of recognizable brands.

42. *Newsweek*, 24 Sept. 1951, p. 57.

43. "Problems of TV Soap Opera," *Sponsor*, Jan. 1951, p. 63; *Broadcasting*, 15 Feb. 1938,

p. 18; Gilbert Seldes, "Darkness before Noon," *Saturday Review of Literature*, 5 Dec. 1953, pp. 53–54.

44. *Newsweek*, 14 July 1952, p. 85; 1 Feb. 1954, p. 74.

45. Stedman, p. 255; *Variety*, 25 Sept. 1957, pp. 38–39, quoted in Stedman, p. 274.

46. Wylie, p. 102.

47. *Broadcasting*, 7 Nov. 1977, p. 35; 11 Aug. 1975, p. 32.

48. "They're Watching," ABC-TV Brochure, 1982.

## CHAPTER 6

1. H. R. Jauss, *Toward an Aesthetic of Reception*, (Minneapolis: University of Minnesota Press, 1982), p. 20.

2. Tony Bennett, "Text and Social Process: The Case of James Bond," *Screen Education* 41 (1982): 6–7.

3. Stuart Hall, "Introduction to Media Studies at the Centre," in Stuart Hall, Dorothy Hobson, Andrew Lowe, and Paul Willis, eds., *Culture, Media, and Language* (London: Hutchinson, 1980), pp. 117–22. See also in the same volume, Hall's "Encoding/Decoding," pp. 128-38; and David Morley's "Texts, Readers, Subjects," pp. 163–73.

4. Hall, "Introduction," p. 134.

5. Unless otherwise noted, information on the social and economic status of women during the 1930s is taken from Susan Ware, *Holding Their Own: American Women in the 1930s* (Boston: Twayne, 1982); Carl Degler, *Against the Odds: Women and the Family in America from the Revolution to the Present* (New York: Oxford University Press, 1980); and Mary W. M. Hargreaves, "Darkness before the Dawn: The Status of Working Women in the Depression Years," in Mabel E. Deutrich and Virginia C. Purdy, eds., *Clio Was a Woman: Studies in the History of American Women* (Washington: Howard University Press, 1980).

6. Hadley Cantril, ed., *Public Opinion, 1935–1946* (Princeton: Princeton University Press, 1951), p. 1044.

7. Robert Lynd and Helen Lynd, *Middletown in Transition: A Study in Cultural Conflicts* (New York: Harcourt, Brace, 1937), p. 176.

8. Ware, pp. 2–7. The Eleanor Roosevelt quotation is from *It's Up to Women* (New York: Frederick A. Stokes, 1933), p. 8, quoted by Ware, p. 2.

9. *Ma Perkins*, 12 Dec. 1933, recorded transcription, Museum of Broadcasting, New York.

10. Muriel G. Cantor and Suzanne Pingree, *The Soap Opera* (Beverly Hills, Ca.: Sage, 1983), pp. 20–22; Raymond William Stedman, "A History of the Broadcasting of Daytime Serials in the United States," Ph.D. dissertation, University of Southern California, 1959, pp. 110–11; Tania Modleski, *Loving with a Vengeance* (Hamden, Conn.: Archon Books, 1982), pp. 88–91.

11. For an overview of the controversy, see Mary Kelley, "The Sentimentalists: Promise and Betrayal in the Home," *Signs* 4 (Spring 1979), pp. 434–46. See also Herbert Ross Brown, *The Sentimental Novel in America, 1789–1860* (Durham: Duke University Press, 1940); Helen Papashvily, *All the Happy Endings: A Study of the Domestic Novel in America, the Women Who Wrote It, the Women Who Read It, in the Nineteenth Century* (New York: Harper and Row, 1956); Ann Douglas, *The Feminization of American Culture* (New York: Knopf, 1977); Nina Baym, *Woman's Fiction: A Guide to Novels by and about Women in*

*America, 1820–1870* (Ithaca, N.Y.: Cornell University Press, 1978); Henry Nash Smith, "The Scribbling Woman and the Cosmic Success Story," *Critical Inquiry* 1 (Sept. 1974): 47–70; Dee Garrison, "Immoral Fiction in the Late Victorian Library," *American Quarterly* 28 (Spring 1976): 71—89; Barbara Welter, "The Cult of True Womanhood, 1820–1860," *American Quarterly* 18 (Summer 1966): 151–74.

12. Nancy Cott, Introduction to *The Roots of Bitterness: Documents of the Social History of American Women*, ed. Nancy Cott (New York: Dutton, 1972), p. 12. See also Degler, pp. 26–28; Douglas, p. 8.

13. Degler, pp. 27–28. As Degler points out, the doctrine of the two spheres was an "ideological construct," rather than a universal description of the way people behaved. Social historians have demonstrated that women were essential actors in the expansion of the nation into the western wilderness, where they assumed tasks that were anything but "lady-like." Also Nancy Cott reminds us that at the same time that women were being represented as angels of the hearth, women were entering the industrial work force for the first time in large numbers: "While the upwardly-mobile middle class cultivated the inspirational domestic role of the female as synonymous with 'the lady,' early factories in the Northeast found female industrial labor available, cheap, and malleable" (p. 12).

14. Douglas, p. 12; Baym, p. 27; Kelley, pp. 437–45. The Augusta Evans Wilson quote is from her novel *St. Elmo* (New York: G. W. Carleton, 1866), p. 526, quoted by Kelley, p. 442.

15. Papashvily, p. 4; Frank Luther Mott, *A History of American Magazines, 1885–1905* (Cambridge: Harvard University Press, 1957), pp. 353, 365.

16. Baym, p. 50; Mary V. Terhune, *Marion Harland's Autobiography* (New York: Harper and Row, 1910), pp. 482–84.

17. Sheila Rothman, *Woman's Proper Place: A History of Changing Ideals and Practices 1870 to the Present* (New York: Basic Books, 1978), pp. 97–217.

18. Douglas, p. 67; Cott, p. 24.

19. Degler, pp. vi–viii; Papashvily, p. 14; Modleski, pp. 15–26.

20. Hall, p. 136.

21. Baym, p. 144.

22. Iser, p. 100–101. The other three types of perspective arrangements, in descending order of hierarchical solidarity, are oppositional, echelon, and serial.

23. Shlomith Rimmon-Kenan, *Narrative Fiction: Contemporary Poetics* (London: Methuen, 1983), pp. 86–100; Seymour Chatman, *Story and Discourse* (Ithaca, N.Y.: Cornell University Press, 1978), p. 151.

24. Quoted in Stedman. p. 164.

25. *Today's Children*, 20 Dec. 1933, "Closing Announcement," typescript, Irna Phillips Collection; *Ma Perkins*, 13 Dec. 1933, recorded transcription, Museum of Broadcasting.

26. *The Guiding Light*, 4 July 1950, script, Phillips Collection.

27. *The Guiding Light*, 10 Jan. 1950, script, Phillips Collection.

28. *The Guiding Light*, 7 May 1952, script, Phillips Collection.

29. *The Guiding Light*, 6 June 1947, 30 May 1956, script, Phillips Collection.

30. *The Guiding Light*, 16 May 1938, script; *Today's Children*, 24 Oct. 1932, audition script, Phillips Collection.

31. The 3 Jan. 1938 episode "concluded" a five-and-one-half-year run of the serial. It was resurrected by Phillips in 1943 and ran for several more years.

32. *Today's Children*, 3 Jan. 1938, script; *The Guiding Light*, n.d., script, Phillips Collection. See also Stedman, pp. 168–69.

33. *The Guiding Light*, 22 Dec. 1950, 7 May 1952, 2 July 1952, and 5 Mar. 1956 scripts, Phillips Collection.

34. Sandy Flitterman, "The *Real* Soap Operas: TV Commercials," in E. Ann Kaplan, ed., *Regarding Television* (Frederick, Md.: University Publications of America, 1983), pp. 84–96.

35. Letter, Irna Phillips to William Ramsey, 3 Mar. 1942, Phillips Collection.

36. Iser, pp. 101–2.

37. Hall, p. 134.

38. Ware, p. 17.

39. Eleanor F. Straub, "Women in the Civilian Labor Force," in *Clio Was a Woman*, pp. 206–26; Degler, p. 418.

40. Rothman, p. 231.

41. Degler, pp. 430–31.

42. Letter, Irna Phillips to William Ramsey, 12 Feb. 1949, Phillips Collection.

43. Hall, p. 134.

## AFTERWORD

1. Robert Holub, *Reception Theory* (London: Methuen, 1984), pp. 141–46; Tony Bennett, "Marxism and Popular Fiction," *Literature and History* 7 (1981): 130–65; Annette Kuhn, "Women's Genres," *Screen* 75 (1984): 18–28.

2. David Morley, *The "Nationwide" Audience* (London: British Film Institute, 1980), p. 14. See also, Charlotte Brunsdon and David Morley, *Everyday Television: "Nationwide"* (London: British Film Institute, 1978).

3. Morley, p. 163.

4. Janice Radway, *Reading the Romance: Women, Patriarchy, and Popular Literature* (Chapel Hill: University of North Carolina Press, 1984), p. 8.

# Bibliography

Adorno, Theodor W. "Scientific Experiences of a European Scholar in America." In *The Intellectual Migration: Europe and America, 1930–1960*, edited by Donald Fleming and Bernard Bailyn, pp. 338–70. Cambridge: Harvard University Press, 1969.

Allen Robert C. "On Reading Soap Operas: A Semiotic Primer." In *Regarding Television*, edited by E. Ann Kaplan, pp. 97–108. Frederick, Md.: University Publications of America, 1983.

Altman, Charles F. "The American Film Musical: Paradigmatic Structure and Mediatory Function." *Wide Angle* 2 (1978): 10–17.

"Among New Words." *American Speech* 20 (1945): 145.

"Are Soap Operas Only Suds?" *New York Times Magazine*, 28 March 1943, pp. 19, 36.

Atkins, Liz, and Jarrett, David. "The Significance of 'Significance Texts.'" In *Demystifying Social Statistics*, edited by John Irvine, Ian Miles, and Jeff Evans. London: Pluto Press, 1979.

Aydelotte, William. *Quantification in History*. Reading, Mass.: Addison-Wesley, 1971.

Barnouw, Eric. *A Tower in Babel*. New York: Oxford University Press, 1966.

———. *Tube of Plenty: The Evolution of American Television*. New York: Oxford University Press, 1975.

Barthes, Roland. *Critique et Verite*. Paris: Seuil, 1966.

———. *S/Z*. Translated by Richard Miller. New York: Hill and Wang, 1974.

Baym, Nina. *Woman's Fiction: A Guide to Novels by and about Women in America, 1820–1870*. Ithaca: Cornell University Press, 1978.

Beard, Charles. "That Noble Dream." In *The Varieties of History*, edited by Fritz Stern, pp. 314–28. New York: Meridian Books, 1956.

Bennett, Tony. "Marxism and Popular Fiction." *Literature and History* 7 (1981): 138–65.

———. "Text and Social Process: The Case of James Bond." *Screen Education* 41 (1982): 3–14.

Benton, Ted. *Philosophical Foundations of the Three Sociologies*. London: Routledge and Kegan Paul, 1977.

Berelson, Bernard. *Content Analysis in Communication Research*. Glencoe, Ill.: Free Press, 1952.

Bernstein, Richard. *The Restructuring of Social and Political Thought*. New York: Harcourt, Brace Jovanovich, 1976.

Best, Katherine. "Literature of the Air." *Saturday Review of Literature*, 20 April 1940, pp. 11–13, 16.

Beville, H. M. "The ABCD's of Radio Audiences." *Public Opinion Quarterly* 4 (1940): 195–206.

————. "Social Stratification of the Radio Audience." Princeton: Princeton Radio Research Project, 1939.

Bhaskar, Roy. *A Realist Theory of Science*. Atlantic Highlands, N.J.: Humanities Press, 1978.

Blank, David. "The Gerbner Violence Profile." *Journal of Broadcasting* 21 (1977): 273–79.

Blumler, Jay, and Katz, Elihu, eds. *The Uses of Mass Communication*. Beverly Hills, Ca.: Sage, 1974.

Booth, Wayne C. *The Rhetoric of Fiction*. Chicago: University of Chicago Press, 1961.

Bordwell, David; Staiger, Janet; and Thompson, Kristin. *The Classical Hollywood Cinema: Film Style and Mode of Production to 1960*. London: Routledge and Kegan Paul, forthcoming.

"Broadcast Serial Audience Not Typed." *Broadcasting*, 26 April 1943, p. 19.

Brown, Herbert Ross. *The Sentimental Novel in America: 1789-1860*. Durham: Duke University Press, 1940.

Brown, Les. *Television: The Business behind the Box*. New York: Harcourt, Brace Jovanovich, 1971.

Brunsdon, Charlotte, and Morley, David. *Everyday Television: "Nationwide."* London: British Film Institute, 1978.

Buerkel-Rothfuss, Nancy L., and Mayes, Sandra. "Soap Opera Viewing: The Cultivation Effect." *Journal of Communication* 31 (Summer 1981): 108–15.

Buermeyer, Laurence. "The Aesthetic Experience." Merion, Pa.: Barnes Foundation Press, 1924.

Cantor, Muriel, and Pingree, Suzanne. *The Soap Opera*. Beverly Hills, Ca.: Sage, 1983.

Cantril, Hadley, ed. *Public Opinion, 1935–46*. Princeton: Princeton University Press, 1951.

Carey, James. "The Origins of the Radical Discourse on Cultural Studies in the United States." *Journal of Communication* 33 (Summer 1983): 311–13.

Carswell, E. A., and Rommelveit, Ragnar. *Social Contexts of Messages*. London: Academic Press, 1971.

Cassata, Mary, and Skill, Thomas, eds. *Life on Daytime Television: Tuning-In American Serial Drama*. Norwood, N.J.: Ablex, 1983.

Cassata, Mary; Skill, Thomas; and Boadu, Samuel O. "Life and Death in the Daytime Television Serial: A Content Analysis." In *Life on Daytime Television: Tuning-In American Serial Drama*, edited by Mary Cassata and Thomas Skill, pp. 23–36. Norwood, N.J.: Ablex, 1983.

Chatman, Seymour. *Story and Discourse*. Ithaca: Cornell University Press, 1979.

Coffin, Thomas E., and Tuchman, Sam. "A Question of Validity: Some Comments on 'Apples, Oranges, and the Kitchen Sink.'" *Journal of Broadcasting* 17 (1972-73): 31–33.

Collins, M., and Riley, Olive L. *Art Appreciation for Junior and Senior High Schools*. New York: Harcourt, Brace, 1937.

Compesi, Ronald J. "Gratifications of Daytime Television Serial Viewers: An Analysis of Fans of the Program *All My Children*." Ph.D. dissertation, University of Oregon, 1976.

Comstock, George. "The Legacy of the Past." *Journal of Communication* 33 (Summer 1983): 42–50.

Cook, Whitfield. "Be Sure to Listen In." *American Mercury*, March 1940, pp. 316–20.

Cott, Nancy, ed. *The Roots of Bitterness: Documents of the Social History of American Women*. New York: Dutton, 1972.

Coward, Rosalind, and Ellis, John. *Language and Materialism*. London: Routledge and Kegan Paul, 1979.

Culler, Jonathan. "Prolegomena to a Theory of Reading." In *The Reader in the Text: Essays in Audience and Interpretation*, edited by Susan Sulieman and Inge Crossman, pp. 44–66. Princeton: Princeton University Press, 1980.

———. *The Pursuit of Signs*. London: Routledge and Kegan Paul, 1981.

"Daylight and Drama—Salesmen for Flour." *Broadcasting*, 1 March 1935, p. 12.

Degler, Carl. *Against the Odds: Women and the Family in America from the Revolution to the Present*. New York: Oxford University Press, 1980.

Dennison, Merrill. "Soap Opera." *Harper's*, April 1940, pp. 498–505.

Doob, Anthony N., and MacDonald, Glenn E. "Television Viewing and Fear of Victimization: Is the Relationship Causal?" *Journal of Personality and Social Psychology* 37 (1979): 170–79.

Douglas, Ann. *The Feminization of American Culture*. New York: Knopf, 1977.

Dyer, Richard. *Stars*. London: British Film Institute, 1979.

Eco, Umberto. *The Role of the Reader: Explorations in the Semiotics of Texts*. Bloomington: Indiana University Press, 1979.

Eleey, Michael; Gerbner, George; and Signorielli, Nancy. "Validity Indeed!" *Journal of Broadcasting* 17 (1972–73): 34–35.

Feuer, Jane. "The Self-Reflexive Musical and the Myth of Entertainment." *Quarterly Review of Film Studies* 2 (1977): 313–26.

Fischer, David Hackett. *Historians' Fallacies*. New York: Harper and Row, 1970.

Flitterman, Sandy. "The Real Soap Operas: TV Commercials." In *Regarding Television*, edited by E. Ann Kaplan, pp. 84–96. Frederick, Md.: University Publications of America, 1983.

Foucault, Michel. *The Order of Things: An Archaeology of the Human Sciences*. New York: Vintage Books, 1973.

Garrison, Dee. "Immoral Fiction in the Late Victorian Library." *American Quarterly* 28 (Spring 1976): 71–89.

Gerbner, George, et al. "Cultural Indicators: Violence Profile #9." *Journal of Communication* 28 (Summer 1978): 207.

———. "A Curious Journey into the Scary World of Paul Hirsch." *Communication Research* 8 (January 1981): 39–72.

———. "The Demonstration of Power: Violence Profile #10." *Journal of Communication* 29 (Summer 1979): 177–96.

———. "Final Reply to Hirsch." *Communication Research* 8 (July 1981): 259–80.

———. "Living with Television: The Violence Profile." *Journal of Communication* 26 (Spring 1976): 173–99.

———. "The Mainstreaming of America: Violence Profile #11." *Journal of Communication* 30 (Summer 1980): 19–29.

———. "TV Violence Profile #8: The Highlights." *Journal of Communication* 27 (Spring 1977): 171–80.

Gitlin, Todd. "Media Sociology: The Dominant Paradigm." *Theory and Society* 6 (1978): 205–53.

Hadjinicolaou, Nicos. *Art History and Class Struggle*. London: Pluto Press, 1978.

# Bibliography

Haight, Timothy R. "The Critical Researcher's Dilemma." *Journal of Communication* 33 (Summer 1983): 226–37.

Hall, Stuart. "Encoding/Decoding." In *Culture, Media, and Language*, edited by Stuart Hall, Dorothy Hobson, Andrew Lowe, and Paul Willis, pp. 128–39. London: Hutchinson, 1980.

———. "Introduction to Media Studies at the Centre." In *Culture, Media, and Language*, edited by Stuart Hall, Dorothy Hobson, Andrew Lowe, and Paul Willis, pp. 117–22. London: Hutchinson, 1980.

Hargreaves, Mary W. M. "Darkness before the Dawn: The Status of Working Women in the Depression Years." In *Clio Was a Woman: Studies in the History of American Women*, edited by Mabel E. Deutrich and Virginia C. Purdy, pp. 178–88. Washington: Howard University Press, 1980.

Harre, Rom. *Philosophies of Science*. Oxford: Oxford University Press, 1972.

Harris, Mark. "Easy Does It Not." In *The Living Novel*, edited by Granville Hicks, pp. 113–16. New York: Macmillan, 1957.

Hempel, Carl. "Reasons and Covering Laws in Historical Explanation." In *The Philosophy of History*, edited by Patrick Gardiner, pp. 90–105. Oxford: Oxford University Press, 1974.

Herzog, Herta. "What Do We Really Know about Daytime Serial Listeners?" In *Radio Research, 1942-43*, edited by Paul Lazarsfeld and Frank Stanton, pp. 3–33. New York: Duell, Sloan and Pearce, 1944.

Hirsch, Paul M. "Distinguishing Good Speculation from Bad Theory." *Communication Research* 8 (January 1981): 73–96.

———. "On Not Learning from One's Own Mistakes." *Communication Research* 8 (January 1981): 3–38.

Holub, Robert. *Reception Theory*. London: Methuen, 1984.

"The Hummert's Super Soaps." *Newsweek*, 10 Jan. 1944, pp. 79–80.

Huyghe, René. *Les Puissances de l'image, bilan d'une psychologie de l'art*. Paris: Flammarion, 1965.

Iser, Wolfgang. *The Act of Reading: A Theory of Aesthetic Response*. Baltimore: Johns Hopkins University Press, 1978.

———. *The Implied Reader: Patterns of Communication in Prose Fiction from Bunyan to Beckett*. Baltimore: Johns Hopkins University Press, 1978.

———. "Indeterminacy and the Reader's Response in Prose Fiction." In *Aspects of Narrative*, edited by J. Hillis Miller, pp. 1–45. New York: Columbia University Press, 1971.

Jameson, Fredric. *The Political Unconscious*. Ithaca: Cornell University Press, 1981.

Jauss, Hans Robert. *Aesthetic Experience and Literary Hermeneutics*. Minneapolis: University of Minnesota Press, 1982.

———. *Toward an Aesthetic of Reception*. Minneapolis: University of Minnesota Press, 1982.

Johnstone, Sally, and Allen, Robert C.. "Functional Analysis of Soap Opera Viewing: A Comparison of Two Populations." Unpublished paper, University of North Carolina, 1981.

Jowett, Garth. *Film: The Democratic Art*. Boston: Little, Brown, 1976.

Kaplan, Abraham. *The Conduct of Inquiry*. New York: Harper and Row, 1968.

# Bibliography

Katz, Elihu, and Lazarsfeld, Paul. *Personal Influence: The Part Played by People in the Flow of Mass Communications*. New York: Free Press, 1955.

Katzman, Natan. "Television Soap Operas: What's Been Going on Anyway?" *Public Opinion Quarterly* 36 (1972): 200–12.

Keat, Russell. "Positivism and Statistics in Social Science." In *Demystifying Social Statistics*, edited by John Irvine, Ian Miles, and Jeff Evans. London: Pluto Books, 1979.

Keat, Russell, and Urry, John. *Social Theory as Science*. London: Routledge and Kegan Paul, 1975.

Kelley, Mary. "The Sentimentalists: Promise and Betrayal in the Home." *Signs* 4 (1979): 434–46.

Kristeva, Julia. "Women's Time." *Signs* 7 (1981): 13–35.

Kuhn, Thomas. *The Structure of Scientific Revolutions*. 2nd edition. Chicago: University of Chicago Press, 1969.

LaGuardia, Robert. *Ma Perkins to Mary Hartman: The Illustrated History of Soap Operas*. New York: Ballantine, 1977.

Lazarsfeld, Paul. "An Episode in the History of Social Research: A Memoir." In *The Intellectual Migration: Europe and America, 1930-1960*, edited by Donald Fleming and Bernard Bailyn, pp. 270–337. Cambridge: Harvard University Press, 1969.

Lazarsfeld, Paul, and Field, Harry. *The People Look at Radio*. Chapel Hill: University of North Carolina Press, 1946.

Lemay, Harding. *Eight Years in Another World*. New York: Atheneum, 1981.

Lief, Alfred. *It Floats*. New York: Rinehart, 1958.

Lovell, Terry. *Pictures of Reality*. London: British Film Institute, 1980.

Lynd, Robert, and Lynd, Helen. *Middletown in Transition: A Study in Cultural Conflicts*. New York: Harcourt, Brace, 1937.

McCoombs, Maxwell, and Shaw, Donald. "The Agenda-Setting Function of the Mass Media." *Public Opinion Quarterly* 36 (1972): 176–87.

MacDonald, Dwight. "A Theory of Mass Culture." *Diogenes* 3 (Summer 1953): 10–17.

Macherey, Pierre. *A Theory of Literary Production*. London: Routledge and Kegan Paul, 1978.

McLennan, Gregor. *Marxism and the Methodologies of History*. London: Verso Books, 1981.

Mailloux, Steven. *Interpretive Conventions: The Reader in the Study of American Literature*. Ithaca: Cornell University Press, 1982.

Mannes, Marya. "Massive Detergence." *Reporter*, 6 July 1961, pp. 39–42.

Margolis, Joseph. *The Language of Art and Art Criticism*. Detroit: Wayne State University Press, 1965.

Melody, William H. and Mansell, Robin E. "The Debate over Critical vs. Administrative Research: Circularity or Challenge." *Journal of Communication* 33 (Summer 1983): 103–16.

Miller, Gerald. "Taking Stock of a Discipline." *Journal of Communication* 33 (Summer 1983): 31–49.

Modleski, Tania. *Loving with a Vengeance: Mass-Produced Fantasies for Women*. Hamden, Conn.: Archon Books, 1982.

Morley, David. *The "Nationwide" Audience*. London: British Film Institute, 1980.

Mott, Frank Luther. *A History of American Magazines, 1885–1905*. Cambridge: Harvard University Press, 1957.

Mulvey, Laura. "Visual Pleasure and Narrative Cinema." *Screen* 16 (Autumn 1975): 6–18.

Newcomb, Horace. *TV: The Most Popular Art*. New York: Doubleday, Anchor, 1974.

Ortega y Gasset, Jose. *The Revolt of the Masses*. London: George Allen and Unwin, 1932.

Papashvily, Helen. *All the Happy Endings: A Study of the Domestic Novel in America, the Women Who Wrote It, the Women Who Read It, in the Nineteenth Century*. New York: Harper and Row, 1956.

Phillips, Irna. Personal and Business Papers. Film and Manuscripts Archive, State Historical Society of Wisconsin, Madison.

Porter, Dennis. "Soap Time: Thoughts on a Commodity Art Form." In *Television: The Critical View*, 3rd ed., edited by Horace Newcomb, pp. 122–31. New York: Oxford University Press, 1982.

"Problems of TV Soap Opera." *Sponsor*, January 1951, p. 63.

Radway, Janice. *Reading the Romance: Women, Patriarchy, and Popular Literature*. Chapel Hill: University of North Carolina Press, 1984.

Rimmon-Kenan, Shlomith. *Narrative Fiction: Contemporary Poetics*. London: Methuen, 1983.

Rodina, Michelle Lynn; Cassata, Mary; and Skill, Thomas. "Placing a 'Lid' on Television Serial Drama: An Analysis of the Lifestyles, Interpersonal Management Skills, and Demography of Daytime's Fictional Population." In *Life on Daytime Television: Tuning-In American Serial Drama*, edited by Mary Cassata and Thomas Skill, pp. 3–22. Norwood, N.J.: Ablex, 1983.

Rogers, Everett M. "The Empirical and the Critical Schools of Communication Research." *Communication Yearbook 5* (1982): 125–43.

Roosevelt, Eleanor. *It's Up to Women*. New York: Frederick A. Stokes, 1933.

Rothman, Sheila. *Woman's Proper Place: A History of Changing Ideals and Practices 1870 to the Present*. New York: Basic Books, 1978.

Schroeder, Fred. "Video Aesthetics and Serial Art." In *Television: The Critical View*, 2nd ed., edited by Horace Newcomb, pp. 407–19. New York: Oxford University Press, 1979.

Seiter, Ellen. "The Role of the Woman Reader: Eco's Narrative Theory and Soap Operas." *Tabloid 6* (1981).

Seldes, Gilbert. "Darkness before Noon." *Saturday Review of Literature*, 5 Dec. 1953, pp. 53–54.

Siepmann, Charles. *Radio's Second Chance*. Boston: Little, Brown, 1946.

Sirota, David. "An Ethnomethodological Study of Soap Opera Writing." Ph.D. dissertation, Ohio State University, 1976.

Slack, Jennifer Daryl, and Allor, Martin. "The Political and Epistemological Constituents of Critical Communication Research." *Journal of Communication* 33 (Summer 1983): 208–18.

Smith, Henry Nash. "The Scribbling Woman and the Cosmic Success Story." *Critical Inquiry* 1 (1974): 47–70.

Smythe, Dallas W., and Dinh, Tran Van. "On Critical and Administrative Research: A New Critical Analysis." *Journal of Communication* 33 (Summer 1983): 117–127.

"Soap Opera." *Fortune*, March 1946, pp. 119–24, 146–48,151–52.

"Soap Operas: Men Are Tuning In." *New York Times*, 21 Feb. 1979, section 3, p. 1.

# Bibliography

Staiger, Janet. "The Hollywood Mode of Production: The Construction of divided Labor in the Film Industry." Ph.D. dissertation, University of Wisconsin, 1981.

Stedman, Raymond William. "A History of the Broadcasting of Daytime Serial Dramas in the United States." Ph.D. dissertation, University of Southern California, 1959.

Straub, Eleanor F. "Women in the Civilian Labor Force." In *Clio Was a Woman: Studies in the History of American Women*, edited by Mabel E. Deutrich and Virginia c. Purdy, pp. 206–26. Washington: Howard University Press, 1980.

Stuart, Fredric. "The Effects of Television on the Motion Picture Industry." In *The American Movie Industry: the Business of Motion Pictures*, edited by Gorham Kindem, pp. 257–407. Carbondale: Southern Illinois University Press, 1982.

Sulieman, Susan, and Crossman, Inge, eds. *The Reader in the Text*. Princeton: Princeton University Press, 1980.

Tegler, Patricia. "The Daytime Serial: A Bibliography of Scholarly Writings,1943–1981." *Journal of Popular Culture* 16 (Winter 1982), reprinted in *Life on Daytime Television: Tuning-In American Serial Drama*, edited by Mary Cassata and Thomas Skill, pp. 187–96. Norwood, N.J.: Ablex, 1983.

Terhune, Mary V. *Marion Harland's Autobiography*. New York: Harper & Row, 1910.

Thayer, Lee. "On 'Doing' Research and 'Explaining' Things." *Journal of Communication* 33 (Summer 1983): 80–91.

"They're Watching." Brochure. ABC-Television Social Research Unit, 1982.

Thomas, Sari. "The Relationship between Daytime Serials and Their Viewers." Ph.D. dissertation, University of Pennsylvania, 1977.

Thurber, James. *The Beast in Me and Other Animals*. New York: Harcourt, Brace, 1948.

Todorov, Tzvetan. *Introduction to Poetics*. Minneapolis: University of Minnesota Press, 1981.

Tompkins, Jane P., ed. *Reader-Response Criticism: From Formalism to Post-Structuralism*. Baltimore: Johns Hopkins University Press, 1980.

van den Haag, Ernest. "Of Happiness and Despair We Have No Measure." In *Mass Media and Mass Society*, edited by Alan Casty, pp. 5–11. New York: Holt, Rinehart, and Winston, 1968.

Wakefield, Dan. *All Her Children*. New York: Avon Books, 1976.

Ware, Susan. *Holding Their Own: American Women in the 1930s*. Boston: Twayne, 1982.

Warner, W. Lloyd, and Henry, William E. "The Radio Day Time Serial: A Symbolic Analysis." *Genetic Psychology Monographs* 37 (1948): 3–71.

Welter, Barbara. "The Cult of True Womanhood, 1820–1860." *American Quarterly* 18 (Summer 1966): 151–74.

White, Hayden. *Metahistory: The Historical Imagination in Nineteenth Century Europe*. Baltimore: Johns Hopkins University Press, 1973.

Wiley, George. "End of an Era: The Daytime Radio Serial." *Journal of Broadcasting* 5 (Spring 1961): 97–115.

Willer, David, and Willer, Judith. *Systematic Empiricism: Critique of a Pseudo-Science*. Englewood Cliffs, N.J.: Prentice-Hall, 1973.

Wilson, Augusta Evans. *St. Elmo*. New York: G. W. Carleton, 1866.

Wollen, Peter. *Signs and Meanings in the Cinema*, 3rd ed., Bloomington: Indiana University Press, 1972.

Wylie, Max. "Dusting Off Dr. Berg." *Printer's Ink*, 12 Feb. 1943, p. 44.

———. "Washboard Weepers." *Harper's*, November 1942, pp. 633–38.

# Index

A&P, 106, 109
A&P Gypsies, 106
A. C. Nielsen Co., 50
Adorno, Theodor, 62, 215 (n. 16), 216 (n. 3),
    221 (n. 8)
Advertising agencies, 103, 105, 107
Aesthetics, "traditional," 12–18, 61–62,
    222–23 (n. 1)
Against the Storm, 159
All My Children, 90
Allen, Robert C., 221 (n. 8)
Althusser, Louis, 226 (n. 9)
Ameche, Don, 124
American Broadcasting Co. (ABC), 124,
    126, 127
American Federation of Radio Artists
    (AFRA), 124
American Home Products, 117
American Mercury, 11
American Speech, 8, 9
American Telephone and Telegraph Co.
    (ATT), 101
Amos and Andy, 104–5, 109, 138
Andrews, Charles Robert Douglas Hardy,
    116
Another World, 49, 127
Arthur Godfrey Show, 121, 122
As the World Turns, 57, 77, 127, 128,
    155, 169
Auteur theory, 214 (n. 12)
Aydelotte, William, 98

Barnouw, Eric, 96–97, 99, 102, 109
Barthes, Roland, 69, 83
Bauer, Charita, 56
Baym, Nora, 141, 142, 143, 144, 146, 150

Beard, Charles, 98
Bell, Clive, 12
Bennett, Tony, 15, 61, 131, 183
Berelson, Bernard, 35
Berg, Louis, 21, 26, 120, 121, 131
Bernstein, Richard, 217 (n. 5)
Best, Katherine, 11
Betty and Bob, 116
Beville, H. M., 19–20
Bhaskar, Roy, 100
Big Sister, 27
Bishop, Hazel, 122
Boadu, Samuel, 36
Breakfast at Sardi's, 121
Breakfast Club, 121
Bricolage, 137
Brighter Day, 169
Broadcasting, 10, 103, 114
Brown, Les, 45
Buerkel-Rothfuss, Nancy L., 218–20 (n. 8)
Buermeyer, Laurence, 13, 215 (n. 15)
Bureau of Applied Social Research, 20–21,
    23, 30, 216 (n. 3)

Cantor, Muriel, 49, 140, 222 (n. 10)
Capitol, 65
Capra, Frank, 128
Cassata, Mary, 36–40
Charles Revson Co., 127
Chatman, Seymour, 154
Chicago Daily News, 116
Chicago Tribune, 101
Cinema: studies of, 5, 7; Hollywood studio
    system, 46, 48; mode of production, 46–
    47, 48; classical Hollywood style, 64–69,
    71–72, 84, 167

Colgate-Palmolive Co., 122, 127

Collins, Wilkie, 14, 78

Columbia Broadcasting System (CBS), 24, 75, 102, 103, 105, 106, 109, 117, 118, 124, 125, 126, 127, 128

Columbia University. *See* Bureau of Applied Social Research

*Comfort*, 145

Comic strips, 108

Compton-Burnett, Ivy, 154

Comstock, George, 5, 42

Conventionalism, 226 (n. 9)

Cook, Whitfield, 11

*Coronation Street*, 3, 66

Cott, Nancy, 142, 229 (n. 13)

*Counterfeiters*, 160

*Couple Next Door*, 117

Crocker, Betty, 139

Crossley Ratings, 118

Culler, Jonathan, 6, 63, 223 (n. 2)

Cummins, Maria S., 140–41

*Dallas*, 57–58

*Days of Our Lives*, 169

Degler, Carl, 142, 173

Denison, Merrill, 25–26

Derrida, Jacques, 226 (n. 9)

Dickens, Charles, 14, 78

*Dictionary of American Slang*, 9

*Doctors*, 127, 169

Domestic ideology, 143–50, 171–73. *See also* Separation of spheres

Domestic novel, 140; as precedent for soap opera, 140–41; representation of women, 141–42; domestic ideology of, 142–45; relationship to Protestantism, 143–45; representation of men, 144; legacies of, 145–46; relationship to advertising, 147–48; establishing women as consumers of narratives, 148–49; relationship to soap opera, 149–50, 178. *See also* Woman's fiction

*Dreams Come True*, 117

Douglas, Ann, 143

Durr, Clifford, 26

Dyer, Richard, 89

Eco, Umberto, 81–84, 89, 91, 92, 93

*Edge of Night*, 77, 169

*Egg and I*, 125

Elder, Robert, 105

Encrustation, 8, 9, 10, 28, 61, 214 (n. 1)

Empiricism, 31; in mass communications research, 5–8, 31–44 passim, 216 (n. 3); in historiography, 6–7, 97–98; role of covering laws, 32, 43; applied to social sciences, 32–34, 35; probabilistic explanation, 33–34; null hypothesis, 33; role of theory, 33–34, 217 (n. 5); distinguished from empirical research, 34, 217 (n. 6); subject/object dichotomy, 41; applied to open systems, 41–42. *See also* Mass communications research, empiricism in

Falken-Smith, Pat, 49, 53

Federal Communications Commission (FCC), 26, 127

Feminist criticism, 91–95

"Fictitious" reader, 151, 152, 163

*First Hundred Years*, 123, 124

Fischer, David Hackett, 42

Fleming, Ian, 82

Flitterman, Sandy, 79, 167–68, 174

Foot, Cone, and Belding, 24

*Fortune*, 15, 105

*42nd Street*, 68

Foucault, Michel, 12

Fox Film Co., 103

Francis, Genie, 78, 89

Franklin, Nancy, 54, 55

Fulton, Eileen, 57

Garroway, Dave, 124

Geary, Tony, 57, 89

General Electric Co. (GE), 101

General Foods Co., 113–14, 117

*General Hospital*, 13, 49, 50, 57, 63, 78, 87, 89, 128, 155

General Mills Co., 139

*General Mills Hour*, 162

Genette, Gérard, 72

Gerbner, George, 218 (n. 8)

Gide, Andre, 160

Gilman, Harry, 111
Gitlin, Todd, 221 (n. 8)
*Godey's Lady's Book*, 145
Godfrey, Arthur, 124
*Good Housekeeping*, 147
*Good Luck Margie*, 111
*Good Morning, America*, 121
Great Depression, 103, 107, 134–36,
    139, 171
Greenburg, Clement, 16
Gross, Larry, 90, 218 (n. 8)
*Guiding Light*, 3, 13, 46, 49, 50, 56, 74, 162;
    writer's role, 53, 54; paradigmatic com-
    plexity, 71–72, 74–75, 80–81; textual
    scope, 76; characters' "deaths," 77;
    "Model Reader," 83; intertextuality, 88;
    radio origins, 117, 119–20; transition to
    television, 125; ownership by Procter and
    Gamble, 127; longevity, 151; role of nar-
    rator, 157–58; characterization in, 159–
    61; narrative structure, 164–66

Hagman, Larry, 57
Hall, Stuart, 132, 149, 174–75, 183
*Happy Hollow*, 105
Harland, Marian. *See* Terhune, Mary
    Virginia
*Harper's*, 25, 145
Harre, Rom, 100
Harris, Mark, 16
Hawthorne, Nathaniel, 140
Hempel, Carl, 98
Henry, William E., 27–28, 41
Herzog, Herta, 23, 24, 30, 134
Historiography, 6–7, 97–98; quantitative
    fallacy, 42; literary, 131–32
Hitchcock, Alfred, 68, 128
Holmes, Mary J., 141
Holub, Robert, 182
*Home Sweet Home*, 117
Horizon of expectations, 134, 137, 140,
    149–50
Horkheimer, Max, 215 (n. 16)
Hummert, Anne, 17, 116, 128, 151, 177
Hummert, Frank, 17, 116, 128, 151,
    177

Husserl, Edmund, 75
Huyghes, René, 15

Ideology, 89; of soap operas, 168–69. *See
    also* Domestic ideology
Iser, Wolfgang, 6, 63, 73, 75, 79, 84,
    91, 151–53, 154, 170–71, 172, 182,
    215 (n. 15)

Jauss, Hans Robert, 6, 75, 86, 91, 99–100,
    131, 182
Jelke Oleomargarine Co., 111
Johnstone, Sally, 221 (n. 8)
*Jollycos, The*, 108
*Journal of Communication*, 5
Joyce, James, 82
*Joyce Jordan, M.D.*, 138

Kaplan, Abraham, 42
*Kate Smith Speaks*, 121
Katz, Elihu, 218 (n. 8)
Katzman, Natan, 30
Keat, Russell, 43
Kelley, Mary, 144
Kitsch, 16–17
*Kitty Keene*, 117
KMBC, 105
Krieger, Murray, 13
Kristeva, Julia, 93
Kuhn, Annette, 183
Kuhn, Thomas, 7

Lacan, Jacques, 226 (n. 9)
*Ladies Home Journal*, 145, 147
*Lady in the Lake*, 84
*Lamplighter*, 140
Langford, Frances, 124
Lazarsfeld, Paul, 19–25, 30, 216 (n. 3),
    218 (n. 8)
Lever Brothers Co., 122
*Life Can Be Beautiful*, 159
Lotman, Juri, 77
*Love of Life*, 75, 125, 127, 169, 171
*Love Is a Many Splendored Thing*, 174
Lynd, Helen, 135
Lynd, Robert, 135

*McCall's*, 117, 145, 147
McCombs, Maxwell, 221 (n. 8)
MacDonald, Dwight, 12, 16–18
Macherey, Pierre, 214 (nn. 1, 6)
Magazines: women's, 138–39, 145–46
*Magnificent Ambersons*, 155
Mailhooks, 111, 112, 114, 116, 119, 160
Mannes, Marya, 14
*Ma Perkins*, 115, 116, 117, 118, 121, 124, 126, 137, 156, 159
Margolis, Joseph, 12, 14
Marcuse, Herbert, 215 (n. 16)
Marland, Douglas, 53
*Mary Noble: Backstage Wife*, 126, 137
*Masquerade*, 118
Mass communications research: empiricism in, 5–8, 30–31, 36–44, 62, 182, 216–17 (n. 3), 218–21 (n. 8); European, 5; critical studies, 5, 7, 62, 216–17 (n. 3); influence of Paul Lazarsfeld on, 19–20, 216 (n. 3); administrative research, 20, 21, 23, 216 (n. 3); and sociology, 20–21; and commercial broadcasters, 20–21; hypodermic theory, 21–23, 218 (n. 8); personal influence theory, 25, 218 (n. 8); content analysis, 35–40; historical, 96–98, 130–31; reception studies, 130–31; textual analysis, 131; uses-and-gratifications research, 218 (n. 8); agenda-setting theory, 218 (n. 8); cultivation paradigm, 218–20 (n. 8); functionalism, 221 (n. 8)
Mass culture, 16–18
Mayes, Sandra, 218–20 (n. 8)
Merton, Robert, 23
Mickleberry Products Co., 112
*Middletown*, 135
Miller, Gerald, 5–6, 35
Minnow, Newton, 127
Modleski, Tania, 91–94, 140, 175, 215 (n. 16)
Montgomery Ward Co., 111–12
Monty, Gloria, 87, 128
Moore, Garry, 124
Morley, David, 183–84, 214 (n. 3)
*Mrs. Blake's Radio Column*, 109
Muncie, Indiana, 135

*Name of the Rose*, 83
National Broadcasting Co. (NBC), 24, 101–2, 103, 108, 109, 114, 115, 121, 124, 126, 127, 162
*Nationwide*, 183–84
Newcomb, Horace, 223 (n. 1)
New criticism, 223 (n. 2)
*Newsweek*, 9, 124
*New York Times*, 12
Nixon, Agnes, 53, 54, 128
*Nouveau roman*, 154

*Office Girl*, 119
Ogiens, Michael, 128
*O'Neills, The*, 117
*One Life to Live*, 46, 52–53, 156
*Open Door*, 155–56
Ortega y Gasset, Jose, 16–18
*Our Gal Sunday*, 126
*Oxol Feature*, 106

*Painted Dreams*, 4, 110–12, 120, 137, 159
Papashvily, Helen, 141, 145, 148
Payne, Virginia, 126
*Pepper Young's Family*, 117
Pepsodent Co., 104, 109
Phillips, Irna, 116, 128, 151, 167, 168, 177; *Painted Dreams*, 110–12; *Today's Children*, 112–14; *Masquerade*, 118–19; *Office Girl*, 119; *Guiding Light*, 119–20, 164; doubts about television soap operas, 123; *Another World*, 127; *Love Is a Many Splendored Thing*, 171
*Pilgrim's Progress*, 152
Pillsbury Co., 19, 114, 117
Pingree, Suzanne, 49–51, 140, 222 (n. 10)
*Poetics*, 6, 61–63, 223 (n. 2); reader-oriented, 6–7, 63
*Point Sublime*, 123
Popular culture: debates over, 16–18
Porter, Dennis, 13
Prentiss, Ed, 162
Princeton University: Radio Research Project, 19–20
Procter and Gamble Co., 19, 48, 174; Procter and Gamble Productions, Inc., 49;

soap opera production strategies, 49–51; soap operas as advertising vehicles for, 50; relations with actors, 89; advertising strategies, 107–10, 122–23; involvement in radio, 108–10; radio advertising budget, 109, 117, 121; sponsorship of soap operas, 115–16, 117, 119–20, 121, 123, 125; involvement in television, 122, 125; ownership of soap operas, 126–27

Protestantism, 143, 145, 159, 172

*Psycho*, 77

*Public Opinion Quarterly*, 19, 30

*Puddle Family*, 115

Radio: networks, 101–3; audience size, 103–4, 105–10, 116, 117; as advertising medium, 103–4, 105, 108–9, 117–18; serials, 103–5, 110–22 passim; variety shows, 104–5; daytime, 105–7, 108–9, 115–16, 118, 120–21; advice shows, 108–10, 139–40; commercials, 118–20; decline of network, 122–26

*Radio Beauty School*, 108

Radio Corporation of America (RCA), 101, 102, 103

*Radio Homemakers' Club*, 108

Radio-Keith-Orpheum (RKO), 103

Ramsey, William, 123, 168

Reader-response theory, 6–7, 72–84 passim; *Rezeptionsästhetik* movement, 6; handling of reading-duration, 72–73; wandering viewpoint, 76–78; horizon of expectations, 76, 85–86, 99; treatment of history, 99–100, 131–32; "actual" readers, 182–85

Realism, 7, 100, 132, 225–26 (n. 9); in historiography, 7, 100; generative mechanisms in, 7, 100, 130, 176, 225–26 (n. 9)

*Redbook*, 147

Rimmon-Kenan, Shlomith, 72, 154, 160

R. J. Reynolds Tobacco Co., 110

*Road of Life*, 117, 126, 159

Rockefeller Foundation, 20

Rodina, Michelle Lynn, 40

Rogers, Everett M., 217 (n. 6)

*Romance of Helen Trent*, 116

Roosevelt, Eleanor, 135

Rothman, Sheila, 147, 172

*Ruth Turner's Washing Talks*, 109

*Ryan's Hope*, 47, 65

*Saturday Review of Literature*, 11

Saussure, Ferdinand de, 9

*Scarface*, 68

Schroeder, Fred, 222 (n. 1)

*Search for Tomorrow*, 73, 125, 127, 169

*Secret Storm*, 169

Sedgwick, Catharine Maria, 141

Seiter, Ellen, 91–92, 93

Seldes, Gilbert, 125

Selinger, Henry, 110, 111

Semiotics, 12

Separation of spheres, 142. *See also* Domestic ideology

Serial fiction: novels, 78–79; in magazines, 138

Shaw, Donald L., 221 (n. 8)

Short, Robert, 222 (n. 4)

Siepmann, Charles, 26

*Sisters of the Skillet*, 109

*$64,000 Question*, 127

Skill, Thomas, 36–40

Smith, Kate, 120, 124. See also *Kate Smith Speaks*

*Soap Opera Digest*, 38, 56, 88–89

Soap operas: popularity of, 3–4; origin of term, 8–9; in broadcasting discourse, 10–11; in aesthetic discourse, 11–18, 58–59, 61–62, 222–23 (n. 1); lack of narrative closure, 13–14, 69, 75–77, 127, 137, 138; authorship of, 14–15, 48–54, 56, 59–60; as kitsch, 16–17; in social science discourse, 18–28, 30–31, 34–44; audience research, 18–29 passim, 35, 50–51, 116, 118, 121, 133–36, 182–83; imputed psychological and physiological effects, 21–23, 38–39, 218–20 (n. 8); women as listeners/viewers, 24–29, 91–95, 133–36, 140, 148–49, 171–73, 177–79; as woman's form, 29, 44, 91–95, 134, 138–39, 149–50, 152, 178–79; content analysis of, 35–40, 61, 64; as adver-

tising vehicle, 45–47, 50, 58–60, 101, 117–22, 124–26, 127, 139, 176–77; mode of production, 46–58; division of labor, 48–51; producer's role, 49–51, 55; writer's role, 51–54, 56; scripts as "blueprints," 51–54; actors, 53, 55; director's role, 55–56; commercials, 58, 79–80, 160–61, 163–64, 167–68, 174, 177; poetics applied to, 61–64; and reader-response theory, 62–63, 72–73, 75–81, 86; stylistic analysis, 64–69, 84; and classical Hollywood film style, 64–69; use of space, 65–66; editing, 66–67; camera movement, 67–68; sound, 68; narrative structure, 69–91 passim, 127, 137; paradigmatic structure, 69–75; social relations in, 73–75, 168–69; syntagmatic structure, 75–81; protensive and retensive dimensions, 76–81; representation of minorities, 74–75; as open/closed text, 81–84; feminist analysis, 82–83; textual codes, 83–91; "stars," 88–89; attributional and inferential decoding of, 90–91; origins on radio, 110–16; "boom" of mid-1930s, 117–20; production costs, 121, 124, 125; transition to television, 122–26, 164–71; survival on television, 126–29; ownership by sponsors, 126–27; college student viewers, 128, 175; ratings, 128; history of soap opera reception, 133–40, 149–50; changes in textual structure, 130–31, 153–71; relationship to domestic novel, 140–51; narrative perspectives, 151–64, 170–72, 173–74; narrator's role, 153–59; narratee, 153, 154, 163–64, 167–68; characters, 153, 158–61, 169–70, 174; changes as result of television, 164–71; "real" readers of, 184
Soap World, 88
Sociology, 31
Song of the City, 117
Southwark, E.D.E.N., 141
Springfield, Rick, 89
Stagefright, 84
Staiger, Janet, 46, 48
Stanton, Frank, 30

State University of New York at Buffalo: "Project Daytime," 36
Stedman, Raymond William, 97, 118, 120, 125, 140
Sterne, Laurence, 152
Stolen Husband, 116
Stuart, Mary, 73
Structuralism, 12
Summers, Leda, 24, 134
Sudds, The, 111
Super-Suds Co., 111

Television: economic basis, 45–46; ratings, 45; advertising, 47, 122–23, 125; habitual viewing, 47; commercials, 79–81, 156, 167–68; viewing situation, 81; daytime, 124–26; production costs, 124; quiz-show scandals, 126–27
Terhune, Mary Virginia (Marian Harland), 141, 146
Thayer, Lee, 5, 42, 43
These Are Today's Children, 123
Thomas, Sari, 90
Thurber, James, 3, 4, 116, 181
Time, 10
Today, 121, 124
Today's Children, 11, 112–14, 121, 123, 137, 156, 159, 160, 161–62
Todorov, Tzvetan, 62
Touch of Evil, 68
Tristram Shandy, 152, 154

Ulysses, 83
University of Birmingham: Centre for Contemporary Cultural Studies, 183–84
University of Pennsylvania, 218 (n. 8)

Van den Haag, Ernest, 16–18
Vane, Edwin, 127
Variety, 8, 10, 11
Vaudeville, 104
Voice of Experience, 110, 140

Ware, Susan, 136, 148, 171
Warner Bros., 103
Warner, Susan, 145

# Index

Warner, W. Lloyd, 27–28, 41

WEAF, 101, 108

Welles, Orson, 155

Westinghouse, 101

WGN, 101, 104

White, Hayden, 98

*Wide, Wide World*, 141, 145, 149, 150

Willer, David, 31, 219–20 (n. 8)

Willer, Judith, 31, 219–20 (n. 8)

Wilson, Augusta Evans, 145

Wiseman, Mark H., 108

WLW, 115

WMAQ, 112–13

Wollen, Peter, 214 (n. 12)

*Woman in White*, 138, 162

Woman's fiction, 140–45; relationship to soap operas, 149–50, 178. *See also* Domestic novel

Wons, Tony, 110

Woolf, Virginia, 82

Worth, Sol, 90

Wylie, Max, 26

*Young and the Restless*, 86, 224 (n. 8)